New Perspectives in Organizational Communication

Series Editors
Milton Mayfield, Texas A&M International University,
Laredo, TX, USA
Jacqueline Mayfield, Texas A&M International University,
Laredo, TX, USA

This series will examine current, emerging, and cutting edge approaches to organizational communication. Throughout this series, authors will present new ideas in – and methods for – conducting organizational communication research. The series will present a variety of topics, giving readers an in-depth understanding of the organizational communication field to develop the skills necessary to engage in field research.

More information about this series at
http://www.palgrave.com/gp/series/16587

Leah M. Omilion-Hodges · Jennifer K. Ptacek

Leader-Member Exchange and Organizational Communication

Facilitating a Healthy Work Environment

palgrave
macmillan

Leah M. Omilion-Hodges
Western Michigan University
Kalamazoo, MI, USA

Jennifer K. Ptacek
University of Dayton
Dayton, OH, USA

ISSN 2730-5333 ISSN 2730-5341 (electronic)
New Perspectives in Organizational Communication
ISBN 978-3-030-68755-7 ISBN 978-3-030-68756-4 (eBook)
https://doi.org/10.1007/978-3-030-68756-4

This Palgrave Macmillan imprint is published by the registered company Springer Nature Switzerland AG
The registered company address is: Gewerbestrasse 11, 6330 Cham, Switzerland

This book is dedicated to employees of all levels and across all industries. The enactment of work and work environments are not without obstacles, but we continue to be inspired and encouraged by the intention, innovation, and resilience of employees.

Additionally, Dr. Omilion-Hodges is deeply grateful for her family's unyielding love, patience, and support. Without you, none of this would be possible. Also, she would like to thank her friends and colleagues for their continued support and so willingly sharing their work experiences so she can geek out over leader–member relationships.

Dr. Ptacek would like to thank her family for their unwavering support and love and for listening to her talk about research all the time. Additionally, she is so thankful to her wonderful colleagues and friends for their encouragement, support, and for being sounding boards for so many things. Thank you so much for all the love and incredible opportunities.

Preface

It is hard to understate the importance of the relationship between a leader and their employees. In fact, employees who share a high-quality relationship with their leader are more likely to earn a higher salary, climb the ranks more quickly, and report higher levels of life satisfaction than their peers who have a less copasetic leader–member relationship. Considering the impact the leader–member relationship has on the employee experience, it is of little surprise that there are over four decades of study on leader–member exchange theory. Moreover, this key area of research shows no signs of slowing down. Part of the reason for the continued study, aside from the obvious impact of the special relationship between leader and member, is that research indicates that the relationship an employee shares with his/her leader also impacts their peer relationships and their overall status within their team. This project synthesizes the academic literature and translates empirical findings into workable solutions for managers and employees.

Unlike other approaches to coaching leaders and employees to higher levels of organizational success, our text takes a communicative perspective. Focusing on communication highlights the relational aspect of the leader–member relationship, which results in more concrete and accessible solutions for employees and positions readers for long-term success in their organizations. Breaking away from a predominant psychological or management perspective, using a communicative lens also better illustrates the theory's complex theoretical underpinnings, such as the importance of social interaction and communicating to achieve organizational goals. In short, by focusing on leadership development via intentional communication, professionals and students can walk away with specific, behavioral solutions for enhancing their workplace experience, whether as a leader or as an employee.

Scholars will also find this text a helpful resource. LMX is a highly communicative theory. However, most management academic work on LMX treats this feature implicitly, glossing over the essential role communication plays in enacting leadership. We believe that researchers can benefit from the communicative lens and the practical implications that the book incorporates. Additionally, we address this enduring leadership theory's strengths and the limitations and critiques to help scholars remain abreast of innovations and sidestep common conceptualization and measurement concerns.

Leader–Member Exchange and Organizational Communication is designed to help you understand the unique and defining role communication plays in organizational settings. This text utilizes the following to provide realistic, evidence-based suggestions for formal leaders, employees, human resources personnel, and teacher-scholars, among others:

- A combination of recent empirical research and theory in an accessible writing style
- The following chapter features:
  - Sharpening your Communication Skills Features
  - Leadership in Action: Organization and Leader Profiles
  - Leadership Moments: Takeaways for Leaders & Members
  - Mini Case Studies

Kalamazoo, USA Leah M. Omilion-Hodges
Dayton, USA Jennifer K. Ptacek

Acknowledgments The authors wish to thank Leah Mcilreavy for her help in proofreading and editing.

Introduction

The primary questions guiding this book are: 1) what is the professional and personal impact of an employee's relationship with their leader? and 2) how do you coach both leaders and followers to integrate everyday communication practices to enhance their organizational experience?

We present empirical findings, practical uses, and theoretical underpinnings of an influential and far-reaching leadership communication theory: leader–member exchange (LMX). Leader–member exchange or LMX acknowledges a fundamental truth about the human nature of leaders and members. Leaders develop relationships of different qualities with each of their followers. Sometimes these relationships are of high quality and benefit the leader, member, and the organization. Other times, the leader–member relationship can be downright counterproductive and even unhealthy for one or both parties. In these instances, we also illustrate how the harmful effects of a low-quality leader–member exchange relationship can bleed over to influence workgroup dynamics and collective output.

Employing a communication-rooted perspective, this book illustrates how leaders and members can harness the power of four decades of LMX research to develop and maintain successful, healthy workplace relationships. The emphasis on employee empowerment is key, as LMX literature shows that the quality of an employee's leader–member relationship is not isolated. That is, the quality of an employee's leader–member relationship also impacts their peer relationships and their place within their team.

Through seminal and contemporary research and theory and mini case studies, we help readers trace how an employee's relationship with their leader shapes who they are likely to befriend in the workplace and shapes their overall standing within the workgroup. Considering the far-reaching effects of the leader–member relationship, we also explore the potential dark side of leader–member exchange theory, such as how LMX tends to encourage homophily or an abundance of demographic similarity between leaders and his/her trusted lieutenants. However, we do not stop at acknowledging the potential downfalls of LMX, but we also offer readers checks and workable solutions to guard against these tendencies. This book considers the implications of differentiated relationships, who stands to benefit, who may lose, and what both leaders and members can do to focus on strengthening the relationship.

A leader can be seen as a trusted mentor and advocate or seen as a gatekeeper and an insurmountable obstacle. However, small but meaningful communication practices can transform transactional workgroup associations into highly functional, intentional relationships. This approach results in an enhanced workplace experience for employees of all ranks. Organizations tend to enjoy increased benefits and reduced turnover and gains in individual workgroups' collective functioning.

This book is written for employees, hiring managers, recruiters, students, and teacher-scholars. In these roles, we ebb and flow between serving as formal leaders and as followers. Most often, however, we find ourselves enacting and juggling the leader and member role simultaneously—either as an advisor and an employee, as a middle manager and an employee, or as a CEO who serves at the pleasure of a board of directors. The point is that taking the time to learn and think about the impact of the leader–member relationship better positions us all to be a) more effective leaders, b) more effective followers, and c) employees who feel equipped to communicate intentionally and ethically for ourselves, our ideas, and for the betterment of the groups and communities we serve. By breaking away from the outmoded concept of communication as a tool that is only necessary when a message has gone awry, we show readers the positive outcomes associated with a constitutive or foundational role of communication. We also provide pragmatic and concrete solutions for commonplace leadership, workgroup, and organizational stumbling blocks. Some of the topics that will be addressed include exploring how organizational members can adjust their communication styles depending on the context and type of organization, how leaders and members can play up their strengths, and how all actors can overcome communication failures.

Contents

Abbreviations

CWX	Coworker Exchange
LMX	Leader–Member Exchange
SET	Socal Exchange Theory
TMX	Team-Member Exchange

List of Tables

PART I

Setting the Foundation: Understanding the Role of Communication in Leader-Member, Peer, and Team Relationships

CHAPTER 1

What is the Leader–Member Exchange (LMX) Theory?

Abstract This chapter introduces leader–member exchange theory and speaks directly to the following question: Why does this theory matter to me? The authors review and summarize the over four decades of related research and tell employees and formal leaders how this theory can help them predict their organizational experience. Additionally, we provide prescriptive suggestions for employees and address how they may make minor changes that may result in major changes to their leader–member relationship quality. This chapter also takes readers on a historical tour of the evolution of LMX from its conception as vertical dyad linkage theory to the dynamic, interdependent relational phenomenon it is today (Sheer, 2015) This chapter also addresses how leader–member relationships are likely to flourish or flounder based on power enactment. French and Raven's (1959) five sources of power (i.e., reward, coercive, expert, legitimate, and referent) are considered with the role of a formal leader. We also highlight how in-group and out-group members may interpret the same situation in different ways. This shows leaders how even their best-laid plans may go awry if they are not mindful of relational differences in their ranks.

Keywords Leader–member exchange · Vertical dyadic linkage model · Leadership making · Sources of power

L. M. Omilion-Hodges and J. K. Ptacek, *Leader-Member Exchange and Organizational Communication*, New Perspectives in Organizational Communication, https://doi.org/10.1007/978-3-030-68756-4_1

First Things First: Why Do I Need to Know About Leader–Member Exchange and Organizational Communication?

The primary questions guiding this book are: (1) what is the professional and personal impact of employees' relationships with their leaders, and (2) how to coach both leaders and followers on how to integrate everyday communication practices to enhance their organizational experience.

This book presents the findings, practical uses, and theoretical underpinnings of an influential and far-reaching leadership communication theory: Leader–member exchange (LMX). Leader–member exchange or LMX acknowledges a fundamental truth about the human nature of leaders and members. Leaders develop relationships of different qualities with each of their followers. The text also shows how an employee's relationship with their leader shapes who they are likely to befriend in the workplace and their overall standing within the workgroup. We will also explore the potential dark side of leader–member exchange theory, such as how LMX tends to encourage homophily or an abundance of demographic similarity between a leader and his/her trusted lieutenants. However, we will not stop at acknowledging the potential downfalls of LMX. We will offer readers checks and workable solutions to guard against these tendencies. This book will consider the implications of differentiated relationships, who stands to benefit, who stands to lose, and what both leaders and members can do to focus on strengthening their relationship.

Focusing on the role of communication, this book illustrates how leaders and members can harness the power of four decades of LMX research to develop and maintain successful, healthy workplace relationships. The emphasis on employee empowerment is key as LMX literature shows that the quality of an employee's leader–member relationship is not isolated. That is, the quality of an employee's leader–member relationship also impacts their peer relationships and their place within their team. Thus, while leader–member exchange originates within each individual leader–member dyad, it bleeds over to influence other key relationships, and can be detrimental to an employee's well-being.

This book begins by considering the theoretical roots of this special leadership theory and then takes a natural progression to integrate research and practical suggestions on how one's leader–member relationship impacts coworker and team exchanges, successes, and potential failures. An organizational communication lens is employed throughout to highlight the power of intentional communication, especially emphasizing that small, but meaningful changes can pay off in terms of allowing leaders and members to engineer the type of relationship and an environment they desire. While other texts have addressed the leader–member relationship, they have done so from solely an academic/theoretical perspective or a psychological perspective. While this treatment of LMX serves a purpose, it does not offer employees tangible and workable communication-rooted solutions. Concrete ways the current text can readily impact readers'/employees' everyday work include chapter features such as sharpening your communication skills, profiles of leaders and organizations, mini case studies or application vignettes, and key takeaways for leaders and members.

Before considering the impact of leader–member relationships in groups, teams, unique contexts (i.e., for-profits, non-profits, start-ups, etc.), and ethical considerations, this first chapter is designed to give readers a solid understanding of the theoretical underpinnings of this pervasive and enduring leadership theory.

What is the Leader–Member Exchange Theory?

The leader–member exchange (LMX) theory is considered to be among the first of the relational approaches to leadership. While adopting a people-centered view of leadership may not seem incredibly innovative today, the shift from focusing on the traits, characteristics, and behaviors of leaders and followers to considering a third domain, relationships, indicated a significant shift in practicing and conceptualizing leadership. Nearly five decades later, attention to this special leadership theory has not waned, likely since it focuses on the three primary domains or elements of leadership: the leader, the follower, and the relationship (Graen & Uhl-Bien, 1995).

Leader–member exchange was formulated initially as the vertical dyad linkage model (VDL; Dansereau et al., 1975; Graen & Cashman, 1975). VDL acknowledged a fundamental human truth that earlier leadership models and theories did not: leaders form unique relationships with each follower. Some of these relationships may be built on a solid foundation of trust and mutual respect. Others may be a formal transactional relationship where leaders and members are loosely coupled only because of their formal roles. Before the vertical dyad linkage model, the consensus was that leaders employed an average leadership style (ALS) using roughly the same approach and generating the same relational and task outcomes with each follower. However, this approach did not account for individual differences. That is, while one employee may see an assertive leader in a positive light, another follower may perceive the same leader as abrasive. The employee who perceives this leader in the positive light may be more committed to workgroup tasks and output than the associate who finds the leader's communication style off-putting. Before providing prescriptive advice for leaders and members, it is necessary to consider the evolution of LMX. Considering the theory's development allows us to point out critical theoretical underpinnings that underscore the practical suggestions and solutions this book is built around.

Evolution of Leader–Member Exchange Theory

Figure 1.1. illustrates the transformation of leader–member exchange theory and details some of each iteration's major components or phases. By examining each developmental phase's key elements, we can illustrate why specific tips are likely to position leaders and members for success.

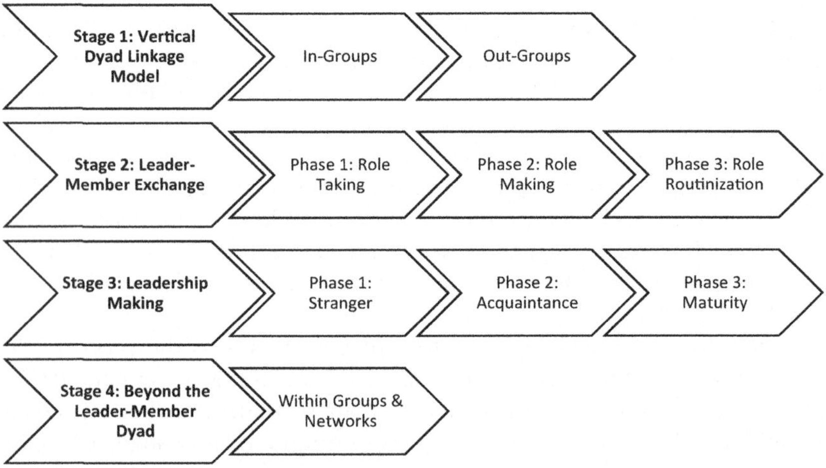

Fig. 1.1 Evolution of leader–member exchange theory

Vertical Dyadic Linkage Model

The key takeaway from the vertical dyadic model is that because leaders treat individual employees differently, followers are likely to hold differing views of their leaders. Research indicates that this differential treatment often created two unique divisions within a workgroup: an in-group and an out-group. As the names imply, in-group members are followers who have developed high-quality, effective relationships with their leader, and out-group members have a leader–member relationship characterized by low trust and limited support.

What determines group membership? Whether an employee becomes a member of the in-group or the out-group is based on several factors, including how well they get along with the leader, which can stem from a similarity in personality, demographics, and values. Follower competence, assimilation to the workgroup, and willingness to take on more responsibility can also impact group membership. One of the main critiques of leader–member exchange relates specifically to the emergence of in- and out-groups described by vertical dyad linkage. Differential treatment may lead to preferential treatment of in-group members, often at the expense of out-group member peers. In some instances, such as when an employee continually submits error-ridden work or does not follow policy and procedures, out-group membership may be fitting. However, suppose a leader is unsure of how to connect and develop a high-quality relationship with a follower because they are different in terms of ages or stages (i.e., new graduate, young kids, empty-nester). In that case, out-group membership may be unwarranted. One of the authors has a friend who took up distance running only because she genuinely felt that it was the only way to become a part of the in-group. Her male manager and his trusted lieutenants (in-group members) would meet for long runs three days per week before work. Even though she did not enjoy running and had recently given birth, she felt that she would not be "heard" until she was seen as a member of the in-group. This friend traces many of her career successes to putting in the effort to run with her leader. Other similar critiques and criticisms of the theory are discussed in greater detail below.

Leader–Member Exchange

While VDL illuminated some initial and important outcomes of differentiated leader–member relationships, leader–member exchange shifted focus to the relationship's quality rather than classification (i.e., in-group or out-group). Thus, instead of taking an either-or approach (i.e., either you are an in-group or out-group member), this change considers relationship quality on a continuum from a low-quality to a high-quality exchange relationship. Just as VDL showed some clear advantages to in-group members, the same is true for those who develop an effective leader–member relationship. LMX literature is replete with positive outcomes for high LMX employees (i.e., those who have a high-quality leader–member exchange relationship). These associates often enjoy more successful careers, remain more committed to their organization, are more satisfied with the communication practices of their leader, their group, and their organization, and report higher levels of motivation among other positive outcomes (Culbertson et al., 2010; Van Dam et al., 2008). Not only do those with high LMX enjoy more perks, but it appears that those with low LMX may be on the receiving end of exclusionary treatment from their leader, including withholding information, gossip, and blocking career advancement (Omilion-Hodges & Baker, 2017). Leader–member exchange literature focuses primarily on the antecedents and consequences of developing relationships of varying quality. One concrete way to consider how some leader–member couplings flourish and others flounder is by considering the role taking, role making, and role routinization process (Cropanzano et al., 2017).

The leader–member relationship takes shape through a three-part process—role taking, role making, and role routinization. The first phase, role taking, is characterized by traditional leader–member exchanges; the leader gives the new employee tasks and responsibilities and assesses how well they complete the work. Assessments of how well the employee is assimilating to the workgroup also occur in the role taking phase. If the first phase is more leader-directed, the second phase—role making—is more member-led. In this phase, the member advocates explicitly and implicitly to engineer the role to fit their skill set better and align with their goals. For example, after six months, an employee may realize that they enjoy client-facing tasks and see client relations as their next career stepping stone. This employee may then offer to take on and lead more client-focused tasks and projects and take care to do these duties exceedingly well to be recognized as an expert in this area. In the role taking phase, employees who volunteer to lead additional projects or chair various tasks may also find themselves in the position to shed or shift some of their initial role responsibilities. That is, if an employee has shown initiative and expertise in areas that are valuable to the workgroup and the organization, the leader may then remove or reassign some of the other tasks the employee was initially hired to complete. While these examples highlight employees experiencing a strong person-position fit, the role making phase may look quite different for an associate who is experiencing a more challenging entry.

In instances where the leader does not believe that the member has done a satisfactory job of completing the tasks in the role taking phase, this employee may never find themselves able to negotiate the tasks and expectations of the role (i.e., the role making phase). The differences exemplified here provide an excellent example of how leader–member communication can vary wildly between leader–member dyads. These distinctions will be more fully explored in Chapter 2. Still, we can see how in the high LMX dyad, the leader is receptive to the follower's desires and suggestions. This relationship is characterized by two-way communication between both parties exemplified through honesty and transparency. The redesigning of one's role responsibilities requires trust, respect, and effective communication. However, in the instance where the employee either fails to meet task demands or otherwise falls short of the leader's expectations, the communication practices in this dyad are likely to remain authoritative and formal. The leader assigns the employee tasks and provides feedback and/or reprimands when necessary and otherwise does not necessarily invest in this association.

Role routinization is the final stage of the LMX relationship development process. In this phase, the relationship has reached a routine. The implicit and explicit bargaining of the role taking and role making phases has concluded as both parties have come to understand what to expect from each other. Once a relationship has progressed to the role routinization phase, it is difficult, if not impossible, to alter the nature of the relationship—both for better or for worse. Thus, if an employee had a challenging entry to the workgroup or organization and took some time to assimilate successfully, they may feel like no matter what they do, their leader still treats them as an out-group member. This can be exceedingly frustrating as this associate attempts to secure additional or new projects or increase their responsibilities and is met with a leader who continues to put off or ignore such requests. Employees in this position may find that they need to switch departments or even move to another organization to get ahead. Just as the routinization phase may "lock" initially low-LMX associates into the out-group regardless of performance enhancements, high-LMX associates may continue to enjoy in-group benefits even if their performance falters. In this instance, an employee who initially made a large and favorable impact may continue to be treated as a trusted colleague and given flexibility and latitude from their leader even if they have begun to perform at a lower or less innovative level. These illustrations represent additional criticisms of the leader–member exchange theory. While the LMX stage of this leadership theory parceled out key differences for high and low-LMX employees, the third phase, leadership making, stresses high-quality relationship development among all members.

Leadership Making

Leadership making research focuses on the practical and ethical benefits of a leader working to develop an individual relationship with each follower, rather than only with a few trusted lieutenants. This may seem like a subtle shift from the LMX process described above; however, leadership making moves away from how a manager may differentiate treatment between members to consider collaborating effectively with each member. The leadership making process has been suggested as a best practice for leaders, members, and the organization (Graen & Uhl-Bien, 1995; Uhl-Bien & Graen, 1993). The focus of leadership making is on connecting and communicating with each member to engineer an effective work environment. Similar to the role taking, making, and routinization phases described earlier, leadership making is often detailed in three unique phases: stranger, acquaintance, and mature partnership. Each dyad progresses through these phases differently, and some do not evolve into the mature partnership phase. The leadership making process considers the leader–member relationship as a partnership rather than in traditional superior–subordinate terms. This transition also implicitly requires more work from both leader and member because of the time and energy it takes to cultivate a trusting, two-way relationship.

Why would leaders and members want to put in the work to get to the mature partnership phase? Research is replete with positive outcomes for members and workgroups who can cultivate these special and dynamic associations. Employees tend to enjoy having a leader who listens to and respects and trusts them (Duchon et al., 1986; Fairhurst, 1993). In turn, when members feel valued, they often engage in additional organizational citizenship behaviors. They are also more likely to remain committed to the organization than employees who have a more contractual relationship with their leader (Graen, 1989).

From Dyads to Groups
Contemporary scholarship considers the fourth phase of leader–member exchange theory: Expansion to the network and group level. While the previous three phases of the theory have focused on individual leader–member relationships, some argue that the theory should be considered beyond the dyadic level to be considered at its fullest potential. Research from this approach seeks to consider how individual leader–member relationships impact group and network-level phenomena such as the development of peer and team relationships (Sherony & Green, 2002), perceptions of how fair or just the leader is (Omilion-Hodges & Baker, 2013), allocation of resources within the group (Omilion-Hodges & Baker, 2017), and workplace attitudes (Bakar & McCann, 2014), among other critical organizational outcomes. Research in this area also considers measurement and theoretical concerns to caution scholars from theorizing at one level and inadvertently measuring at another level. For example, some researchers may employ a theoretical foundation that considers the individual, dyadic leader–member relationship, and then measures outcomes at the group level. Others have also begun to consider how leader–member relationships may impact groups and networks differently based on cultural and geographic differences (Terpstra-Tong et al., 2020). This book, especially chapters three and four, focuses on the impact individual leader–member relationships have on coworker and team relationships and outcomes.

Why Does This Theory Matter to Me?

Most adults spend more time at work than they do with their family members and their friends. If things are not going well at work, feelings of frustration and anger can spill over into one's personal life. Frequently, the leader–member relationship is the deciding factor in how well or how challenging one's professional life is going.

Whether you are a formal, titled leader or a member, leader–member exchange theory directly impacts you. This is especially true for middle managers who find themselves toggling between directives from their leader and approaching the relationship they share with their followers.

As a manager, considering LMX will show you how your communication behaviors directly impact the relationships you develop and maintain in the workplace. As a manager, you are likely in the position to have to juggle many demands, some of them competing, and all needing your attention at the same time. We will translate theoretical findings from nearly 50 years of communication and leadership literature to show you how investment in your employees is likely to pay off in terms of workgroup and organizational successes. In this sense, reviewing leader–member exchange literature will help you consider how different situations may play out in your unique organizational setting (makeup of your work team, member maturity, nature of the task, etc.) and how you can communicate and relate to your employees in a way that will allow you to realize group goals. Moreover, Chapter 6 illustrates how a leader may practice inclusion in meaningful ways to help leaders to be mindful of individuals' unique identities and as it relates to employee retention and turnover. Just as considering LMX and communication can help a titled leader facilitate effective relationships with their members, the same literature and practical solutions can help them broker a copasetic relationship with their leader. Enacting mindful relationships with one's followers and their leader sounds easy enough on paper. Still, for anyone who has done this or is currently attempting to do this, you know that it can be anything but. As leadership communication experts, we make a point to draw out specifics and provide clear-cut suggestions on how to integrate these ideas into practice.

Just as leader–member exchange theory can help titled leaders, understanding the theory's potential can dramatically change members' work experiences. Study after study has reiterated the positive outcomes high-LMX members enjoy. From enhanced mentorship, more professional development opportunities, rapid career, salary growth, and overall work satisfaction, employees who cultivate and maintain effective relationships with their leaders enjoy a plethora of additional advantages (see Omilion-Hodges et al., 2016 for review). It is one thing to know that an effective leader relationship leads to a positive outcome. Still, it is another thing to have prescriptive advice for developing that relationship, especially if there are demographic, value, or other differences that seem to stand in the way of the development of a trusting, high functioning leader–member relationship. As a member, being aware of how your leader–member relationship may make you predisposed to befriend some peers and exclude others can also help you to avoid autopilot and actively consider how to navigate these associations.

Knowing that the theory has a direct impact on you is the first step. The second step is considering the potential advantages and disadvantages of this theory and its effects in very real ways.

Looking up: Benefits of the Leader–Member Relationship
The dedication to and continued exploration of leader–member exchange theory reiterate countless advantages of cultivating an effective, two-way relationship. Some of those benefits for members who have a high-LMX relationship include (e.g., Audenaert et al., 2020; Culbertson et al., 2010; Martin et al., 2016; Naidoo et al., 2011; Omilion-Hodges & Baker, 2017; Zagenczyk et al., 2015; Zhou et al., 2020):

- Increased role autonomy
- Greater influence with the leader and in the workplace
- Enhanced employee voice, social currency, and work currency
- Satisfaction with leader and organizational communication
- More challenging and engaging work assignments
- Access to a wealth of positive leadership and organizational resources
    - Mentoring, professional development, feedback, access to the leader
- Increased career satisfaction
- Enactment of more organizational citizenship behaviors
- More frequent promotions and higher earning potential
- Increased organizational commitment

At first glance, the above list appears to be focused solely or primarily on member benefits. What about the leader? By taking a step back, it becomes more apparent how taking the time to cultivate high-quality exchange relationships with all (or most) members benefits the leader. Consider leading a team of employees who are poised to take on more complex projects, can do so independently, and go above and beyond to help you and their peers? Leaders who put in the work to develop individual relationships with each member may also find that some of their followers have become trusted confidants and advisors, helping to ease the solitude or loneliness that can surround titled or formal leadership positions. In summary, it is hard to overstate the benefits imbued within a high-quality leader–member relationship. Additionally, as this list above begins to illustrate, the benefits impact employees (individual level), workgroups (team level), and the organization (organizational level).

Potential Disadvantages of the Leader–Member Relationship
While numerous clear benefits stem from the development of high-LMX relationships, the theory is not without critique. The theory has long been criticized for being a shortcut and measuring leader likeability (Seers et al., 2006; Sheer, 2015). That is, does my leader like me, or does my leader not like me?

Part of the binary (high or low LMX; in-group or out-group) traces back to LMX homophily or that it is often easier to grow a relationship with someone similar. Thus, if you share values that are analogous to those held by your leader, or if you are in a comparable station in life (i.e., new parents, empty nesters, etc.), or you are simply alike demographically (i.e., age, gender, race, hobbies, religion, etc.) then it is easier to connect on those shared elements. However, what can happen is that leaders can build a workgroup with little to no diversity. Relatedly, members who are different from the leader may inadvertently find themselves in the out-group or with low LMX simply because the interpersonal connection is not as apparent as it may be with other workgroup peers.

Other downfalls or challenges of the leader–member exchange approach to leadership, particularly for those who have low LMX, include (e.g., Byron & Landis, 2020; Bolino & Turnley, 2009; Chaudhry et al., 2020; Matta & Van Dyne, 2020; Omilion-Hodges & Baker, 2017):

- Decreased workgroup diversity
- Feeling unsupported by their leader
- Less engaged and satisfied with work
- Decreased organizational commitment
- Mundane assignments
- Limited or no career advancement
- Decreased voice or feedback behavior
- Development of fewer high-quality peer relationships
- Recipient of exclusionary and/or retaliatory leader behavior
- Being micromanaged or feeling as though your manager does not trust your work
- Limited or no professional development including mentorship from the leader

These are just a few of the adverse outcomes or disadvantages that can stem from a low-quality leader–member relationship. At its worst, LMX can lead to an abundance of demographic similarity reminiscent of the old boy network. This can stem from unethical and even illegal behavior where individual members are overlooked or disregarded for promotions or salary increases because they are different from the leader and not based on their work quality. Low LMX has also been linked to leaders engaging in unethical behaviors such as withholding information employees need to do their jobs, taking credit for associates' work, and having the leader gossip about them to their peers or higher-ups (Omilion-Hodges & Baker, 2017). As discussed earlier in the chapter, once a leader–member dyadic relationship reaches the role routinization phase, it tends to remain of that quality for better or worse. Considering this, employees who find themselves in a low-quality exchange relationship with their leader may consider internal transfers or seeking new employment if continued attempts to engage with their leader result in the adverse outcomes noted above.

LMX and Power: How Relationships Flourish or Flounder

Those in titled leadership positions are not always right or moral or immune to bad decision-making. However, in this section, we link position power to thoughtful, other- and group-oriented communication and decision-making processes. Reflecting on how they use their position power can help leaders to become more mindful of the weight of their authority and illuminate their go-to communication tools. After considering traditional sources of power, we conclude the chapter by illustrating how members may perceive the same message differently based on the quality of the relationship they share with their leader. This helps to exemplify further the influential role that communication plays in the enactment and perceptions of leadership.

As indicated in Table 1.1, part of why some followers may have flocked toward Steve Jobs and thrived under his direction could be his approach to communication. One concrete way to illuminate Jobs', and all leaders for that matter, communication tendencies is by considering how frequently and for what means he drew from various sources of power. Additionally, Table 1.2 offers some communication tips for using LMX to your advantage.

Table 1.1 Leadership in action—leader profile: Steve Jobs

What made Steve Jobs such a great leader? Industry titan Richard Branson (2011) summed Jobs' success as a leader as follows "... [he] surrounded himself with like-minded people to follow his lead."
Jobs' approach to leadership has been lauded and criticized. Leaders who provoke such a polarized response illustrate a fundamental tenet of leader-member exchange theory. Those who are similar to the leader in a variety of ways tend to fare better than those who are not.
This does not mean that the "like-minded people" who Jobs surrounded himself with were necessarily male and of the same age and background, but rather they may have also preferred direct and authoritative communication and a high-stakes, competitive work environment.
Though LMX has evolved to consider unique contexts and outcomes at the group and network level, the heart of the theory reminds us that leaders develop unique relationships with each follower. Like Steve Jobs, it is often easier to work collaboratively with those that we can relate to and understand on an interpersonal level.

Source Branson (2011)

Sources of Power: The Potential to Influence the Behavior of Others

French and Raven (1959) outlined five predominant sources of position power that remain applicable today: legitimate, reward, coercive, expert, and referent. In this sense, power is considered as the potential to influence the behavior of others. Like any other tool, these sources of power are not particularly impactful on their own. That is, a hammer lying in a toolbox is neither good nor bad. It is the motive or intent, however, that colors the action. Using a hammer to assist with a community garden effort is qualitatively different than a hammer being used to inflict bodily harm to another. The same is true for the enactment of the various sources of position power.

Legitimate Power

Legitimate power stems from the position rather than the person in the post. Simply stated, position power describes the extent to which an individual can enact authority and autonomy based on their organizational (or social) role. What does this look like in the workgroup? Even when we do not necessarily agree with our leader, we often go along with the plan and even help them enact the idea simply because they are the ranking member. Indeed, parents and children can relate to perhaps the most frequent application of legitimate power: "Because I said so." In

Table 1.2 Sharpening your communication skills: using LMX to your advantage

Now that you know how influential LMX can be for your career, how can you use this theory to your advantage? Below we offer some communication tips: • **Relationship Development**: The importance of relationships is hard to overstate – especially considering that many jobs require long hours and increased team-based project work. Workplace relationships, those with peers or with your leader, are linked to increased employee satisfaction, production, and retention (Dotan, 2009). Taking the time to get to know your leader, your peers, and your employees (if you're a titled leader) will not only facilitate a more welcoming culture, but can also innovate employee creativity and innovation (Omilion-Hodges & Ackerman, 2017). Asking questions, listening, sharing information and tasks, and enacting positive and affirming communication are among the most often used and most recommended strategies for developing and maintaining workgroup relationships (Madlock & Booth-Butterfield, 2012). • **Listening**: Dotan (2009) identified a number of reasons why employees seek to develop high-quality workplace relationships such as work trust/safety, sanity check, and work-values/life-interest similarity, among others. What do these have in common? They all require a bedrock of active listening to develop and to be maintained. Active listening is more than simply hearing the other person. Active listening includes nonverbals such as eye contact, nodding, and opening your body to lean into the speaker. Active listening also entails a number of verbal communication behaviors such as asking questions, summarizing, and paraphrasing as a means to demonstrate that you are listening and also that you are interpreting the messages as they are intended. • **Mirroring**: Part of enacting and demonstrating active listening is mirroring your posture and movements to match those of your conversational partner. If they lean in, you lean in. If they uncross their arms, you can do the same. How does this help relationship development and maintenance? The synchronicity of the movements can help people to feel a sense of ease and belongingness because mirroring promotes feelings of similarity.

Source Dotan (2009), Madlock and Booth-Butterfield (2012), and Omilion-Hodges and Ackerman (2017)

the organizational setting, employees may recognize this enactment by a particular look their leader gives them or when a leader delegates tasks or issues orders without seeking or listening to employee feedback.

Organizations are often structured around legitimate power as it provides a scaffolding, clear reporting structure, and can be incorporated organization-wide. In short, legitimate power helps organizations, large and small, function by giving clarity via structure. While there are clear benefits to this power source, relying on legitimate power can become less effective over time. It can also prompt lower task performance and satisfaction among followers. Why? Because it doesn't feel good or incredibly empowering to continue to hear your manager say, "because I said so."

Reward Power

Reward power does not necessarily stem from being in a titled role, though organizational leaders are often positioned to offer the most attractive rewards. As the name suggests, reward power describes the ability to use desired items to influence others' behavior. Enacting this source of power can help a leader to quickly motivate employees for a short-term performance boost or as a means to focus attention on specific group priorities.

On the surface, reward power can seem like a win–win. However, there are some potential drawbacks to consider. For example, followers do not all respond the same to rewards. One employee may value a $100 gift card after a particularly trying project or event, whereas another employee may feel offended and would have instead received a handwritten thank you card. Additionally, over time rewards may lead to escalating financial costs and may become the primary or sole motivator for employee contribution.

Coercive Power

While reward power addresses the ability to bestow desired items to followers, coercive power describes a leader's ability to administer punishment. Certainly, this can align with the use of legitimate power, but it can go a step further. While legitimate power may include a leader's ability to document issues in an employee's file or reduce their salary or downgrade a follower's title, coercive power can also include punishment by excluding followers from certain information from choice projects or engaging in the silent treatment.

Coercive power often leads to quick follower obedience and might be the right choice if an employee's behavior requires disciplinary action. This communication approach can also be useful in high turnover industries (i.e., retail, food industry, etc.) to set clear expectations and achieve quick results for a new manager. Naturally, some costs are associated with the continued or predominant use of coercive power, including a drain of physical and emotional energy from the leader, lowered follower task satisfaction, and likely a negative workgroup culture that lacks trust and commitment.

Expert Power

Titled leaders who possess specialized knowledge and experience in the area they lead can also enact expert power. Unlike the forms of power discussed above, expert power resides in the individual and not in the position. While it seems like a no-brainer that a leader would have experience in the particular area they work in, consider how often CEOs jump between industries.

Use of expert power leads to high follower task satisfaction and performance while also requiring very little extra work or emotional or physical drain from the leader. Expert power takes time and dedication to develop. Without other role-based sources of power (i.e., reward, coercive, and legitimate), an employee with expertise may still not generate the desired results.

Referent Power

The fifth source of power also resides in the person rather than in the formal leadership position. Individuals who have referent power are often charismatic, and others want to listen to them and hear their thoughts and opinions. Individuals with referent power can be extremely influential due to the feelings of esteem, affection, and respect that they inspire in others.

You do not need a formal titled leadership position to enact referent power. Sometimes one of the leader's trusted advisers becomes the "face" of the department and becomes a proxy for the titled leader. A few challenges come with referent power such as using charisma to influence others to engage in conduct or stand by causes intended to harm or exclude others. Cult leaders are guilty of this application of referent power.

Taking the time to reflect on the five sources of power is helpful for both leader and member. As a leader, reviewing the power sources provides some insight into how leaders attempt to inspire, relate to, and align followers. Suppose a manager realizes that they primarily use coercive power. Reflecting on this tendency allows them to consider why that has become their go-to communicative approach and evaluate whether it is still useful. Conducing a personal communication audit also allows leaders to consider what approach(es) would motivate their followers and engineer their preferred work culture.

On the other hand, members can consider their manager's communication as a barometer to understand a given situation. For example, suppose the manager tends to draw from the referent, expert, and reward power predominantly, and they approach a particular concern with coercive power. In that case, the member can draw some conclusions about the depth of emotion and pressure the manager feels toward the event.

Another important outcome of reviewing the sources of power is the opportunity to consider how various messages may be interpreted differently based on the quality of an employee's leader–member relationship.

Lost in Translation: How In-Group and Out-Group Members May Perceive Messages Differently

LMX is about differences; Differences in every leader–member dyad, differences in how these relationships influence the workgroup, and differences in how LMX variance can impact networks and organizational functioning. Knowing that this pervasive leadership theory is rooted in differences reminds us to consider how members may experience unique interpretations of the same message based on their leader–member relationship quality (Table 1.3).

Leadership Moments: Takeaways for Leaders & Members

- **LMX Theory is Your Friend:** Part of the reason for the theory's longevity lies in its simplicity. The theory is not particularly hard to apply or to understand, while at the same time, it illuminates fundamental truths about the development and impact of leader–member relationships.
- **Leaders Should Strive to Develop High-LMX Relationships with Each Follower:** While it was originally thought that leaders could or should only seek to develop mature relationships with select followers, as the theory evolved it became clear that an attempt to cultivate a unique relationship with each follower is best. Taking this approach results in benefits for the leader, members, the workgroup, and the organization. No one said this process would be easy, and it indeed asks a lot of titled leaders, but it is perceived as the ethical and equitable course of action, and it also positions the leader to align their team for the best outcomes.
- **A Leader's Communication Patterns are Telling for the Leader and for Members:** Becoming aware of your leader's communication tendencies helps followers become aware of how to interpret messages and situational factors, such as organizational pressures or deadlines.

Table 1.3 Lost in Translation: Possible variations in member interpretation based on LMX level

Organizational Scenario	*Leader message*	*High-LMX interpretation*	*Moderate LMX interpretation*	*Low-LMX interpretation*
Team Meeting	"Let's thank Hadley for leading this project. Hadley, hopefully you can engage some of your peers for the next stage of the project."	My manager appreciates me and continues to help me to grow.	This feels like a mixed message. I guess I will chat with some peers to try to get their feedback and buy in.	Wow. I really had thought I had done a good job. Maybe I need to think about transitioning this project to someone else.
Performance Evaluation	"Johnny, you're right where I would expect you to be at this point. Now I would like to see you begin to propose and develop some of your own projects."	My manager and I are in lockstep.	I am adjusting fairly well, but should do a bit more so that my manager sees me as a leader.	I don't know what else I could possibly do to be recognized or get ahead here.
Providing Feedback	"Olivia, thanks for putting this draft together so we have something to react to. I have a number of edits that will need to be addressed and integrated before we move forward."	I'm glad my efforts are noticed and appreciated.	I am glad that my manager is taking the time to give specific feedback to keep this project moving along.	It feels like I can't do anything right in her eyes.

Mini Case Study: The New Employee

Your friend has recently started a new job. She likes the work that she is doing and told you that she could see herself happy in the organization for years to come. The only issue, she said, is that she isn't quite sure that her manager likes her. She tells you that it's not so much that he doesn't like her, but instead, they really could not be more different. She is a single woman in her late 20s who enjoys traveling and reading. Her manager has four young children and jokes that the only travel he does is to work, daycare, and errands. After telling you about her manager, she shrugs and suggests that he won't play much of a role in her career trajectory aside from signing her paycheck.

1. What advice do you have for your friend?
2. How can you help her to understand the importance of an effective leader–member relationship?
3. What 3 pieces of tangible advice can you give your friend that will set her up for success in this new role?

References

Audenaert, M., Van der Heijden, B., Rombaut, T., & Van Thielen, T. (2020). The role of feedback quality and organizational cynicism for affective commitment through leader-member exchange. *Review of Public Personnel Administration*, 1–23. https://doi.org/10.1177/0734371X20923010.

Bakar, H., & McCann, R. M. (2014). Matters of demographic similarity and dissimilarity in supervisor–subordinate relationships and workplace attitudes. *International Journal of Intercultural Relations, 41,* 1–16. https://doi.org/10.1016/j.ijintrel.2014.04.004.

Bolino, M. C., & Turnley, W. H. (2009). Relative deprivation among employees in lower-quality leader-member exchange relationships. *The Leadership Quarterly, 20*(3), 276–286. https://doi.org/10.1016/j.leaqua.2009.03.001.

Branson, R. (2011, October 6). Apple boss Steve Jobs was the entrepreneur I admired most. *The Telegraph.* https://www.telegraph.co.uk/technology/steve-jobs/8811232/Virgins-Richard-Branson-Apple-boss-Steve-Jobs-was-the-entrepreneur-I-most-admired.html.

Byron, K., & Landis, B. (2020). Relational misperceptions in the workplace: New frontiers and challenges. *Organization Science, 31*(1), 223–242. https://doi.org/10.1287/orsc.2019.1285.

Chaudhry, A., Vidyarthi, P. R., Liden, R. C., & Wayne, S. J. (2020). Two to tango? Implications of alignment and miss alignment in leader and follower perceptions of LMX. *Journal of Business and Psychology, 2020,* 1–17. https://doi.org/10.1007/s10869-020-09690-8.

Cropanzano, R., Dasborough, M. T., & Weiss, H. M. (2017). Affective events and the development of leader-member exchange. *Academy of Management Review, 42*(2), 233–258. https://doi.org/10.5465/amr.2014.0384.

Culbertson, S. S., Fullagar, C. J., & Mills, M. J. (2010). Feeling good and doing great: The relationship between psychological capital and well-being. *Journal of Occupational Health Psychology, 15*(4), 421. https://psycnet.apa.org/doi/10.1037/a0020720.

Dansereau, F., Graen, G., & Haga, W. J. (1975). A vertical dyad linkage approach to leadership within formal organizations: A longitudinal investigation of the role making process. *Organizational Behavior and Human Performance, 13,* 46–78. https://doi.org/10.1016/0030-5073(75)90005-7.

Dotan, H. (2009). Workplace friendships: Origins and consequences for managerial effectiveness. *Academy of Management Proceedings, 86,* 1–6. https://doi.org/10.5465/ambpp.2009.44244633.

Duchon, D., Green, S. G., & Taber, T. D. (1986). Vertical dyad linkage: A longitudinal assessment of antecedents, measures, and cosequences. *Journal of Applied Psychology, 71,* 56–60. https://psycnet.apa.org/doi/10.1037/0021-9010.71.1.56.

Fairhurst, G. T. (1993). The leader-member exchange patterns of women leaders in industry: A discourse analysis. *Communications Monographs, 60*(4), 321–351. https://doi.org/10.1080/03637759309376316.

French, J., & Raven, B. H. (1959). The bases of social power. In D. Cartwright (Ed.), *Studies in social power* (pp. 150–167). Institute for Social Research.

Graen, G. B. (1989). *Unwritten rules for your career: The 15 secrets for fast-track success.* New York: Wiley.

Graen, G. B., & Cashman, J. F. (1975). A role-making approach model of leadership in formal organizations: A developmental approach. *Leadership Frontiers, 143,* 165.

Graen, G. B., & Uhl-Bien, M. (1995). Relationship-based approach to leadership: Development of leader-member exchange (LMX) theory of leadership over 25 years: Applying a multi-level multi-domain perspective. *The Leadership Quarterly, 6*(2), 219–247. https://doi.org/10.1016/1048-9843(95)90036-5.

Madlock, P. E., & Booth-Butterfield, M. (2012). The influence of relational maintenance strategies among coworkers. *Journal of Business Communication, 49*(1), 21–47. https://doi.org/10.1177/0021943611425237.

Martin, R., Guillaume, Y., Thomas, G., Lee, A., & Epitropaki, O. (2016). Leader–member exchange (LMX) and performance: A meta-analytic review. *Personnel Psychology, 69*(1), 67–121. https://doi.org/10.1111/peps.12100.

Matta, F. K., & Van Dyne, L. (2020). Understanding the disparate behavioral consequences of LMX differentiation: The role of social comparison emotions. *Academy of Management Review, 45*(1), 154–180. https://doi.org/10.5465/amr.2016.0264.

Naidoo, L. J., Scherbaum, C. A., Goldstein, H. W., & Graen, G. B. (2011). Longitudinal examination of the effects of LMX, ability, and differentiation on team performance. *Journal of Business and Psychology, 26,* 347–357. https://doi.org/10.1007/s10869-010-9193-2.

Omilion-Hodges, L. M., & Ackerman, C. D. (2017). From the technical know-how to the free flow of ideas: Exploring the effects of leader, peer, and team communication on employee creativity. *Communication Quarterly, 66*, 38–57. https://doi.org/10.1080/01463373.2017.1325385.

Omilion-Hodges, L. M., & Baker, C. R. (2013). Contextualizing LMX within the workgroup: The effects of LMX and justice on relationship quality and resource sharing among peers. *The Leadership Quarterly, 24*(6), 935–951. https://doi.org/10.1016/j.leaqua.2013.10.004.

Omilion-Hodges, L. M., & Baker, C. R. (2017). Communicating leader-member relationship quality: The development of leader communication exchange scales to measure relationship building and maintenance through the exchange of communication-based goods. *International Journal of Business Communication, 54*(2), 115–145. https://doi.org/10.1177/2329488416687052.

Omilion-Hodges, L. M., Ptacek, J. K., & Zerilli, D. H. (2016). A comprehensive review and communication research agenda of the contextualized workgroup: The evolution and future of leader-member exchange, coworker exchange, and team-member exchange. *Annals of the International Communication Association, 40*(1), 343–377. https://doi.org/10.1080/23808985.2015.11735265.

Seers, A., Wilkerson, J. M., & Grubb, W. L. (2006). Toward measurement of social exchange resources: Reciprocal contributions and receipts. *Psychological Reports, 98*, 508–510.

Sheer, V. C. (2015). "Exchange lost" in leader-member exchange theory and research: A critique and a reconceptualization. *Leadership, 11*(2), 213–229. https://doi.org/10.1177/1742715014530935.

Sherony, K. M., & Green, S. G. (2002). Coworker exchange: relationships between coworkers, leader-member exchange, and work attitudes. *Journal of Applied Psychology, 87*(3), 542. https://psycnet.apa.org/doi/10.1037/0021-9010.87.3.542.

Terpstra-Tong, J., Ralston, D. A., Treviño, L. J., Naoumova, I., de la Garza Carranza, M. T., Furrer, O., Li, Y., & Darder, F. L. (2020). The quality of leader-member exchange (LMX): A multilevel analysis of individual-level, organizational-level and societal-level antecedents. *Journal of International Management*, *26*(3), 1–18. https://doi.org.libproxy.library.wmich.edu/10.1016/j.intman.2020.100760.

Uhl-Bien, M., & Graen, G. B. (1993). Leadership-making in self-managing professional work teams: An empirical investigation. In K. E. Clark, M. B. Clark, & D. P. Campbell (Eds.), *The impact of leadership* (pp. 379–387). Leadership Library of America.

Van Dam, K., Oreg, S., & Schyns, B. (2008). Daily work contexts and resistance to organisational change: The role of leader-member exchange, development climate, and change process characteristics. *Applied Psychology: An International Review, 57*(2), 313–334.

Zagenczyk, T. J., Purvis, R. L., Shoss, M. K., Scott, K. L., & Cruz, K. S. (2015). Social influence and leader perceptions: Multiplex social network ties and similarity in leader–member exchange. *Journal of Business and Psychology, 30,* 105–117. https://doi.org/10.1007/s10869-013-9332-7.

Zhou, Q., Huo, D., & Wu, F. (2020). Different workplace currencies and employee voice: From the multidimensional approach of leader-member exchange. *Frontiers in Psychology, 11,* 589. https://doi.org/10.3389/fpsyg.2020.00589.

CHAPTER 2

Leadership & Communication: Demystifying the Steps to Success

Abstract Leadership is in the eye of the beholder (Fairhurst, 2016). And often the main criterion used to determine the quality of one's leadership is one's communication ability. Without adept communication skills in place, the leader is not likely to rack up too many successes, or those wins are likely to be short-lived. At its heart, leadership means to influence. Moreover, as the employee with more position power, the leader is charged with communicating on behalf of their team to argue for additional resources or remove organizational obstacles. This chapter provides leaders and employees with concrete steps to sharpen their communication skills. This chapter coaches readers on how active listening differs from simply hearing and presents the myriad benefits research shows of active listening. In addition to focusing on active listening and intentional word choice, immediacy behaviors—or nonverbal behaviors—are also presented to translate empirical data for immediate integration into the workplace. This chapter also provides readers with tangible solutions on how to navigate conflict between a leader and a member, among two or more members, and gives leaders tips for how to approach interpersonal challenges they may have with their own leader.

Keyword Leadership communication · Intentional verbal and nonverbal communication · Relationship development and maintenance · Conflict management

L. M. Omilion-Hodges and J. K. Ptacek, *Leader-Member Exchange and Organizational Communication*, New Perspectives in Organizational Communication, https://doi.org/10.1007/978-3-030-68756-4_2

Leadership is in the eye of the beholder (Fairhurst, 2016). And often, the main criterion used to determine the quality of one's leadership is one's communication ability. Why not a leader's output or organizational successes? Well, in short, because without adept communication skills in place, the leader is not likely to rack up too many successes or those wins are likely to be short-lived. At its heart, leadership means to influence. If a leader cannot communicate a clear vision, develop productive and trusting relationships with members, listen to their concerns, etc., then his or her tenure is likely to be brief. Moreover, as the workgroup employee with the most position power, the leader is charged with communicating on behalf of their team to argue for additional resources or alleviate organizational obstacles.

In concert with proactive leadership communication skills, this chapter also begins the conversation about successfully addressing and navigating conflict. Ignoring conflict does not mean that the misunderstanding is resolved or that it will simply go away. Unaddressed conflict often tends to grow legs and attach itself to other initially unrelated aspects of work. For example, a follower, harboring resentment at how a leader talked to them in a team meeting, may find themselves snapping at a peer or ignoring their leader's advice on a different project. Therefore, part and parcel of leadership communication are acknowledging conflict, facilitating dialogue, and helping parties move to resolution. This chapter leaves readers with tangible solutions for navigating the conflict between a leader and a member and among two or more members and gives leaders tips for approaching interpersonal challenges they may have with their leader.

Leader–Member Exchange Theory is Rooted and Enacted via Communication

Leader–member exchange is primarily seen as a leadership theory. Having the term "leader" as part of its name doesn't hurt, nor does the fact that the theory was designed to describe an approach to management from the leader's perspective. However, as leadership communication scholars, we argue that the theory could just as easily be cast as a communication theory.

Through the dyadic communicative exchanges enacted between leader and member, a relationship emerges, develops, and is maintained. Put simply, through a series of incremental leader–member interactions, from role taking to role routinization, varied interpersonal relationships arise between a leader and their members (Omilion-Hodges & Baker, 2017). This means that leader–member connections are produced by and are a product of communication. This also means that communication is among a leader's and a follower's most essential tools. Despite the clear and deciding role that communication plays in leader–member relationship development, early LMX research has been critiqued for assuming the role of communication rather than exploring it (Sheer, 2015).

Classic leader–member exchange research (Scandura et al., 1986; Uhl-Bien, 2006) acknowledges that these special dyadic associations develop through a series of "interacts," but does little to recognize the literal nature of these social exchanges. Numerous scholars (Seers et al., 2006; Sheer, 2015) have suggested that "the exchange in LMX suggests the need to assess actual exchanges between leader and member" (Liden & Maslyn, 1998, p. 67). In a review of LMX literature, communication researcher Vivian Sheer, suggested that "exchange is lost" in LMX theory (2015). Taken together, these calls highlight that communication is the foundation and scaffolding of leader–member exchange theory.

Relationships = Communication

Not only is communication the foundation and scaffolding of LMX, but communication fuels (and can deflate) relationships. Applying a communication lens to leader–member exchange theory helps to fill in some of the holes or cracks that scholars have pointed out in LMX over the years. Two primary areas that have received the most notable critiques include ambiguity in terms of literal leader–member communicative exchanges and the argument that the theory is nothing more than a measure of leader likeability.

Again, while the theory is built on the idea of exchange until recently, little was known about the concrete verbal and nonverbal communication interactions between leader and member. Glossing over the communication nuances not only conceals the exchange element of the theory, but it limits the potential of this theory to offer prescriptive advice to both leaders and members. Put simply, until specific exchanges were studied, scholars and practitioners could only provide general guidance on what to do and what not to do to broker an effective relationship with your leader or with your members. Thus, in the absence of specific communication exchanges, LMX stalled at the descriptive level of theory, which effectively limited its degree of usefulness, particularly for organizational members. An organizational theory that is more helpful to academics than toward practitioners is limited indeed.

The other lasting critique that LMX has suffered is being perceived as a measure of leader likeability or a binary indicator (high or low) of relationship quality. However, employing a communicative view provides breadth and depth in understanding how these unique dyadic relationships develop and may differ in nuanced ways even among high-quality and low-quality associations. A communicative lens rejects a rudimentary dichotomous view of leader–member relationships (e.g., either high or low-quality), and instead considers these partnerships on a continuum.

In sum, a communicative view of leader–member exchange addresses two long-standing critiques of the theory. Focusing on the fact that a leader and a member interact over time to accomplish organizational tasks allows us to consider the social and professional exchanges that naturally occur (Sheer, 2015). Taking this approach moves away from the broad strokes that have long been used to help explain leader–member relationships. While these macro means of organizing were helpful when the theory was in its initial stages of development in the 1970s, more nuanced ways of understanding the intricacies in relationship development are needed. Considering that a member's employee experience can differ greatly based on the quality of their relationship with their leader, it is important to offer as specific and prescriptive advice as possible. It has been suggested that if managers value their workgroup's collective functioning, they need to be aware of their relationships, their resource distribution, and member perceptions of relationships and resource distribution practices (Omilion-Hodges & Baker, 2013).

Employees Are Savvy Discerners of Managerial Behavior

Considering that relationships are built and sustained through communicative exchanges, workgroup members are privy to a general understanding of the quality and quantity of interactions between their leader and peers. Different conclusions can be drawn from the leader–member dyad that involves banter, laughter, and numerous formal and informal meetings, in contrast to the dyad that interacts only when necessary to address a work-related issue. These exchanges do not happen in a silo and as such, do not go unnoticed. This means that employees can compare their relationship with their leader to those their coworkers share with the leader. Employees may consider how frequently a manager engages with employees, their tone, and the exchanges' content and nature.

Omilion-Hodges and Baker (2013, 2017) studied LMX within the context of workgroups, especially concerning how employees made sense of their leader–member relationship in relation to their peers'. Through a series of experiments, focus groups, and surveys, the researchers found that employees are acutely aware of their peers' LMX levels and engage in sensemaking communication with each other to consider how the perceived equity of a colleague's LMX relationship. If an employee consistently produces high-quality results, then members generally accept that the leader would hold this employee in high regard. However, it gets fuzzier when members are not as clear on an employee's contributions, particularly if they seem to enjoy a high-status LMX relationship. Considering this, Omilion-Hodges and Baker (2017) offered three pieces of advice to managers:

1. **Manage Relationships:** Managers who strive to build unique interpersonal relationships with each employee will always fare better than those who do not. Yes, it is a lot of work, and it is asking a lot of managers who have role obligations above and beyond managing followers. However, taking the time to get to know each employee, their career and personal development goals, what motivates them, and what discourages them is likely to make the manager's work more effortless in the long run. This approach allows managers to align employees more strategically by harnessing employees' strengths and goals to meet workgroup and organizational demands. Managers would also be well served to ask questions such as what can I do to make your job easier, what have managers done in the past that has not worked, and how do you learn best.
2. **Manage Resources:** Managers are often the sole or at least guiding steward of their workgroup's resources. Resources can be considered as tangibles such as performance increases and support for professional development opportunities (i.e., travel to conferences, seminar tuition, training, etc.) or less tangible, but still, highly coveted entities like a flexible work schedule, being brought into prized projects, or mentorship. Research (Omilion-Hodges & Baker, 2017) found that managers can enact various positive resources *and* negative resources. Positive communication exchanges include bestowing or instilling a sense of the manager's

professional trust in an associate, professional development, affective communication that shows care, positive communication, intentional non-verbal communication behavior, and being accessible to employees. Negative communication exchanges a manager can enact include hindering an employee's ability to develop professionally, indicating a lack of trust in the employee's work, communicating verbally and nonverbally in a way that is perceived as disrespectful, and can also include betraying or excluding a follower.

3. **Manage Perceptions of Relationships and Resources:** Because leader–member relationships emerge and occur in a workgroup setting, it is naïve and just plain wrong to assume that followers are not aware of who is receiving what from the leader. Leaders do not have to feel as though they are working under a microscope. However, by being mindful of their language and actions and communicating clear expectations, managers can cultivate a workgroup that employees see as fair. Transparency is key. When employees know that two of their peers landed the prized account because their sales numbers were 15% higher than everyone else's, then the decision makes sense. Linking preferred behaviors with rewards and linking discouraged behaviors with consequences shows members the expectations and illustrates that their leader treats everyone equitably. With this approach, employees do not have to like a decision, but it becomes more palatable if they understand why it was made.

Taken together, leaders who are thoughtful about their verbal and nonverbal communication behaviors are likely to cultivate a much more inclusive and productive workgroup than those who look at leader–member relationships as a series of ad-hoc interactions. The following section dives more deeply into the influential role that communication plays in shaping a healthy work environment.

Addressing Organizational Obstacles with Communication

Although communication is anything but a one-size-fits-all endeavor, the thoughtful and tailored use of communication can solve or improve just about any work-related issue. From considering how to best onboard and assimilate new employees to create individual relationships with each member, pitch new ideas, and resolve interpersonal conflict, communication is more than a tool. Instead, it shapes the way employees experience and navigate work.

This section translates communication research and literature for non-communication experts to offer easy to integrate practices for employees of all levels, tenures, and across industries. After exploring the impact of a foundational view of communication, we discuss the connection between the leader and organizational communication, and employee engagement. We then narrow our focus to consider best practices for interpersonal relationship development and how using various channels (i.e., face to face, video meetings, conference calls, social media, etc.) may require leaders and members to flex their communication style to convey active listening and effective verbal and nonverbal behaviors. Consideration is also given to context, where we offer some guidance for how to match the message, the audience, the channel, and the situation effectively.

The Foundational Role of Communication

Communication scholars often talk about communication as foundational. You may also hear communicators talk about communication as meaning-making. These approaches suggest the importance of moving away from the antiquated view of communication as a tool.

Early conceptualizations of communication suggested that communication was essentially an instrument used to fix a faux pas or pull out only when a message went awry. However, this view severely limits the pervasive role, and impact communication plays in our everyday lives. Adopting a view of communication as foundational encourages us to view all interactions and interpretations of others' verbal and nonverbal behavior as relational and interdependent. Thus, a leader and a member who continues to be at odds on a particular project are not likely to come to a shared understanding by merely stating their arguments in different words or by annunciating more clearly or speaking louder. Yet, these tend to be the most frequent and first used approaches to being understood. However, it is not likely that the leader or member did not hear the other or did not understand the basis of the other's argument. Instead, the conflict stems from a disagreement in meaning-making. Put simply, because they both come from different perspectives and may possess slightly different goals and values, they each see their suggestion as the "right" one. Yet, adopting a foundational view of communication would help each member take a step back and seek to understand before being understood. Even if one of the parties can do this, it can diffuse tension and allow the dyad (or group) to reorient around the shared goal.

A foundational view of communication often allows parties to realize and connect over shared values or other similarities. In the instance above, if either the leader or member were to adopt a foundational role of communication, they would likely point out that the disagreement stems from the fact that they are each passionate about the project and want to see it executed well. Taking a moment to reflect on their shared goal also allows them to discuss other primary or secondary goals. For example, the leader may be making specific suggestions because they have additional information about what the C-suit or board members expect. On the other hand, the employee may be pushing for their recommendations to be implemented to illustrate to their leader that they are deserving of more responsibility or a promotion. As they communicate from this perspective, they can move to a meaning-centered approach.

Imes et al. (2021, pp. 15–16) considered the foundational role of communication in team-based environments. Though they focused on specific advice for those in the healthcare setting, the suggestions will elevate anyone's ability to communicate and relate across industries. These suggestions include:

- **Intentional Language:** One of the authors (Imes et al., 2021) had a manager who would refer to her followers as "rock stars" in team meetings and other workgroup interactions. However, anytime the manager's peers or her leader would visit the department, the "rock stars" were always referred to as "just my staff." This turn may seem slight, and some may argue that it would have been inappropriate for the manager to use the term "rock stars," yet other terms would be viewed as both professional and inclusive. Substituting "team" or even "group" for "staff" would have helped to promote continued trust and respect at all levels. Thinking about how it could feel to be on the receiving end of various comments helps all employees.
- **Tone:** This communication tip can be boiled down to not necessarily what is said, but how it is said. Continuing with the example above, if the manager had said "my staff" with warmth and affection in her voice, it would have certainly evoked different responses in her members than when she would say it dryly and often with a

dismissive shrug. It becomes imperative to be aware of tone when delivering bad or unexpected news, during times of constructive criticism, and when engaging with preferred and least preferred coworkers. Leader–member exchange theory does not suggest that leaders have to become best friends with all members. Instead, it means that leaders should *try* to develop effective relationships with each member. However, it is often easier to communicate with warmth and patience with those we like than those we find more challenging or have a harder time connecting with. Considering this, titled leaders should reflect on their member relationships to be mindful of how these distinctions may become even more pronounced based on their go-to tone with each follower.

- **Other-Oriented Focus:** In many ways, this one communicative approach illustrates the foundational role of communication. This is a macro approach to considering relationships and communication. It is easier said than done, but when some become practiced at taking an other-oriented focus, it can help minimize misunderstandings and reduce conflict. As the name suggests, this communication practice means focusing on the other person's perspective rather than figuring out how to bolster your argument. It's not easy to put someone else's needs first, particularly when it feels like something is at stake (such as a project's success). However, by taking an other-oriented approach, perceived conflict can often be quickly diffused. A shared understanding (i.e., we both want what is best for the project) emerges more rapidly than if we continue to reiterate our stance repeatedly and likely, more loudly. An other-oriented approach does not mean that you are not heard or walked all over; contrarily, those who take an other-oriented approach tend to be highly regarded. Why is that? Because it shows complexity in thought and problem-solving while simultaneously enacting a relational approach.
- **Active Listening:** Briefly discussed in Chapter 1, active listening often offers a practical and direct route to successful relationship development and maintenance. Active listening certainly includes hearing your conversational partner, but it ensures that you're on the same page more than anything. In addition to attending to the content of a message, active listening includes asking questions, paraphrasing, and summarizing to indicate that you are interpreting

messages as they are intended. This approach helps to guard against messages being lost in translation.

- **Meaning-Centered Approach:** A meaning-centered approach is the apex of a foundational view of communication. A meaning-centered approach infuses active listening, intentional language, tone, and as a result, is the ultimate enactment of an other-oriented perspective. Meaning-centered communicators are cognitively complex and work hard to observe and engage with others and their environments in thoughtful and meaningful ways. A meaning-centered approach also means that communicators take responsibility for what they say, including owning mistakes and missteps. This approach does not mean that communicators are exempt from the occasional faux pas, but rather when it occurs, they acknowledge the error and take steps to rectify the situation.

Considering the foundational role of communication makes it easier to see the link between intentional leadership and organizational communication, and employee engagement. Table 2.1 provides additional examples of how to enact meaning-centered communication.

Making the Connection: Communication and Employee Engagement

Historically, organizations have spent most of their time and financial and human resources on their communications to external stakeholders. Of course, this makes good sense as they need clients and the community's interest and trust to remain in business. However, this view may be a bit short-sighted as it overlooks the importance of communicating to and connecting with employees.

In many ways, titled leaders serve as a proxy for the organization itself. Especially in large and structurally complex organizations, employees at certain levels may never have the opportunity to interact with individuals in the C-suite or other high-level executives. Even in mid-sized or smaller organizations, status distinctions or the way departments and projects are organized may prohibit employees from all levels from interacting in meaningful ways. This means that an employee's manager becomes a stand-in for the organization as a whole. However, several issues stem from this setup. For example, if an employee does not like or trust their manager, all messages may be interpreted with suspicion. Employees may also feel like they are left out or overlooked when messages are

Table 2.1 Say this, not that: moving to a meaning-centered view of communication

Reactive response	*Meaning-centered response*	*The difference*
"You just don't understand."	"How can I best support you?"	There is a good chance that the employee already knows that they are falling short of expectations. It will be more productive to engage in a conversation about what resources they need to be successful.
"Failure is not an option."	"What safeguards do we have built in if we're not able to fulfill the project in its entirety by the deadline?"	The reactive response frames work output as an either or: either we succeed or we fail. A more productive approach is to strive to innovate, while also being realistic about moving parts. This approach also allows employees to celebrate mini victories and triumphs throughout the project rather than making it feel like an all or nothing situation.
"That's not important. Forget about it."	"It sounds like you've thought of some potential concerns. Let's talk about them."	The reactive response assumes the leader has thought of everything and the member's ideas are worthless. It is important to remember, especially when you're immersed in a project, that others will likely have helpful suggestions because they are approaching it from a different perspective.
"Time off? It feels like you just took time off."	"I'm glad to see you're using your vacation days. Good for you. It's important to take time off."	Shaming employees for using the time off that they earned is not okay. While an employee may have planned a vacation in a less than ideal time for work matters, it is important to encourage and support work/life balance.

(continued)

Table 2.1 (continued)

Reactive response	*Meaning-centered response*	*The difference*
"Because that is the way it has always been done."	"There is a lot of history and tradition in this project, but it's important to always consider how to improve and innovate. I'd love to hear your suggestions."	The reactive response is reminiscent of the traditional parenting response, "because I said so." It effectively shuts down conversation and implicitly tells employees that their opinions do not matter.

Source Adapted from Blink (n.d.), Desjardins (2019), and Young Entrepreneur Council (2015)

directed externally first or if their concerns and suggestions continue to go unanswered.

Communication researchers (Omilion-Hodges & Baker, 2014) explored this issue. They found several standard organizational stumbling blocks that leaders fall prey to in attempting to deliver or, worse yet, overlooking the importance of internal communication with members. The stumbling blocks include:

- **Misleading or withholding information:** Not being transparent or forthcoming about information, especially when it directly impacts employees (e.g., reorganizations, layoffs, etc.).
- **Organizational dishonesty:** This may stem from a poor reputation, increased employee surveillance, and mismatch with employee values.
- **Pseudo open-door policy:** Many CEOs and executives tout the open-door policy, encouraging members of all levels to stop by at any time. However, very few can accommodate this claim.
- **Invisible leaders:** Due to the nature of their work, leaders may find themselves in a series of closed-door meetings for the bulk of the workday. However, this does little to connect with other employees or role model preferred behaviors in the organization .

The good news is that there are many communicative stepping stones that leaders and organizations can take to foster employee engagement and sidestep the stumbling blocks. One of the most effective and quickest ways to promote employee engagement is by having titled leaders model intentional and inclusive communication. If the organization wants employees to engage in active listening and employ an other-oriented focus, training leaders to do so will go a long way. Additionally, when supervisors and directors lead by example, it tells employees what is expected, and it provides a clear demonstration of the desired behaviors. It is one thing to tell someone how to be an effective communicator by giving them a list or a verbal directive. Still, it is another to have a leader who is patient, who actively listens, and who focuses on meaning-making rather than being heard.

Another way to connect with employees and to encourage employee engagement is by building an internal brand. The antiquated view was to brand for external audiences, but a more contemporary approach suggests that employees should also be viewed as an essential audience. Building an internal brand helps establish a community and helps employees connect with their organization and its mission. This also means that organizations and leaders are thoughtful in considering how best to reach employees of all levels. Stagecoach, for example, created an employee app to provide information and resources to associates. Not only did this help to make work easier for their employees, but considering that up to 30,000 Stagecoach employees interface directly with patrons, but it has also helped to enhance customer service ("11 Companies with Great Organizational Communication and How You Can Follow Suit," 2019). Apps and other virtual and face-to-face communication tools provide employees with opportunities to collaborate, problem solve, and innovate within and across teams. Moreover, organizations like 3M afford employees up to 15% of their workdays to engage in ideation and innovation individually and collaboratively. This gives employees space to explore new ideas, but one of the underlying takeaways is that employees are appreciated and encouraged to work autonomously.

Employees are vital to an organization's success or instrumental in its failure. Employing strategic organizational and leadership communication to facilitate an effective, productive, and satisfied workplace often has little to no financial cost but often results in a healthy work environment and may reduce turnover. Table 2.2 presents an organizational profile highlighting a successful internal communication campaign.

Table 2.2 Leadership in action—organizational profile: Thomson Reuters

With the goal to innovate and to engage employees in strategic change, Thomson Reuters introduced the #dare2disrupt campaign. The campaign stemmed from a realization that innovation organization-wide was lagging.
The campaign had three main foci:
1. Cultivating innovation
2. Collaboration between teams
3. Creating and disrupting
How did they engage 50,000 global employees in this internal communication campaign? They met employees where they were—virtually and face to face.
Team lunches and inspiration sessions were held regularly and boards were put up electronically and in office locations so employees could leave positive or inspiring messages for peers. Thomas Reuters also sponsored innovation challenges, startup bootcamps, and brought in coder dojos to assist with teaching new skills and sparking creativity.
The result? By communicating with employees and bringing them into strategic decision-making processes, Thomson Reuters has already seen an increase in the number of innovation project requests submitted across the organization. The company is also reshaping their culture to be one grounded in open and frequent communication and innovation.

Source Thomson Reuters (2020)

Reading the Room: Context Matters

While Chapter 7 focuses exclusively on this topic, we want to introduce context early in the book. Beginning to think about some of the fundamental aspects of communication can help to inform the link between LMX and organizational communication in subsequent chapters.

Since leadership is synonymous with influence and influence is enacted or stalled via communication, it is crucial to consider some communication fundamentals.

One way to consider communication fundamentals is as an equation. Unlike a traditional math problem, you are not solving for one correct answer. However, there are still some constants to be considered: audience, message, and channel. By reflecting on these elements, you are considering the context of the situation and making intentional decisions regarding:

1. What am I communicating?
2. To whom am I communicating?
3. And how can I best communicate my message?

By starting with the content of the message, it helps managers to make decisions about whom to communicate and how to deliver the news. News of organizational layoffs, for example, may best be given to individual members based on the details of the event rather than to the workgroup as a whole. This is especially true if layoffs are likely to impact individual members more directly than other workgroup members. After considering the message's content and to whom the message is intended, managers can decide if a face-to-face conversation is appropriate or if the news should be documented in an email or official memo. Some messages, such as a quick touch base on a project's detail, might best be delivered via an organizational instant messaging system or another internal informal communication channel like email.

When leaders (and members) consider the questions above, it becomes easier to see that communication is fluid and that so long as some thought is given to the audience, content, and channel that even the delivery of bad news can be done tactfully and in a way that preserves the integrity of message receivers. Relatedly, reflecting on these questions can also help show leaders the quality of their various leader–member relationships. For example, suppose a leader always selects a formal organizational channel such as email or memo. In that case, it can be an indicator of a low-quality exchange relationship that the manager wishes to formally document. On the other hand, if the manager finds that they reach out to a follower via text or an IM-based platform, it may reiterate that they share a high-quality relationship based on mutual trust and respect. For more specifics and details regarding the communication context, see Chapter 7. Table 2.3 explores how leaders can enact immediacy behaviors—verbal and nonverbal expressions of warmth—via various communication channels.

Communicating Through Muddy Waters: Communication Accommodation and Conflict Management

Even the most thoughtful messages may not be interpreted as such or may otherwise miss their mark. This is part of communication. However, it is after a miscommunication occurs that becomes the most important. Unaddressed communication or relational missteps generally do not resolve on their own. Worse yet, if communication issues persist in dyads

Table 2.3 Sharpening your communication skills: enacting immediacy or warmth behaviors across channels & contexts

Immediacy behaviors are verbal and nonverbal communication behaviors that indicate engagement and inspire positive feelings such as liking and closeness. These behaviors can be modeled through active listening, open and attentive body language, vocal tone, etc. While you may have an idea of how to show coworkers that you're engaged and listening in a face to face conversation, you may not be quite as confident in what this looks like in other channels or contexts.
• **Face-to-Face:** Making eye contact, taking an audience-centered approach regarding delivery of message content, paraphrasing others' statements, asking questions, arms unfolded, body angled toward speaker
• **Face-to-Face—Delivery of Bad or Challenging News:** Even vocal tone, thoughtful audience analysis in terms of audience needs, expectations, feelings, and enacting empathy through eye contact and open body language
• **Text Message/Instant Message:** Consider if content would be better delivered through a face to face or telephone conversation, avoid sarcasm, review for accuracy, use positive language and greeting. If you receive text or IM messages, respond in a timely manner
• **Phone Call:** Positive vocal tone, asking questions, paraphrase, and summarize
• **Video Chat:** Similar to face to face suggestions, but be mindful to stay engaged and focused on the other

or groups, it can exacerbate challenges and make slight communication gaps feel like insurmountable obstacles.

One theory that can help both leaders and members be more successful in their workplace communication is communication accommodation theory (CAT; Giles & Ogay, 2007). CAT addresses how individuals may modify their verbal and nonverbal communication behaviors to minimize or increase the social connection between themselves and others. Giles and colleagues (Giles & Coupland, 1991; Giles & Ogay, 2007) found that in communicating with another or within groups, individuals tend to alter their communication tendencies to either emphasize their connection and similarity to others, or they can use their communication behaviors as a way to emphasize differences, thereby increasing social distance.

The theory highlights communication complexity in dyads and groups by pointing out that we may not always be successful in our communication. Does this mean that the theorists suggest that we should hide or otherwise conceal our unique identity? No, not in the slightest. Instead, CAT suggests that we return to the three questions addressed above: What am I communicating? To whom am I communicating? And how am I going to share the message? Considering this, a manager may decide it is better to address one follower's performance review from the communicative perspective as the formal manager. For another follower, it may behoove the situation to address the performance evaluation as a friend.

Coupling communication fundamentals with CAT, the following section highlights some things to consider when encountering conflict in various workgroup relationships. Chapter 8 dives more deeply into conflict management and conflict styles within the context of leadership failures; however, the basics are addressed below. General guidelines for managing conflict (Edwards et al., 2019) are considered before reviewing specific scenarios:

- **Address the conflict promptly:** If tempers are high, it is vital to take a step back and allow everyone to cool off so they can approach a conversation with a level-head. However, waiting too long to address conflict can give the impression that it is resolved when it is not. Also, failing to address the issue may leave one, or both parties feeling disrespected or unvalued.
- **Talk about the issue face to face if possible:** While it may feel more comfortable to retreat to one's desk or office and rattle off an apology via email or text, this introduces an increased risk of misunderstanding. Face-to-face communication integrates nonverbal behaviors and tone, which can go a long way in portraying empathy and sincerity.
- **Use I statements:** Using I statements is routinely ranked as a best communication practice and becomes essential in times of conflict. Using I language allows you to avoid blaming or shaming language, instead allowing parties to express their feelings. Thus, instead of saying, "You make me so angry," a manager may say, "I feel frustrated about the outcome of the client meeting."
- **Focus on the issue, not the person:** By focusing on the issue, perhaps an important project, instead of the other person, organizational members can keep the discussion professional. Also, by returning to the project's goals, employees may be able to connect on their shared interests instead of their frustration with each other or their various work styles.
- **Practice active listening:** This suggestion will continue to pop up throughout the book because practicing active listening can efficiently nip conflict in the bud (in addition to help build and maintain relationships). Active listening means focusing on the other's

content, tone, and body language(s). It does not mean appearing to listen while actually formulating a mental rebuttal. When you're engaging in active listening, it becomes easier to understand the other's perspective, which may allow you to focus on similarities or, at the very least, to know where the other person is coming from.

Conflict Between Leader and Member

In addition to enacting the conflict resolution guidelines addressed above, leaders and members are encouraged to put themselves in the other's shoes. As Edwards and colleagues (2020, p. 149) acknowledge, "most of the time, each person is correct about at least part of the problem." Enacting empathy can allow both leader and a member the opportunity to try to understand where the other is coming from and to acknowledge the potential benefits of each party's point of view.

Unresolved conflict between leader and member can lead to infrequent or hostile communication. This is akin to losing an arm of the workgroup. It is in the best interest of the leader, the member, and the workgroup as a whole for dyads to engage in open, honest, and collaborative communication.

Research indicates that if members feel their leader has mistreated a coworker or the leader is otherwise wrong and has not attempted to rectify the situation, employees will come together to make sense of the issue. Leaving members to try to make sense of negative events on their own, especially those that appear to stem from the leader's behavior, is likely to damage the workgroup's climate (Hooper & Martin, 2008; see Sias & Jablin, 1995 for seminal communication perspective).

Conflict Between Members

Conflict between members can also prove toxic to a workgroup. Lateral communication, like that between members, can be incredibly challenging if several members are vying for one promotion or otherwise feel like they are in competition rather than working in concert. Part of the reason that this type of workgroup conflict can be particularly disastrous is that members may start to withhold or distort information from each other as a means to get ahead. One way that leaders can guard against such behavior is to reward collaboration. That means doing more than giving lip service to working together, but perhaps even tying bonuses and performance goals to collaborative successes. Suppose a manager becomes aware of employees withholding information or otherwise engaging in behavior that does not promote the group's values and goals. In that case, the leader should act decisively and swiftly link said behavior to consequences.

Conflict Between Leaders

This describes a situation when a titled leader is experiencing conflict with their leader. How is this different from the leader–member conflict described above? When a titled leader is experiencing discord in their leader–member relationship, it can easily bleed over into their workgroup relationships. This may look like the leader being short or less patient with followers, or it may reduce resources to the workgroup because the manager's manager disagrees with the direction the team is headed. Thus, not only does this type of conflict embody traditional leader–member challenges, but it also can present unique challenges for other organizational members. It may interfere with their ability to meet organizational goals.

Leadership Moments: Takeaways for Leaders & Members

- **Leadership and Communication are Part and Parcel:** Leadership involves the act and art of influence. Influence is modeled and articulated through verbal and nonverbal communication. Leaders who fail to reflect on their communication strengths and weaknesses cap their leadership potential. Focusing on communication allows leaders to develop stronger workgroup relationships, reach goals more quickly, and successfully navigate conflict.
- **Model the Behaviors You Want to Encourage:** Social learning theory (Bandura, 1977) suggests that those in positions of influence (i.e., leaders, parents, teachers, older siblings, etc.) should model the behaviors they want to encourage. While titled leaders are trained on their jobs' task-related elements, the relational or communicative aspects are often ignored or presumed. However, if an organization or a specific leader wishes for members to use intentional, inclusive, and other-oriented communication, then this behavior has to start with those in titled leadership positions.

- **Meaning-Making is the Gold Standard, but Any Mindfulness in Speech and Deed Will Go Far:** Subscribing to a meaning-making view of communication is the first step. There are many, many other steps between valuing a meaning-making view and developing the expertise to continually enact it. While modeling this gold standard of communication behavior is challenging, the good news is that practicing mindfulness and reflection in one's communication will make a difference. Meaning-making is like any other communication skill, like public speaking, for example; the more often the skill is utilized, the more comfortable and natural it becomes. The more time you take to practice active listening, audience analysis, and remaining present during exchanges, the closer you are to a meaning-making view of communication.

Mini Case Study: "I Wasn't Hired to Make Friends."

As the HR manager, you find yourself in a predicament. Your organization landed the prized computer engineer that they had been headhunting for years. Everyone was excited about how the engineer would elevate the organization, and employees were giddy at the chance to work with and learn from this industry leader. However, just six weeks in, there are a slew of complaints and concerns. While everyone is quick to acknowledge the engineer's skill and know-how, they are just as quick to acknowledge how "challenging," "abrasive," and "borderline rude," the new employee is. When you brought the employee into your office to discuss these concerns, the engineer replied, "I wasn't hired to make friends," before standing up and walking out of the meeting. You're left considering what to do next.

1. How can you help the engineer to understand the impact of intentional communication?
2. What are three concrete tips you could give the engineer about improving one's workplace communication skills?
3. How could you convince the engineer that working on their communication skills would increase their leadership ability?

References

Bandura, A. (1977). *Social learning theory*. Englewood Cliffs, NJ: Prentice-Hall.

Bently-Edwards, K. L., Stevenson, H. C., Thomas, D. E., Adams-Bass, V. N., & Coleman-King, C. (2020). Teaching sacred: Pre-service teacher appraisals of racial stress, socialization and classroom management self-efficiency. *Social Psychology of Education, 23,* 1233–1257. https://doi.org/10.1007/s11218-020-09578-8.

Blink (n.d.) *The companies nailing internal communication today: 11 inspiring examples*. https://joinblink.com/blog/11-companies-with-great-organizational-communication-and-how-you-can-follow-suit.

Desjardins, J. (2019, May 27). *11 Things Leaders Should Never Say to Their Teams*. Visual Capitalist. https://www.visualcapitalist.com/11-things-leaders-should-never-say-to-their-team/.

Edwards, A., Edwards, C., Wahl, S.T., & Myers, S.A. (2019). *The communication age: Connecting and engaging* (3rd ed.). Sage Publishing.

Fairhurst, G. T. (2016). Reflections on leadership and ethics in complex times. *Atlantic Journal of Communication, 24*(1), 61–69.

Giles, H., & Coupland, N. (1991). *Language: Contexts and consequences.* Thomson Brooks/Cole Publishing Co.

Giles, H., & Ogay, T. (2007). Communication accommodation theory. In B. B. Whaley & W. Samter (Eds.), *Explaining communication: Contemporary theories and exemplars* (pp. 293–310). Mahwah, NJ: Lawrence Erlbaum. Retrieved from: https://doc.rero.ch/record/306556/files/2007_gilesogay_cat.pdf.

Hooper, D. T., & Martin, R. (2008). Beyond personal leader-member exchange (LMX) quality: The effects of perceived LMX variability on employee reactions. *The Leadership Quarterly, 19*(1), 20–30.

Imes, R. S., Omilion-Hodges, L.M., & Hester, J.D.B. (2021), *Communication and care coordination for the palliative care team: A handbook for building and maintaining optimal teams*. Spring Publishing Company.

Liden, R. C., & Maslyn, J. M. (1998). Multidimensionafity of leader-member exchange: An empirical assessment through scale development. *Journal of Management, 24,* 43–72. https://doi.org/10.1177/014920639802400105.

Omilion-Hodges, L. M., & Baker, C. R. (2013). Contextualizing LMX within the workgroup: The effects of LMX and justice on relationship quality and resource sharing among peers. *Leadership Quarterly, 24*(6), 935–951.

Omilion-Hodges, L. M., & Baker, C. R. (2014). Everyday talk and convincing conversations: Utilizing strategic internal communication. *Business Horizons, 57*(3), 435–445. https://doi.org/10.1016/j.bushor.2014.02.002.

Omilion-Hodges, L. M., & Baker, C. R. (2017). Communicating leader-member relationship quality: The development of leader communication exchange scales to measure relationship building and maintenance through the exchange of communication-based goods. *International Journal of Business Communication, 54*(2), 115–145. https://doi.org/10.1177/2329488416687052.

Scandura, T. A., Graen, G. B., & Novak, M. A. (1986). When managers decide not to decide autocratically: An investigation of leader–member exchange and decision influence. *Journal of Applied Psychology, 71*(4), 579–579. https://doi.org/10.5465/AMBPP.1986.4980620.

Seers, A., Wilkerson, J. M., & Grubb, W. L. (2006). Toward measurement of social exchange resources: Reciprocal contributions and receipts. *Psychological Reports, 98,* 508–510.

Sheer, V. C. (2015). "Exchange lost" in leader-member exchange theory and research: A critique and a reconceptualization. *Leadership, 11*(2), 213–229. https://doi.org/10.1177/1742715014530935.

Sias, P. M., & Jablin, F. M. (1995). Differential superior-subordinate relations, perceptions of fairness, and coworker communication. *Human Communication Research, 22*(1), 5–38. https://doi.org/10.1111/j.1468-2958.1995.tb00360.x.

Thomson Reuters. (2020, November 17). *Top 10 reasons to join Thomas Reuters.* https://www.thomsonreuters.com/en/careers/careers-blog/top-10-reasons-to-join-thomson-reuters.html.

Uhl-Bien, M. (2006). Relational leadership theory: Exploring the social processes of leadership and organizing. *Leadership Quarterly, 17*(6), 654–676. https://doi.org/10.1016/j.leaqua.2006.10.007.

Young Entrepreneur Council. (2015, July 6). *9 Things Good Leaders Never Say.* Success. https://www.success.com/9-things-good-leaders-never-say/.

CHAPTER 3

Coworkers: Sources of Support or Relationships Gone Sour

Abstract It has been argued that peers make the place (Chiaburu & Harrison, 2008). For many, developing relationships with their coworkers can be a source of informational and social support and a trusted sounding board (Madlock & Booth-Butterfield, 2012). However, research illustrates that developing strong relationships with peers may not be as easy as it seems on the surface. Instead, the quality of the relationship one shares with their leader largely dictates who they are likely to befriend. Namely, those with high-quality leader-member relationships tend to develop trusted associations with each other, and the same goes for those with less effective leader-member relationships. Life for in-group members, those who have high-quality leader-member relationships, tends to continue to look up in the form of their peer relationships. This also means that out-group members receive fewer positive resources from their leaders and collectively have less to share or exchange with other out-group members. This suggests that once someone has become an out-group member, it becomes difficult if not impossible, to transform their employee experience. After translating relevant coworker-exchange literature for readers, this chapter focuses on providing practical tips for employees to enhance their peer relationships.

Keywords Coworker exchange theory · Peer relationships · Generational cohorts · Career stage · Mentoring

L. M. Omilion-Hodges and J. K. Ptacek, *Leader-Member Exchange and Organizational Communication*, New Perspectives in Organizational Communication, https://doi.org/10.1007/978-3-030-68756-4_3

LMX and CWX: How and Why LMX Affects Your Peer Relationships

Coworker exchange theory (CWX; Sherony & Green, 2002) describes the quality of the relationship shared by two coworkers who report to the same leader. Like leader–member exchange (LMX), CWX rests on the theoretical foundation of social exchange theory (SET; Blau, 1964). Social exchange theory describes the interdependent social interactions in relationships, noting that individuals often undergo a relatively complex set of cost and benefit analyses in these exchanges. Exchange relationships tend to be marked by fairly even exchange among parties, where members tend to keep a mental tally of what has been given in contrast to what has been received. This quid pro quo approach to relationships tends to fall away as relationships mature into friendships or associations built on mutual trust and respect.

LMX and CWX go hand in hand. Because leaders develop relationships of different quality with each follower, members can look around the workgroup and make social comparisons about their leader–member relationship in contrast to their peers'. Sherony and Green (2002) first explained the link through balance theory (Heider, 1958). The researchers (2002) suggested that coworker dyads would be in balance when two employees shared a similar (either low, moderate, or high-quality) relationship with their leader. Their (Sherony & Green, 2002) empirical research reiterated this hypothesis. Others' findings (i.e., Bornay-Barrachina & Herrero, 2018; Erdogan & Bauer, 2014; Omilion-Hodges & Baker, 2013) have also demonstrated that coworkers tend to prefer peers who share a relationship with the leader that is similar to their own. Why is this? For better or worse, it is likely that these two coworkers have somewhat similar workplace experiences. If they are in-group members, they likely enjoy access to high-status projects, frequent and positive leader–member communication, and increased organizational and personal resources (i.e., professional development, mentoring, role latitude, etc.). Those who have less copasetic leader–member relationships may commiserate over feeling micromanaged by their leader, stunted in their career progress, or left out of more desirable projects.

The fact that research continues to show consistent links between LMX and CWX reiterates the power communication plays in leadership and workgroup dynamics. Again, relationships flourish or flounder as a result of a series of communicative interactions. What's more? In workgroup settings, these exchanges, whether between a leader and a member or among peers, are visible and observed by others. When it's not clear why an individual member receives more of the leader's praise or attention, workgroup members engage in dialogue and try to make sense of the preferential treatment and the quality of the relationship (Omilion-Hodges & Baker, 2017; Sias & Jablin, 1995). This sets off additional dialogue and opportunities to kindle or distance relationships. In short, leader–member and peer relationships are interconnected in a web that is impossible to disentangle. While Chapter 4 looks specifically at team-member exchange or the sum of all workgroup relationships, this chapter dives more deeply into dyadic peer or coworker exchange relationships.

The Impact of Peer Relationships

Peer relationships have been linked to many positive personal and organizational outcomes such as job satisfaction, organizational commitment, communication satisfaction, and decreases in workplace alienation (Madlock & Booth-Butterfield, 2012). While the literature skews positive, there are some potential challenges or drawbacks associated with peer relationships, such as emotional exhaustion (Methot et al., 2016).

Part of the reason that peers are as influential as they are is because of the variety of needs they help meet and the variety of roles they fulfill. Like those we develop with workplace peers, interpersonal relationships help to satisfy our inclusion, control, and affective needs (Schutz, 1966). In the theory of interpersonal needs, Schutz suggests that we are hard-wired to connect with others and develop relationships to meet these needs. Dotan (2009) uncovered additional reasons why we may seek to develop friendships with peers: work safety/trust, to fill a missing role, sanity check, work values/life-interests similarity, proximity, and instrumentality. These reasons cover affective, and belongingness needs, such as when one develops a workplace friendship to fill the role a friend or family member fulfills outside of work. Dotan's workplace friendship formation framework also highlights strategic or professional reasons for establishing friendships at work, from having a validation and affirmation source to having greater access to promotions or increased social capital.

Peer relationships can also be consistent sources of social support. Typically considered in three distinct veins, access to social support can radically transform a workplace from hell to heaven (Chiaburu &

Harrison, 2008). Peers can lend emotional support by responding empathetically to a frustrated coworker or by listening to their ideas. This type of support is characterized by trusting communication. As is suggested by the name, informational support describes situations where you approach a coworker for their advice, expertise, or know-how. The third type of social support—instrumental—explains scenarios when peers provide tangible aid. Examples of instrumental support include a peer attending a meeting in your stead or volunteering to lead event set-up or clean-up so that you can attend to other matters.

With a working understanding of the impact and role peer relationships play in the workplace, we now consider empirical benefits and potential challenges associated with peer relationships. We will discuss some foundational outcomes of peer relationships but focus primarily on the coworker exchange relationship as it relates to leader–member exchange.

Benefits of Peer Relationships

In a meta-analysis of peer-related workplace outcomes, Chiaburu and Harrison (2008) suggested that peers make the place, adding unique influence above and beyond that of the leader. The authors found that peers serve as a "rich source of help and information, which is associated with a reduction in their colleagues' role ambiguity, conflict, and overload" (p. 1094). Chiaburu and Harrison revealed that peers also inspired higher levels of organizational commitment in each other in addition to job satisfaction and role engagement in ways that a leader's influence alone could not. Similarly, research has also indicated that peer relationships are the most pivotal (in contrast to the leader) in inspiring employee creativity and innovation (Choi, 2012; Omilion-Hodges & Ackerman, 2018).

Supportive peer relationships are also linked to prosocial behavioral outcomes, including role performance and increased organizational citizenship behaviors. Others (Madlock & Booth-Butterfield, 2012) have found that by communicating and connecting in specific ways, such as through effective conflict management, shared tasks, and positivity, individuals' inclusion needs are fulfilled (Schutz, 1958, 1966). Madlock and Booth-Butterfield (2012) point out that engaging in positive communication with peers can satisfy affection needs, sharing task-related information aligns with inclusion needs, and conflict management parallels control needs. In short, engaging in positive communication with peers can lead to social support and help realize our interpersonal needs when we are away from family members and friends (Dotan, 2009). When employees feel supported, and their task and relational needs are met, they remain more committed to their employer and experience increased job, role, and communication satisfaction (Chiaburu & Harrison, 2008; Madlock & Booth-Butterfield, 2012).

Not only can peer relationships lead to increases in intangibles such as satisfaction and creativity, but they can also lead to more tangible outcomes such as augmented access to various resources. Omilion-Hodges and Baker (2013, 2017) found that employees exchange resources with workgroup peers. However, they don't exchange with just any peer. Employees report (Omilion-Hodges & Baker, 2017) sharing information, feedback, validation, and mentoring advice with the peers they share a high-quality CWX relationship with. This can undoubtedly be viewed as a benefit of peer relationships—especially for in-group members. These employees likely already have increased access to resources via their high-quality leader–member exchange relationship, which becomes compounded through their associations with other high-status actors. What does this look like in the workplace? Through a series of focus groups (Omilion-Hodges & Baker, 2017), employees reported being aware of who (which member) received what (which resource) from the leader. This means that you may ask one employee to pop into the leader's office to ask a question when the door is closed, where you may be the go-to if employees want to learn about the leader's thoughts or feedback on a task. Trusting peer relationships can help employees personally and professionally.

Considering the overwhelmingly positive outcomes associated with supportive peer relationships, it is of little surprise that some have suggested that peer relationships may have the most substantial effect of all the workplace relationships (Baker & Omilion-Hodges, 2013; Takeuchi et al., 2011). Why has it been suggested that peer relationships may be the most crucial of all workgroup relationships? Peers tend to be perceived as more accessible and more approachable than leaders. Additionally, peers can provide unique feedback and insight that may provide unparalleled support or motivation that employees may not have formulated fully on their own or in limited interactions with their leader (Chen et al., 2014). These findings do not take away from the leader's role, but rather because of the multiple role demands and status distinction, peers are better aligned to form friendships and likely have more time to engage in discussion and ideation than leader–member dyads do.

While peer associations tend to act as buffers against the stress of work by providing support and offering additional sources of information and resources, employees should consider potential challenges in or because of peer relationships.

Potential Challenges of Peer Relationships

Just as peer relationships can augment an employee's workplace experience, they can also detract from it. Below we discuss some of the reasons that peer relationships sour; however, it is important to point out the link between LMX and CWX. As discussed above, workgroup members tend to gravitate toward peers who share a relationship with the leader that is similar to their own. This alone should give leaders all of the reasoning they need to develop high-quality relationships with each employee. In workgroups with high-LMX variance, low-LMX members may feel relatively deprived compared to high-LMX peers (Bolino & Turnley, 2009). They may experience lower job satisfaction and overall decreases in their well-being (Hooper & Martin, 2008), which is likely to explain why members are less likely to remain committed to the organization (Wikaningrum, 2007). Moreover, considerable variation in the quality of leader–member exchange relationships in workgroups is linked to increases in team conflict (Boies & Howell, 2006) and feelings of contempt from low-LMX employees for their high-LMX peers. In sum, while it may not be possible to develop high-LMX relationships with all members, it is undoubtedly in the leader's best interest and the employees to attempt to do so.

Sias and colleagues (Sias et al., 2004, 2012; Sias, 2005) have explored various communication phenomena related to differences in leader and peer relationships, including the maintenance of peer relationships, dialogue surrounding differential treatment, and the employee information experience. Sias et al. (2004) uncovered five primary reasons why workplace relationships deteriorate, including distracting life events, conflicting expectations, promotion, betrayal, and personality. On the surface, it may seem as though workplace relationships aren't that important, especially in contrast to "real" relationships with family members and friends outside of work. Yet, considering the amount of time (*One Third of Your Life Is Spent at Work—Gettysburg College*, n.d.) that employees spend at work, the development of trusting interpersonal relationships is key to meeting belongingness and inclusion needs (Schutz, 1958). Relatedly, the development of high-quality peer relationships may provide a safeguard against workplace antagonism, which is linked to employees engaging in counterproductive workplace behaviors such as retaliation (Chiaburu & Harrison, 2008; de Jong et al., 2014; Duffy et al., 2012).

While a benefit of peer relationships is having additional access to intangible and tangible resources, it can lead to animosity and exclusion of low-LMX peers (Omilion-Hodges & Baker, 2017). In a series of focus groups with managers and non-managers, employees admitted to actively withholding help from certain coworkers because of their peer's leader–member relationship. In these focus groups (Omilion-Hodges & Baker, 2017, p. 54), one participant revealed, "It's not that I don't want to help certain people, it just wouldn't look good if I spent a lot of time with them." Other participants echoed this sentiment by suggesting that they don't share resources with those at a lower LMX- status level because "it feels good to be top dog" and because they don't exchange with people "that I don't like." Not only may differences arise in workgroups, especially in peer relationships, owing to leader–member quality, but also because employees may find it challenging to connect with others in different life stages.

Connecting Across Different Ages & Stages

With many employees choosing to continue working into their late sixties and seventies, four generations may be working side-by-side. This brings a wealth of benefits, such as different perspectives and the opportunity for enhanced mentoring. Still, it can also introduce some challenges in the form of connecting across ages and stages.

First, it is important to note that researchers continue to point out several similarities across generations in the workplace. Some scholars (Lester et al., 2012) have conducted empirical research that showed no generational differences. Mencl and Lester (2014) conducted a study with employees from Generation Y, Generation X, and Baby Boomers and found that the cohorts were more alike than different when it came to 7 out of 10 work values. The biggest difference the researchers found was that career advancement tended to be more strongly valued by members of Generation Y in contrast to Baby Boomers or Generation X employees. Differences were also found among generational cohorts when it came to items related to diversity climate and immediate recognition and feedback.

Others have uncovered differences between employees from different generations in terms of workplace expectations and perceptions. Communication scholars (O'Connor & Raile, 2015) found that Millennials place a higher value on personally meaningful work and are more likely to consider the benefits package in contrast to salary alone than members of previous generations. Others (Omilion-Hodges et al., 2019; Omilion-Hodges & Sugg, 2019) have also found that Millennials tend to expect and appreciate more frequent and more detailed feedback from their leader and other high-status actors. This expectation may come from the sheer amount of time new employees spend in closely coupled leader–member-like dyads, such as with parents, teachers, professors, and coaches, before entering into industry full-time.

Reverse Mentoring

One way that organizations are flexing to meet young adults' communicative needs is through a process known as reverse mentoring. Reverse mentoring is when younger employees are partnered with senior colleagues, and each member is expected to teach and learn from the other (Marcinkus Murphy, 2012). This approach has been lauded as a best practice because it is a cost-effective means to assimilate new employees and teach seasoned employees innovations while creating interpersonal relationships that span departments and generations. This approach can be critical in organizations with a lot of generational diversity; as the adage goes, "birds of a feather flock together." It has also been pointed out that mentoring is traditionally a dyadic exchange relationship similar to LMX. Just as LMX relationships can mature to relationships built on trust and respect, so can reverse mentoring dyads. This can stem from the fact that in addition to helping each other grow cognitively and enhance or develop specific skills, mentoring relationships can also result in affective outcomes (Wanberg et al., 2003). These findings illustrate that these associations can exceed the simple transfer of knowledge to include changes in the other's perspective or attitude and enhance motivation.

Career Stage

In addition to considering an employee's age or generational cohort, it is also important to consider their career stage and position (*Engage by Stage—SMS Research Advisors*, n.d.). That is, a 45-year-old who recently switched industries is likely to encounter many of the same challenges a 22-year-old employee encounters. In a national study, SMS Research

Advisors considered how career/position stage impacts employee engagement. Participants were considered in four different stages: newbie (three or fewer years on the job), straddler (four to seven years), seasoned (eight to ten years), and sage (eleven or more years). The researchers found that each stage had distinct needs, which could be addressed by developing close peer (and leader) relationships.

Those newest to the position, newbies, need to feel engaged in the work and accepted within the organization. The goal of this stage is to make sure that newbies feel supported. Leaders can do this by being mindful of giving newbies additional individual attention and pairing them with a peer mentor. Employees are questioning if the organization has invested enough to keep them engaged and growing at the straddler stage. The researchers pointed out that a team-focus is especially important for straddlers so they can continue to feel involved and begin to develop and exercise their leadership skills. Members of the seasoned cohort may feel reenergized by picking up additional projects or, better yet, being encouraged to innovate extant work and pitch new ideas. Leaders and peers can reaffirm seasoned employees of their contributions and how they make a difference at the group and organizational level. Sages, the final career stage, are focused on legacy building. This stage, then, becomes about giving sage employees the latitude to consider how to leave the organization better off than when they entered it. While the leader can play a large role in motivating employees across career stages, it is also essential to consider the role that peer relationships can play. Peers in the same stage can empathize and encourage each other in ways that others in different stages may not. Like reverse mentoring, it may also be helpful to consider how to pair peers across stages to keep them engaged and developing professionally and personally.

Connecting in Competitive Environments

Just as it can feel challenging to connect across generations or career stages, it can feel especially precarious to form trusting relationships in a competitive environment. Some positions, such as that of an astronaut or a Navy SEAL, are expected to be highly competitive because of the requisite skills and the scarcity in the number of positions available. Other jobs, such as a creative director, may not seem as competitive as they are on the surface. When employees need to explicitly or implicitly vie for customers or a client-base, it doesn't exactly encourage peer affection or collaboration. This model varies across industries but is the norm for employees who work in fitness, mental health, real estate, and financial planning. Considering how widespread this employment model is, many employees and leaders have wondered how to cultivate trust and comradery in such competitive conditions.

Business owners, organizations, and leaders who wish to facilitate a collaborative culture in competitive or client-driven work have several options. Leaders can highlight excellent work and potentially foster collaboration to highlight each employee's expertise. This may be in the form of a monthly spotlight or asking each member to host a brown bag lunch talk to teach their peers about a specific approach or skill. In addition to celebrating and learning from each other's strengths, members may connect over the position's shared challenges. For example, in healthcare, providers may convene at weekly or bi-monthly meetings to discuss challenging cases to collaboratively develop patient-centered solutions. Depending on the organization's size and structure, leaders may decide to change the earning system to a more traditional model where employees earn stable salaries compared to having to compete for clients. Indeed, there are pros and cons associated with this shift, but it may attract like-minded employees who are more naturally collaborative.

Developing and Disbanding Peer Relationships

There are numerous models of relationship formation. One of the most widely used and easiest to grasp is social penetration theory (SPT; Altman & Taylor, 1973). This theory describes relationship development as a process that occurs through communication exchanges that peel back "layers" as partners, friends, peers, etc., build greater intimacy. The model posits that we each have a core personality that we tend to guard until we have established mutual trust and respect with the other exchange partner. This explains why when we are first introduced to someone, we begin by discussing superficial level content such as our job title and perhaps some of our favorites (i.e., movies, hobbies, vacation destinations, etc.). As we get to know the other person and as they continue to disclose as well, we peel back the superficial layer, to move to the middle layers, and the inner layers, to finally arrive at one's core personality. A study by communication researchers, Sias and Cahill (1998), illustrates SPT through the development of peer relationships.

In a seminal study, Sias and Cahill (1998) traced the development of coworker relationships from transactional professional roles to close friendships. The researchers found that peer relationships typically underwent three distinct transitions: from acquaintance to friend, from a friend to close friend, and from close friend to best friend. In addition to parceling out the three transitions, Sias and Cahill (1998) also explored the type of communication associated with each stage. Moving from coworker to friend (transition 1) is typified by broad communication that stems from working together in close proximity. In this stage, coworkers may begin to bond over shared organizational experiences and start to spend time together outside of work. The second transition from a friend to a close friend involves communicative exchanges centered on each party seeking affirmation and advice regarding professional and personal endeavors. In moving from friend to close friend, the researchers found that coworkers shifted their communication from general, superficial levels to more intimate and less cautious conversations. Some peer associations made a final transition from a close friend to an "almost best friend." In this scenario, coworkers played integral roles in each other's lives, personally and professionally, and these relationships were built on a long-term foundation of mutual trust.

This research helps to show how workgroup peers can move from acquaintances to trusted confidants. Paired with social penetration theory, the takeaway is that relationship development takes time. It is advised and expected that you start cautiously in terms of self-disclosure. As the other reciprocates by sharing information about themselves, you begin to disclose more to build the relationship further. What happens if your coworker is unresponsive or does not disclose in turn? This is often a signal that they are not ready or willing to move beyond the acquaintance phase. Below we discuss some steps for enhancing peer relationships and indicators that a peer relationship is ending or being renegotiated.

Enhancing Peer Relationships

Several communication behaviors can be enacted to facilitate effective and healthy peer relationships. The tips (BlogIn, n.d.) discussed below are all free and are likely communication behaviors that individuals are already using in other relationships. This is not an exhaustive list, but just some concrete ideas to help employees begin to model more other-oriented relationship behaviors. While this section focuses on peer relationships, these suggestions can be applied to other workplaces (i.e., leader–member, proteges, mentors, etc.) and personal (i.e., romantic partner, kids, friends, etc.) relationships. Table 3.1 also includes some tips for enhancing your conversational skills.

- **Acknowledge others' expertise:** One easy way to develop a peer relationship is to look to them for advice and role modeling. Now, this doesn't mean expecting them to hand-hold you or other new employees, but rather it can be as simple as highlighting their unique

Table 3.1 Sharpening your communication skills: enhancing your conversational skills

Relationships develop through incremental communication exchanges. Sometimes relationships stay at the acquaintance level, whereas other times they progress and grow into friendships. We show our conversational partners our intention for the relationship, that is for it to be maintained or to grow, through our verbal and nonverbal communication behaviors. Below we offer some general tips for enhancing your conversational skills:
• **Ask Questions:** This tip can help to start a conversation or to keep one going. This suggestion is also especially helpful for individuals who identify as introverts. Journalists talk about the 5 Ws and the H. This refers to asking questions regarding: who, what, where, when, why, and how. Keeping this in mind allows you to pose thoughtful and relevant follow-up questions.
• **Practice Active Listening:** It probably feels like this book should include "Active Listening" somewhere in the title. But the truth of the matter is that without practicing active listening, individuals will not be seen or succeed as leaders or as successful conversational partners. While it can be tempting to think of responses or worry about what to say next when someone else is talking, doing so actually makes it more likely that you'll drop the conversational ball. Instead, by actually listening to what the other is saying, it makes responding more natural because you have remained engaged in the conversation.
• **Prepare an Elevator Speech:** At networking events or in large organizations, it may be helpful to have a brief (30s or so) elevator speech ready to go. The trick is to be ready to introduce yourself, your role, and provide any necessary context that can be delivered conversationally. This allows you to feel comfortable with how you introduced and positioned yourself and the confidence associated with getting the conversation off on the right foot.
• **Know When to Wrap it Up:** Just as active listening and thoughtful questions can sustain a conversation, having a concise and direct way to end the chat is needed to end it effectively. We have all been in situations where a thoughtful conversation goes awry because of the awkwardness of trying to wrap it up. If you have another meeting or time-restriction, acknowledging it up front can be helpful. In other instances, if it feels like the conversation is winding down naturally it can be helpful to thank the other person for the chat and politely tell them to enjoy their day/night/conference etc. If you exchanged cards or information, it can also be helpful to thank them and tell them when you will reach out. For example, "Great chatting with you. I look forward to talking about mentoring in the future. I will email you early next week."

skills and contributions. Besides seeking their guidance for problem-solving, coworkers can also take a more passive route by watching how their peer navigates various relational or task scenarios and then model similar behavior. This can be the ultimate compliment.

- **Respect others' time:** While you (and others) may see a peer as *the* go-to group person, you may broker a better relationship with them if you demonstrate respect for their time. This means enacting a problem-solving approach where you try to seek solutions before asking others. You may ask your peer if they prefer quick, informal check-ins or if scheduling time with them is preferred. Showing that you are mindful of their time highlights that you respect their opinion *and* their role demands.
- **Remain transparent:** One of the surest ways to damage a peer relationship is to withhold or distort information. Committing to transparency, even when the news is distressing, demonstrates respect for the other and continues to preserve the trust in a relationship. Though it may seem like concealing bad news or information that could hurt your peer's feelings is the better course, it undermines the relationship's integrity. It implies that the other person is not mature enough or capable of handling the information in question.
- **Use intentional communication at work and on social media:** This suggestion involves using tact in your verbal and written communication both in the workplace and on social media. Social media can feel like a safe place to vent or process challenging work-place events; however, as the name implies—it is social. While it may provide momentary relief to complain about your leader, a peer, or a project, that sense of relief is likely to be fleeting. Releasing such concerns on social media is akin to airing your workgroup's dirty laundry in a public space. It is helpful to consider how others may interpret a message or where a message may end up (if it's forwarded, for example) before communicating. A quick litmus test is if you wouldn't say it or present it to the CEO as is, the message should be revised.
- **Take responsibility:** Miscommunications happen to the best of us. We also overlook details or forget to complete an aspect of a task here and there. Instead of brushing the error under the rug, or worse yet, putting it on another coworker, it is best to acknowledge the misstep and discuss what steps you are taking to make sure it doesn't happen again. This is especially important if you talk

out of turn or let a workplace friend down. Since these relationships have transitioned from acquaintance roles and center around trust, acknowledging an error or faux pas is essential.

Ending Peer Relationships

Just as romantic relationships and other friendships may reach a natural breaking point, so can peer associations. Sias and colleagues (2004) explored how and why workplace friendships may deteriorate. The researchers identified five primary reasons workplace friendships may breakdown, including personality, distracting life events, conflicting expectations, promotion, and betrayal. These findings align with more contemporary research (Methot et al., 2016) that indicates that peer relationships can lead to emotional exhaustion, Sias et al. (2004) found that as peer friendships declined if they resulted in turnover, interfered with employees' ability to complete their jobs, and or increased emotional stress.

While strengthening relationships involves sharing in greater depth and frequency, renegotiating relationships consists of the opposite. As a relationship begins to dissolve, parties tend to move from more intimate, core topics to more general and superficial issues. Through in-depth interviews, Sias et al. (2004) revealed specific communication maneuvers employees reported engaging in or endured from peers through the renegotiation of workplace friendships. These communication strategies were mostly indirect. Instead of having a direct conversation about the relationship, employees are more likely to avoid talking about nonwork matters and attempt to add additional social distance by turning down nonwork-related invitations to spend time together.

While this section considered benefits and potential obstacles embedded within peer relationships, the final section addresses how peers may emerge as informal leaders or otherwise practice their leadership skills.

Informal Leaders: Peers as Leaders in Training

While the benefits of peer relationships were addressed above, another outcome of the peer role is the ability to emerge as an informal leader in the workgroup. Relatedly, others have discussed how peers are in a unique spot to support and or mentor colleagues in ways that a leader cannot. Below we highlight how peers may enact referent power and how that can play out in the workgroup. The formal process of leadership emergence is discussed in Chapter 4.

Leadership scholars (Fairhurst, 2008; Fairhurst & Connaughton, 2014) argue that leadership is in the eye of the beholder. One does not require a formal title to act as a leader or to be seen as a leader. Since leadership is a communicative and relational endeavor, those who communicate clearly and with respect and take an other-oriented, meaning-centered approach are likely to be perceived as leaders regardless of title. Peers can serve as unique sources of social support, inspiration, and mentoring through their communication and referent power (French & Raven, 1958). Referent power is when you can influence others because you are seen as interpersonally attractive, and others want your attention, respect, and opinion. Additionally, peers are often easier to approach than leaders because the perceived social cost is less. That is, it is easier to ask a peer a "dumb question" or ask them to remind you of a process that you keep forgetting than it is to approach the leader with the same inquiry.

Considering the special role that peers can play in a workgroup and organizational settings, it allows career-minded employees the opportunity to consider how to grow their leadership abilities. Some (Raabe & Beehr, 2003) have suggested that if organizations value job satisfaction, organizational commitment, and reduced turnover intentions, peer mentoring functions are of the utmost importance. Research (Omilion-Hodges & Ackerman, 2018) has reiterated this finding in highlighting that employees cited their peers as their greatest sources of innovation and creativity in the workplace. Employees in the video game industry acknowledged that while their leaders could be and often were sources of support, their peers played the most pivotal role in shaping their workplace experience and encouraging their creative output. It was often through informal chats with peers over coffee or in doorways or during shared lunch breaks, that employees reported as spurring the most creative stimulation. Taken together, these findings illustrate the important role that peers play in the workgroup setting above and beyond what a leader can fulfill (see Table 3.2) for an organizational example.

Leadership Moments: Takeaways for Leaders & Members

- **Leaders and Members Should Strive to Develop High-Quality Relationships with all Workgroup Members:** The research is clear;

Table 3.2 Leadership in action—organizational profile: BNY Mellon's Pershing

BNY Mellon's Pershing was experiencing a common organizational issue; Millennials were leaving the company at high rates. This also left the company wondering if they would have difficulty in reaching and remaining relevant with younger consumers (Jordan & Sorell, 2019).
While earlier reverse mentoring programs were focused on technology, BNY Mellon's Pershing's focus was on generating new perspectives and increasing Millennial retention. Three guidelines were offered:
1. Regular, confidential meetings should be held
2. Open communication is key
3. Pairs should approach the meetings as equals
This focus allowed the dyads to exchange in dialogue designed to be mutually beneficial. While the pairings could exchange skill-based abilities (i.e., how to set up a LinkedIn profile), they often addressed broader questions such as how to approach strategic decision making, leadership, and work mindsets. Younger participants were asked about how they would like to connect with peers and the organization and what would help to keep them engaged and committed.
The company is now reporting retention rates of 95% of Millennials who have taken part in the reverse mentoring program.

Source BNY Mellon's Pershing (n.d.) and Jordan and Sorell (2019)

Developing high-quality relationships with your leader and your workgroup peers (and followers if applicable) is beneficial for myriad reasons. Not only do these relationships help to fulfill our interpersonal needs for inclusion and belongingness, but they also expand our access to resources. From various forms of social support to more tangible resources, the development of workplace relationships makes it easier for us to exchange and collaborate with others to achieve organizational goals.

- **Peer Relationships are Not Idle Chatter or Time Wasted:** Classic approaches to management suggested that employees didn't necessarily like to work and needed to be micromanaged to motivate them to complete their role responsibilities. This is an antiquated view of employees and workgroup relationships. Research continues to reiterate the critical and unique role that peers play in the workgroup. From increasing innovation and creativity to serving as effective mentors, some have asserted that peers truly make the place (Chiaburu & Harrison, 2008; Omilion-Hodges & Ackerman, 2018; Raabe & Beehr, 2003). While members certainly need to satisfy deadlines and complete organizational tasks, leaders should give members latitude and space to get to know each other. This will provide employees with the chance to transition from acquaintances to friends. It is essential to keep in mind that part and parcel of friendship is trust and respect. Therefore, it can make it easier for peers to lean on each other and provide feedback, guidance, and motivation.

- **Relationship Development is Systematic and Takes Time:** Relationship development takes time. As is demonstrated by social penetration theory, some layers or steps have to take place to move from superficial connections to more intimate ones. Relationships mature as parties disclose personal information. Some people tend to reveal more quickly, and others take more time. The key is to let people communicate and relate at a pace they are comfortable with, rather than expecting or nudging them to move on your schedule.

Mini Case Study: "Relationships-First Culture"

You have finally earned the promotion that you have been working for. You've had some great managers in the past and some that, well, maybe weren't so great. However, now you are in charge, and you're able to make a real difference in your employees' lives. You didn't get to this position by being a slouch. You were always in early and had no issue staying late when the situation called for it. You also, somewhat reluctantly at first, stayed back when coworkers went to lunch or grabbed coffee together on their breaks. It always seemed like a better time investment to focus on the work than the workplace relationship.

In your onboarding meeting with the CEO, she tells you how happy they are to have you and impresses on you that she is sure that you'll be an excellent fit for their relationships-first focused culture. The CEO presents some statistics about how workplace friendships lead to increased creativity, innovation, and other positive outcomes for employees and the organization. You realize that this means that you are going to have to pivot and do so quickly.

1. What is one concrete solution that you can immediately implement with your new workgroup to enact a relationship-first culture?

2. What can you do to transfer some of your previous work-first successes into an environment that values the power of the leader and peer relationships?
3. How can you enlist your new team's help to help you mold a relationships-first culture for your department?

References

Altman, I., & Taylor, D. A. (1973). *Social penetration: The development of interpersonal relationships*. Holt, Rinehart & Winston.

Baker, C. R., & Omilion-Hodges, L. M. (2013). The effect of leader-member exchange differentiation within work units on coworker exchange and organizational citizenship behaviors. *Communication Research Reports, 30*(4), 313–322. https://doi.org/10.1080/08824096.2013.837387B.

Blau, P. M. (1964). Justice in social exchange. *Sociological Inquiry, 34*(2), 193–206. https://doi.org/10.1111/j.1475-682X.1964.tb00583.x.

BlogIn. (n.d.). Transparent team communication: Why and how to embrace it. https://blogin.co/blog/transparent-team-communication-why-and-how-to-embrace-it-69/.

BNY Mellon's Pershing. (n.d.). Reversing the generation equation: Mentoring in the new age of work. https://www.pershing.com/perspectives/reversing-the-generation-equation-mentoring-in-the-new-age-of-work.

Boies, K., & Howell, J. M. (2006). Leader-member exchange in teams: An examination of the interaction between relationship differentiation and mean LMX in explaining team-level outcomes. *Leadership Quarterly, 17*(3), 246–257. https://doi.org/10.1016/j.leaqua.2006.02.004.

Bolino, M. C., & Turnley, W. H. (2009). Relative deprivation among employees in lower-quality leader-member exchange relationships. *Leadership Quarterly, 20*(3), 276–286. https://doi.org/10.1016/j.leaqua.2009.03.001.

Bornay-Barrachina, M., & Herrero, I. (2018). Team creative environment as a mediator between CWX and R&D team perfromance and moderating boundary conditions. *Journal of Business and Psychology, 33*(2), 311–323. https://doi.org/10.1007/s10869-017-9495-8.

Chen, Y., Yu, E., & Son, J. (2014). Beyond leader–member exchange (LMX) differentiation: An indigenous approach to leader–member relationship differentiation. *the Leadership Quarterly, 25*, 611–627. https://doi.org/10.1016/j.leaqua.2013.12.004.

Chiaburu, D. S., & Harrison, D. A. (2008). Do peers make the place? Conceptual synthesis and meta-analysis of coworker effects on perceptions, attitudes, OCBs, and performance. *The Journal of Applied Psychology, 93*(5), 1082–1103. https://doi.org/10.1037/0021-9010.93.5.1082.

Choi, J. N. (2012). Context and creativity: The theory of planned behavior as an alternative mechanism. *Social Behavior and Personality, 40*, 681–692. https://doi.org/10.2224/sbp.2012.40.4.681.

de Jong, J. P., Curşeu, P. L., & Leenders, R. T. A. J. (2014). When do bad apples not spoil the barrel? Negative relationships in teams, team performance, and buffering mechanisms. *The Journal of Applied Psychology, 99*(3), 514–522. https://doi.org/10.1037/a0036284.

Dotan, H. (2009, August). Workplace friendships: Origins and conequences for managerial effectiveness. In *Academy of Management Proceedings, 2009* (pp. 1–6). Briarcliff Manor, NY: Academy of Management.

Duffy, R. D., Steger, M. F., & Dik, B. J. (2012). Measuring meaningful work: The work and meaning inventory (WAMI). *Journal of Career Assessment, 20*(3), 322–337. https://doi.org/10.1177/1069072711436160.

Engage by Stage—SMS Research Advisors. (n.d.). Retrieved June 16, 2020, from https://smsresearch.com/misc/engage-by-stage/.

Erdogan, B., & Bauer, T. N. (2014). Leader-member exchange (LMX) theory: The relational approach to leadership. In D. V. Day (Ed.), *The Oxford handbook of leadership and organizations* (pp. 407–434). Oxford University Press.

Fairhurst, G. T. (2008). Discursive leadership: A communication alternative to leadership psychology. *Management Communication Quarterly, 21*(4), 510–521. https://doi.org/10.1177/0893318907313714.

Fairhurst, G. T., & Connaughton, S. L. (2014). Leadership: A communicative perspective. *Leadership, 10*(1), 7–35. https://doi.org/10.1177/1742715013509396.

French, J. R., Jr., & Raven, B. H. (1958). Group support, legitimate power, and social influence. *Journal of Personality, 26*(3), 400–409. https://doi.org/10.1111/j.1467-6494.1958.tb01595.

Heider, F. (1958). *The psychology of interpersonal relations*. New York: Wiley. https://doi.org/10.1037/10628-000.

Hooper, D. T., & Martin, R. (2008). Beyond personal leader-member exchange (LMX) quality: The effects of perceived LMX variability on employee reactions. *Leadership Quarterly, 19*(1), 20–30. https://doi.org/10.1016/j.leaqua.2007.12.002.

Jordan, J., & Sorell, M. (2019, November 18). *Why reverse mentoring works and how to do it right*. American Association for Physician Leadership. https://www.physicianleaders.org/news/reverse-mentoring-works.

Lester, S. W., Standifer, R. L., Schultz, N. J., & Windsor, J. M. (2012). Actual versus perceived generational differences at work: An empirical examination. *Journal of Leadership & Organizational Studies, 19*(3), 341–354.

Madlock, P. E., & Booth-Butterfield, M. (2012). The influence of relational maintenance strategies among woworkers. *Journal of Business Communication, 49*(1), 21–47. https://doi.org/10.1177/0021943611425237.

Marcinkus Murphy, W. (2012). Reverse mentoring at work: Fostering cross-generational learning and developing millennial leaders. *Human Resource Management, 51*(4), 549–573. https://doi.org/10.1002/hrm.21489.

Mencl, J. & Lester, S. W. (2014). More alike than different: What generations value and how the values affect employee workplace perceptions. *Journal of Leadership & Organizational Studies, 21*(3), 257–272. https://doi.org/10.1177/1548051814529825.

Methot, J. R., Lepine, J. A., Podsakoff, N. P., & Christian, J. S. (2016). Are workplace friendships a mixed blessing? Exploring tradeoffs of multiplex relationships and their associations with job performance. *Personnel Psychology, 69*(2), 311–355. https://doi.org/10.1111/peps.12109.

O'Connor, A., & Raile, A. N. W. (2015). Millennials' "get a 'real job'": Exploring generational shifts in the colloquialism's characteristics and meanings. *Management Communication Quarterly, 29*(2), 276–290. https://doi.org/10.1177/0893318915580153.

Omilion-Hodges, L. M., & Ackerman, C. D. (2018). From the technical know-how to the free flow of ideas: Exploring the effects of leader, peer, and team communication on employee creativity. *Communication Quarterly, 66*(1), 38–57. https://doi.org/10.1080/01463373.2017.1325385.

Omilion-Hodges, L. M., & Baker, C. R. (2013). Contextualizing LMX within the workgroup: The effects of LMX and justice on relationship quality and resource sharing among peers. *The Leadership Quarterly, 24,* 935–951. https://doi.org/10.1016/j.leaqua.2013.10.004.

Omilion-Hodges, L. M., & Baker, C. R. (2017). Communicating leader-member relationship quality: The development of leader communication exchange scales to measure relationship building and maintenance through the exchange of communication-based goods. *International Journal of Business Communication, 54*(2), 115–145. https://doi.org/10.1177/2329488416687052.

Omilion-Hodges, L. M., Shank, S. E., & Packard, C. M. (2019). What young adults want: A multistudy examination of vocational anticipatory socialization through the lens of students' desired managerial communication behaviors. *Management Communication Quarterly, 33*(4), 512–547. https://doi.org/10.1177/0893318919851177.

Omilion-Hodges, L. M., & Sugg, C. E. (2019). Millennials' views and expectations regarding the communicative and relational behaviors of leaders: Exploring young adults' talk about work. *Business and Professional Communication Quarterly, 82*(1), 74–100. https://doi.org/10.1177/2329490618808043.

One third of your life is spent at work—Gettysburg College. (n.d.). Retrieved June 15, 2020, from https://www.gettysburg.edu/news/stories?id=79db7b34-630c-4f49-ad32-4ab9ea48e72b&pageTitle=1%2F3+of+your+life+is+spent+at+work.

Raabe, B., & Beehr, T. A. (2003). Formal mentoring versus supervisor and coworker relationships: Differences in perceptions and impact. *Source: Journal of Organizational Behavior*, *24*(3), 271–293. https://doi.org/10.1002/job.193.

Schutz, W. (1958). *FIRO: A three-dimensional theory of interpersonal behavior*. New York, NY: Rinehart.

Schutz, W. (1966). *The Interpersonal World*. Palo Alto, CA: Science and Behavior Books.

Sherony, K. M., & Green, S. G. (2002). Coworker exchange: Relationships between coworkers, leader-member exchange, and work attitudes. *Journal of Applied Psychology, 87*(3), 542–548. https://doi.org/10.1037/0021-9010.87.3.542.

Sias, P. M. (2005). Workplace relationship quality and employee information experiences. *Communication Studies, 56*(4), 375–395. https://doi.org/10.1080/10510970500319450.

Sias, P. M., & Cahill, D. J. (1998). From coworkers to friends: The development of peer friendships in the workplace. *Western Journal of Communication (includes Communication Reports), 62*(3), 273–299. https://doi.org/10.1080/10570319809374611.

Sias, P. M., Heath, R. G., Perry, T., Silva, D., & Fix, B. (2004). Narratives of workplace friendship deterioration. *Journal of Social and Personal Relationships, 21*(3), 321–340. https://doi.org/10.1177/0265407504042835.

Sias, P. M., Pederson, H., Gallagher, E. B., & Kopaneva, I. (2012). Workplace friendship in the electronically connected organization. *Human Communication Research, 38*(3), 253–279. https://doi.org/10.1111/j.1468-2958.2012.01428.x.

Sias, P. M. P., & Jablin, F. F. M. (1995). Differential superior-subordinate relations, perceptions of fairness, and coworker communication. *Human Communication Research, 22*(1), 5–37. https://doi.org/10.1111/j.1468-2958.1995.tb00360.x.

Takeuchi, R., Yun, S., & Wong, K. F. E. (2011). Social influence of a coworker: A test of the effect of employee and coworker exchange ideologies on employees' exchange qualities. *Organizational Behavior and Human Decision Processes, 115,* 226–237. https://doi.org/10.1016/j.obhdp.2011.02.004.

Wanberg, C. R., Welsh, E. T., & Hezlett, S. A. (2003). Mentoring research: A review and dynamic process model. In J. J. Martocchio & G. R. Ferris

(Eds.), *Research in personnel and human resources management, 22* (pp. 39–124). Elsevier Science Ltd. https://psycnet.apa.org/doi/10.1016/S0742-7301(03)22002-8.

Wikaningrum, T. (2007). Coworker exchange, leader-member exchange, and work attitudes: A study of coworker dyads. *Gadjah Mada International Journal of Business*, *9*(2), 187. https://doi.org/10.22146/gamaijb.5596.

CHAPTER 4

Fitting into the Workgroup: Relationships Within the Team

Abstract The natural extension of leader–member and peer relationships is considering how they individually and collectively impact workgroup functioning. Leaders may not be aware of how their communication tendencies may impact the culture and output of their workgroup as a whole. This chapter reviews and summarizes scholarly literature at the intersection of leader, peer, and team relationships and functioning. Addressing potential best-case and worst-case scenarios, this chapter shows leaders and members how individual relationships can propel workgroups to greater success or on the other hand, tamper with their accomplishments. This chapter also leans into the potential downfalls of LMX theory—the potential for leaders to assemble a special inner circle of trusted employees who are demographically similar to themselves. Considering this, this chapter addresses some of the natural communication challenges that arise when attempting to communicate across differences and among a group and how to be successful in these potentially trying scenarios. Traditional face-to-face workgroups, virtual teams, self- and co-lead teams, and teams with an ambiguous leadership structure are also considered.

Keywords Team-member exchange · Group roles · Employee engagement · Groupthink · Team environments

L. M. Omilion-Hodges and J. K. Ptacek, *Leader-Member Exchange and Organizational Communication*, New Perspectives in Organizational Communication, https://doi.org/10.1007/978-3-030-68756-4_4

LMX and TMX: How and Why LMX Affects Team Relationships and Functioning

Team-member exchange (Seers, 1989) is arguably the most complex of the workgroup exchange relationships as it encompasses LMX and CWX relationships. That is, team-member exchange or TMX accounts for the sum of all workgroup relationships (i.e., all LMXs and CWXs). Thus, TMX illustrates the intricacies of communication and relationships in a workgroup, reiterating it is virtually impossible to disentangle various dyadic associations without impacting the other dyadic and group affiliations.

What does TMX mean for individual employees? TMX describes how an associate fits within the team. TMX includes how employees feel in their workgroups and how others perceive them relative to their contributions and their relationships with others. Like LMX and CWX, TMX reiterates that how an employee feels in their workgroup can have a significant impact on the quality of their work, their intention to remain in the role and organization, and their overall well-being (Bakar & Sheer, 2013; Hooper & Martin, 2008; Omilion-Hodges et al., 2016; Seers et al., 1995). Relatedly, research (Farmer et al., 2015) has found that TMX functions at the between- and within-group levels of analysis where when members feel like they are part of the group, but still contribute in unique ways, they engage in more prosocial, helping behaviors. However, just as high TMX in a group is linked to prosocial behavior, employees report refraining from engaging in extra citizenship behaviors when the team's overall exchange relationships are of lower quality. This finding reinforces the fact that workgroup relationships are interdependent, and low-quality leader–member or coworker relationships can swell to negatively impact the collective functioning and climate.

At first glance, it may seem like a low-quality leader–member relationship or a couple of distant coworker exchange relationships may not fundamentally alter an employee's place within the team or reach to impact their overall workplace experience. However, decades of TMX-focused studies trace team-level outcomes back to an employee's LMX and CWX relationships. Employees who share a high-quality relationship with their leader are more likely to be granted the latitude to engage in relational, task, and cognitive job crafting (Lee, 2020), and also enjoy increased use of cooperative communication (Bakar & Sheer, 2013), and more resources (Omilion-Hodges & Baker, 2017; Tse, 2014) which enables employees to perform at their highest level, and can kindle employee creativity (Chen & Liu, 2020). In turn, this also means that low-LMX employees do not have the opportunity to reshape or renegotiate their roles, their leader tends to use more directive and task-focused communication, and they have access to fewer positive resources. They may also be more likely to be excluded from workgroup social activities or even be betrayed by their leader (Omilion-Hodges & Baker, 2017). The strength of coworker relationships also plays a deciding role in the employee experience where high-quality exchanges are met with mutual trust, assistance, and obligation (Sherony & Green, 2002) and are characterized by open communication (Vinarski-Peretz et al., 2010). A high-quality peer exchange relationship can also help an employee perform at even higher levels by reducing role ambiguity and providing additional support (Chen et al., 2013; Li et al., 2014). In the absence of close peer relationships, employees are left to wrestle with role questions alone.

This chapter addresses potential benefits and hindrances of TMX, while also highlighting how team-member exchange may look and function differently in various (i.e., face to face, virtual, start-ups, etc.) contexts. However, TMX literature illustrates that leader–member and peer relationships and communication matter in tangible and vital ways. Before turning our attention to antecedents and outcomes of team-member exchange, we review systems theory to provide a theoretical foundation for how LMX, CWX, and TMX function in concert.

Systems Theory

Systems theory uses the human body metaphor to explain how various organizational processes and components function interdependently (Weick et al., 2005). Systems theory has often been used to articulate how leader–member, peer, and team relationships operate within workgroups (Li & Liao, 2014; Omilion-Hodges et al., 2016). Considering how bodies function at their fullest when all internal systems work efficiently, workgroups are also at their best when leader–member, peer, and team associations are in good health. Systems theory underscores the importance of leaders working to develop individual high-quality exchange relationships with each member. These associations may then bloom into trusting CWXs and sum to a high-functioning TMX.

Employing systems theory as a lens for understanding the various relationships imbued within workgroups also highlights the key role communication plays in workgroups. Not only is communication the leader's primary means to influence and motivate members, but it is also the vehicle used to develop relationships, navigate conflict, and collaborate to achieve task demands. Overlooking the importance of communication can quickly lead to deteriorating relationships, which in turn, can hurt productivity, retention, helping behaviors, and innovation (Banks et al., 2013; Terpstra-Tong et al., 2020). Omilion-Hodges et al. (2016, p. 345) used the imagery of a teepee to argue that while leader, member, and team associations serve as stand-alone relationships, they are most potent and most effective when united like the top of a teepee. Earlier conceptualizations and studies of these exchange relationships positioned the associations as points on a triangle. This approach implicitly suggests that these relationships develop and function in isolation, rather than the interconnected, communicative phenomena that they are. Thus, shifting focus to the top of the teepee, where LMX, CWX, and TMX meet illustrates the importance of these relationships, but reiterates that a three-dimensional view is not only more comprehensive, but also more reflective of how these relationships interact and play out in the workplace.

Systems theory is not only helpful in exemplifying the potential strength of leader, peer, and team relationships, but it can also show what happens when relationships or employee behaviors detract from optimal team functioning. The positive and potentially negative outcomes associated with LMX, CWX, and TMX will be explored. Still, first, it is helpful to consider the various roles that employees may play within teams. Effective and ineffective roles that are commonly enacted in groups are explored as they also help illustrate the impact employees can have on the system or unit.

Group Roles

There are many different roles that members play within groups. These are not to be confused with formal titles, and instead, group roles are often fluid, where members take turns ebbing and flowing between them. Scholars often consider group roles by parsing them out and focusing on either communication behaviors that facilitate task progress or on employee and team social needs. The following functions are drawn from *Communication in the Real World: An Introduction to Communication*

Studies (n.d.). This text is highly recommended for a foundational and pragmatic view of the role communication plays in organizations and how communication impacts our relationships at home, with friends, in groups, and within our communities.

Typical task-related roles and behaviors enacted within teams include:

- **Leader:** In this role, the leader does not have to have a formal leadership title. Team members who have expertise or experience in certain areas may set a vision and align other team members to achieve a goal or fulfill project needs. This role allows employees to showcase their unique skills and knowledge.
- **Expediter:** The expediter keeps the group focused on meeting goals and deadlines.
- **Information Seeker:** This role serves to ask questions, seek opinions, and seek clarification regarding group decisions. Appointing someone to serve as the information seeker can prevent groupthink and help the team consider potential unintended consequences.
- **Gatekeeper:** The gatekeeper manages the flow of group discussion, ensuring that everyone contributes and no one dominates the conversation.
- **Recorder:** While formal meetings often appoint an employee to keep minutes, having someone serve as a recorder during informal or ad hoc meetings can help preserve discussions and activities for posterity's sake.

Common relational roles and behaviors are explored next. Though it is important to note that while some roles, such as a recorder or gatekeeper, can be appointed for specific times and contexts (i.e., weekly team meetings), other functions, such as the supporter, may be enacted at any time and by any member:

- **Supporter:** Enactment of this role often aligns with employees' personalities and communication behaviors. For example, an employee serving as a "supporter" may do so by developing meaningful interpersonal relationships complete with thoughtful, other-oriented communication. The supporter may also be there to encourage a peer during a trying project or provide emotional support.

- **Tension Releaser:** Someone in this role has likely always been told that they are naturally funny and witty. The tension releaser has their finger on the pulse of workgroup dynamics and is typically able to communicate in a way that encourages fellowship.
- **Harmonizer:** The harmonizer is an incredibly adept communicator. In this role, the harmonizer can help peers effectively navigate conflict or interpersonal differences.
- **Interpreter:** Interpreters are also highly complex communicators as they can help build bridges by mediating intercultural conflict. Organizations can help employees by training to reduce ethnocentrism and increase employees' awareness of other cultures and value systems. The interpreter role is exceedingly essential, considering the increase in multinational corporations and diverse workgroups.

The roles described above highlight prosocial communicative behaviors that employees enact to facilitate productive team functioning. While it would be optimistic to believe or hope that these are the only roles that team members enact, there are also some negative group role behaviors that employees perform. Cragan et al. (2009) point out that these negative roles stem from employees engaging in self-centered communication behaviors.

Common negative roles and behaviors enacted within teams include:

- **Central Negative:** Often, but not always, the central negative emerges from an employee who wanted to lead but was not selected. The central negative tends to find fault with all leader-initiated ideas and directives.
- **Monopolizer:** The monopolizer tends to dominate conversations, which often leads to others not speaking up either because they cannot join the discussion or fear that the monopolizer will speak over them. The gatekeeper role is designed to keep monopolizers in check.
- **Self-Confessor:** This individual tends to reveal too much personal information to peers, often because they need support, advice, or to alleviate loneliness. The gatekeeper role and or supporters can help manage self-confessors.
- **Insecure Compliment Seeker:** This group member seeks continuous feedback, validation, and praise from peers. This employee

needs continual affirmation that they are needed and valued by the group.

- **Joker:** Unlike the tension-reliever who uses humor effectively and thoughtfully, the joker is perceived as childish and distracting. The joker may play pranks or tell jokes that detract from team functioning and well-being.

In addition to negative roles, some group roles can be downright counterproductive to group functioning. These roles include:

- **Blocker:** A blocker may intentionally or inadvertently prevent work from being completed in a timely manner. Those who block may invoke procedural rules or stall by seeking additional feedback from others. Those who unintentionally block progress may do so by missing deadlines, meetings, or other decision-making ventures.
- **Withdrawer:** This individual intentionally avoids participating and or engaging in group activities. Chances of having a withdrawer on staff increase as group sizes increase. These employees tend to partake in group discussions and events only when required.
- **Aggressor:** An aggressor can dramatically alter the culture or feel of a workgroup because they communicate in ways that block others' ideas or communicate in a manner that leaves others feeling attacked or belittled. This role is especially damaging to group morale and should be addressed quickly and likely reported to Human Resources.
- **Doormat:** Not to be confused with an introvert, the doormat allows group members to dismiss their ideas, suggestions, and contributions to the detriment of the collective functioning of the group.

With a formative understanding of group roles, it now possible to appreciate the complexity and depth of team-member exchange.

Advantages of Team-Member Exchange

The advantages of high team-member exchange are plenty. This should be of little surprise because high TMX is built on a foundation of high-quality dyadic peer and leader–member relationships. Thus, the team enjoys the benefits of working collaboratively with colleagues who share mutual respect, trust, and obligation (Liden et al., 2000) and has been linked to sharing accurate perceptions among workgroup members (Liao et al., 2010). High-quality team-member exchange can also lead to higher levels of positive emotions in teams, including increased member satisfaction (Golden, 2006; Tse et al., 2008). Similarly, a metanalysis (Banks et al., 2013) of LMX and TMX research found positive relationships between TMX and employee job performance, job satisfaction, and organizational commitment. The study also found that in instances where TMX was high, members were less prone to turnover. The authors (Banks et al., 2013) also found that above and beyond LMX, an employee's TMX level explained unique variance in their job satisfaction and their commitment to their organization. Additional research has also indicated that high-quality TMX can not only explain employee outcomes outside of the scope of LMX, but in some instances, TMX can even guard against the potentially damaging effects of a low-LMX relationship.

Recent research (Wang & Hollenbeck, 2019) has demonstrated that a high-quality TMX can extinguish the negative ripples that often stem from a low-LMX relationship. This research (Wang & Hollenbeck, 2019) also indicated that in workgroups where team collaboration was frequent and members worked well together, the leader–member relationship became less impactful, mainly if there was low authority differential and high skill differential. This means that in teams where members are empowered to make decisions and do not need to defer to or go to the leader, LMX has less of an effect on employee performance. This is also the case when members have high skill differentiation, meaning that when members have highly specialized skills and knowledge and are not easily replaceable or interchangeable, the otherwise positive effects of LMX become moot on employee performance. The takeaway message is that TMX can override the potentially harmful effects of low LMX (and may also hamper the positive effects of LMX), in the case that TMX is high. This is great news for employees and leaders who got off on the wrong foot or otherwise continue to experience challenges in connecting above and beyond the transactional superior-subordinate relationship.

In addition to potentially serving as a buffer against lower-quality leader–member relationships, team-member exchange has continually been associated with increased ideation, innovation, and creativity. These positive outcomes likely stem from the fact that TMX is an antecedent of employee engagement and is generally linked to supportive, collegial behavior.

Support, Helping Behaviors, and Employee Engagement

TMX can be a precursor of employee engagement (Liao et al., 2013). Considering this, researchers have suggested that leaders not only encourage employees to spend time together to develop interpersonal relationships but give them the time and space to do so (Omilion-Hodges & Ackerman, 2017). Thus, in place of seeing employee socialization as idle chatter, leaders should instead consider it an investment in team climate and functioning. Additionally, others have found that in groups where TMX is high, employees have the latitude and trusting relationship in place to engage in job crafting, or molding their role requirements to suit their skill sets or other needs better. These findings reiterate the social aspect of workgroups and illustrate that relationships are interdependent. Strong relationships at every level (leader, peer, and team) result in increased employee support. Case in point, in teams that are characterized by high-quality exchanges, helping behaviors are increased too (Farmer et al., 2015). Other research (Omilion-Hodges & Baker, 2013) showed that peers and teams could also play a supporting or buffering position in instances when they believe that a leader mistreats an employee. In such cases, when peers think another's LMX is unfairly low, the team steps into shore up the focal employee. This aligns with findings (Schermuly & Meyer, 2015) that indicate that TMX is just as crucial as LMX in preventing associates' psychological health issues. As was discussed in Chapter 3, peers really do make the place (Chiaburu & Harrison, 2008).

Ideation, Innovation, and Creativity

Team-member exchange has also frequently been linked to increased ideation, innovation, and employee creativity. The underlying reason may have something to do with the fact that in workgroups with high TMX, there is additional support imbued within a grouping of strong horizontal relationships. Banks and colleagues (2013, p. 273) conducted a metanalysis to seek to answer the following question: is an employee's time best spent developing vertical relationships with their leader or horizontal relationships among workgroup members? While they reiterated the importance of LMX, they found that team relationships impacted employee job satisfaction and organizational commitment beyond what the leader–member relationship could predict. This finding helps to explain why high team-member exchange may spark employee innovation. That is, when employees feel supported and accepted by their peers, it becomes easier to think outside of the box, ask questions, and be inspired by others (Martins & Shalley, 2011; Muñoz-Doyague & Nieto, 2012). Through a series of in-depth interviews, Omilion-Hodges and Ackerman (2017) found that high-quality, trusting team interactions are part and parcel of increased creative results while also helping to bolster individual employee contributions rather than concealing or superseding them. This shows that teams can be harnessed to capitalize on the interconnected interpersonal relationships to offer additional social support increasing innovation and output.

Potential Disadvantages or Challenges Associated with Team-Member Exchange

While team-member exchange benefits outweigh the negatives, there are some drawbacks or potential challenges to consider. For instance, in workgroups where the leader is verbally abusive, members tend to retreat to their silos and do not discuss or report the behavior because of feelings of emotional exhaustion (Xu et al., 2015). This effectively cuts employees off from social support and empowerment that stems from high-quality team relationships (Schermuly & Meyer, 2015). Communication across members may also decrease among members when leaders intentionally or inadvertently build a homogeneous team. Doing so can tamper with unique ideas and perspectives, but it can lead to groupthink and isolating out-group employees.

LMX Homophily: Building a Team That Looks and Thinks Just Like You

A lingering critique of leader–member exchange theory is that it is merely a measure of leader likeability. That is, some suggest that LMX results in separating employees into a group that the leader likes and a group that the leader does not like (Liden & Maslyn, 1998; Seers et al., 2006; Sheer, 2015).

Everyone has likely heard the adage that "birds of a feather flock together." This saying illuminates the aspect of human nature to be drawn to similar people. This can promote a sense of familiarity and produce liking. Considering this tendency, it is not likely nefarious motives that propel managers to hire employees similar to themselves or others in their workgroup. Yet, it can limit the group's ability to offer innovative solutions as they likely share similar backgrounds and training and make them less capable of meeting the needs of diverse groups and clients. With the rise of multinational corporations and the increased need to work with peers and clients from different cultures, having a homogeneous team is undoubtedly detrimental. Moreover, building a team where the majority of members are similar to the exclusion of one or two employees, there is more likely to be turnover (Seo et al., 2018) and fissures in the group as members communicate in an attempt to make sense of the differential treatment (Sias & Jablin, 1995; Omilion-Hodges & Baker, 2017).

It is important to remember that the leader is usually the driving force in shaping the group's culture. Leaders should think carefully about their team's driving values and then consider how to structure their group based on its underlying value system. This includes using intentional and inclusive communication but also considers the employee and client experience. Leaders may ask themselves the following questions:

- What does it mean to be a member of this team?
- What does it feel like to be a member of this team?
- What do our clients/stakeholders expect from us?
- What does it feel like to be our client/stakeholder?

These simple questions can help leaders consider if changes are necessary to various processes or procedures to align team goals with member and client/stakeholder experiences. Modifications may include new or updated onboarding procedures, team identity or building sessions, and feedback opportunities for members and stakeholders. Organizations may recruit for differences to ensure fresh perspectives and unique voices are contributing to work processes. Leaders may also have the ability to transform physical workspaces to make them more conducive to collaboration or simply more comfortable. Even refreshing the paint can go a long way in showing employees that their leader and organization care about their experience. Table 4.1 includes some characteristics of healthy teams.

Groupthink

Groupthink describes types of faulty decision-making generated by a group prioritizing unanimous agreement above all else, especially thoughtful discussion of other considerations (Janis, 1972). Janis identified eight signs of groupthink that stem from either overconfidence, closemindedness, or internal group pressures.

Table 4.1 Sharpening your communication skills: team building skills

After studying more than 75 different types of teams, Larson and LaFasto (1989) found eight characteristics of healthy teams:

- **Establish clear goals:** Goals should be SMART (specific, measurable, attainable, relevant, and time-based) and resonate with each team member. Goals that are challenging, but attainable keep members committed, engaged, and focused on the results.
- **Focus on results:** Creating a results-driven culture means that everyone is accountable and has clearly defined role responsibilities. Establishing and following team processes can also help provide members with the structure necessary to be successful individually and collectively.
- **Recruit and align able members:** A high-functioning team is better than the sum of individual members, but only in cases where members are able to fulfill I role responsibilities and collaborate effectively with others.
- **Facilitate member commitment:** Engage members by having them play an active role in setting group goals and helping to shape group procedures. Members who feel personal ownership of group goals and successes are more likely to remain committed and put in the effort necessary to help the group be successful.
- **Maintain a collaborative environment:** Set up physical spaces and time for collaboration and interpersonal relationship building. This allows members to establish and maintain open communication.
- **Establish standards of excellence:** Create a culture of individual and group achievement where members are rewarded for meeting goals and consequences are clear for those who continually under-perform or miss deadlines.
- **Opportunities for external support and recognition:** In addition to basic role benefits (i.e., salary, fringe benefits) members have the opportunity to be rewarded for exemplary work. This may be in the form of financial bonuses, but hard work can also be acknowledged through praise, promotion, or professional development opportunities.
- **Enact principled leadership:** By role modeling desired behavior, titled leaders are able to illustrate ethical behavior while upholding a standard of excellence. This is easier said than done, but the most effective way to motivate employees and get them to adopt these team building skills is to enact them yourself.

Source Larson and LaFasto (1989)

Internal Group Pressures

- **Pressure on dissenters:** Whether implicit or explicit, coercing or applying pressure for members to agree can prove extremely detrimental to group decision-making.
- **Illusion of unanimity:** Members inadvertently assume that everyone is on the same page. This can happen because no one voices concerns or because decisions are made hastily without a dedicated space (i.e., meeting) for discussion.

- **Self-appointed mindguards:** Just as Dwight Schrute seeks to shield manager Michael Scott from any dissent, self-appointed mindguards censor information before it reaches the leader.
- **Self-censorship:** For various reasons, members may decide not to share concerns, considerations, or dissent with the group.

Closemindedness

- **Stereotyping outside groups:** Some groups may adopt an us vs. them mentality. This competitive/combative approach allows them to believe that their decisions are inherently correct compared to the other group's.
- **Collective rationalization:** Group members may come up with reasons to justify or rationalize particular decisions. This behavior can become systematic and often leads to self-deception.

Overconfidence

- **Belief in the group's inherent morality:** Groups who fail to question their decisions and how decisions align with their values may succumb to groupthink because their group choices are founded on assumptions.
- **The illusion of invulnerability:** After a series of successes, groups may develop a "can't lose" attitude, leading them to take unnecessary or unfounded risks.

Leadership in Different Teams

Leadership looks and feels different in every team. However, groups can look and feel different based on the leader and based on the context of the team. Some standard team configurations and contexts concerning how team-member exchange and leadership may look different are reviewed. Chapter 5 provides more depth in terms of leadership in various work contexts, such as healthcare, education, military, etc.

Traditional, Face-to-Face, Leader-Led Teams

Most employees have had at least some experience with the traditional, face-to-face, single-leader led team. In this situation, leaders can build a high-functioning workgroup by being mindful of how they distribute resources among members, the quality of their leader–member relationships, and managing member perceptions of their relationships and resources (Omilion-Hodges & Baker, 2013). Leaders can help engineer a workgroup that employees perceive as fair by committing to transparency and frequently communicating to members about group goals and individual performance. Leaders will also do well to link prosocial employee behaviors to rewards and damaging behaviors with consequences to set and maintain clear expectations. One additional benefit of a traditional, face-to-face team is that leaders can provide members with time and the physical space to engage in team building and interpersonal relationship development. In this setting, leaders should take advantage of face-to-face communication as opposed to relying on email, IM, or other mediated channels as a means to increase dialogue, rapport, and enhance group decision-making.

Virtual Teams

These teams are becoming more prevalent as organizations realize that it is possible to meet organizational goals when employees work remotely while also saving organizations the costs associated with brick and mortar buildings. Recent research suggests that more than two-thirds of professionals globally telecommute at least one day per week, and over 50% report working from home at least half of the week (IWG Global Workspace Survey, 2019). Gallup studies (Mann & Adkins, 2017) have also reported steady increases over the past decade regarding the number of Americans who complete some or all of their work remotely.

In these settings, it is recommended that leaders and members lean toward over-communicating rather than assuming everyone is on the same page. This likely means more frequent, but not necessarily time-consuming, mediated meetings over Teams or WebEx or a similar instant messaging and video system. In these settings, members automatically have more autonomy over their time and physical surroundings because they are not required to report to a specific location at a particular time. Expectations should be clear and communicated in writing, in terms of work-hour expectations, dress, availability, etc. Leaders and members are both cautioned about having work bleed over into home life, as it can be tempting to respond to emails that come in after hours. It is recommended that leaders set an example for members or, at the very least, provide guidance on what is expected of them in terms of response time and after-hours availability.

Team building in virtual teams is a must. However, in the absence of routine face-to-face encounters, interpersonal relationships may take longer to develop. One way to begin to broker trusting peer relationships is through clear role responsibilities and useful online tools. Depending on the scope and nature of the team's work, it may be helpful to use a service such as Slack to centralize tasks and mimic aspects of the face-to-face environment. In this sense, chat rooms replace traditional conference rooms, for example. Other apps or software similarly allow users to share files, maintain a searchable database, and give members opportunities to meet in dyads or groups. Once the tools are in place, it becomes easier to develop trusting relationships than to feel frustrated about project management or get hung up because a peer did not upload a file.

Co-lead Teams

The key to success in co-lead teams are clearly defined role expectations and boundaries, but with a joint focus on shared ownership (Newton, 2015). This is not only true for the leaders, but members should also be aware of the scope of each leader's role and related responsibilities. Role responsibilities may require renegotiating as the team grows or contracts and as projects or circumstances change. It is also essential that roles and responsibilities are divided and agreed upon by the co-leaders.

In co-lead teams, the formal leaders must maintain open and frequent communication. Doing so will help them remain abreast of the task and relational developments among members and make sure that they are united in their messaging and actions. While this may sound and feel a little like parenting, it is! You do not want to inadvertently create a situation where members know that one leader is more lenient with procedures or another is more likely to blindly sign-off on projects because they are inundated. Co-lead teams can be incredibly productive and effective, yet the leaders need to remain committed to an integrated approach. A united face may prove challenging as the co-leaders develop relationships of varying strengths with each member. Depending on personality differences and working styles, members may find that one leader is better to approach mentoring, whereas the other can provide tactical support, for example.

Self-Directed Teams

There are many variations concerning self-directed teams. The common denominator, however, is the focus on employee agency. In self-directed teams, members often assume and share the responsibilities that traditional leaders would in terms of goal setting, individual and group responsibilities, and in some cases, are even charged with dividing performance bonuses. For these teams to be successful, employees must be committed to the group and the organization. Organizations must also approach work from the perspective of high leadership-employee trust (Prykucki, 2012). Many organizations that utilize self-directed work teams go a step further to make employees owners or provide other incentives. For example, Johnsonville Foods empowered employees to decide whether the company would take on a new product line. While the benefits were clear, the decision would require employees to work 6- to 7-days per week for months on end. When the employees voted (nearly unanimously), product quality rose. The company continues to be recognized as one of *HR Magazine's* 50 best companies to work for (see Table 4.2 for related Organizational Profile). Google offers another excellent example in affording engineering employees up to 20% of their time on pet projects. Granting this autonomy shows employees that they are trusted and valued and often results in increased employee commitment and reduced turnover.

Table 4.2 Leadership in action—organizational profile: Johnsonville Foods

Ralph Stayer, CEO of Johnsonville Foods Inc., instituted a self-management structure in the early 1990s. Stayer built the new organizational structure around the idea that employees want to be successful, they want to contribute, and if given the chance, they will rise to the occasion. Johnsonville Foods is still consistently rated as a top local and national place to work and is the No. 1 national sausage brand in the United States.
How did Johnsonville Foods achieve and maintain this external and internal success? They invested in members and treated them as colleagues, rather than hired hands. Employees are taught about the organization and its history, short-term and long-term goals, and members define their own goals and propose strategies for reaching them. This approach requires the organization to relinquish some traditional control and embrace more flexibility, but it appears that it works considering the decades of success Johnsonville has enjoyed.

Source Stayer (1990)

Um, Who Is My Leader?

This can be a very challenging team situation in which to find yourself. The below section on leadership emergence offers insight into how formal and informal leaders can arise in groups. However, in instances where no traditional leader is appointed, communication is king. Members can organize to create a self-directed workgroup, perhaps without the organizational benefits discussed above, but with enough structure and clarity to thrive. Members should discuss and outline group goals, deadlines, and responsibilities. Members can discuss specific roles and processes for achieving group goals after ground rules are established. It is important to discuss expectations for where files will be stored and what communication tools (i.e., Microsoft Teams, Slack, etc.) are preferred. Discussing expectations for handling interpersonal conflict early on is also essential to promote the group's collective functioning and well-being.

Leading in Some Teams and not in Others: Becoming a Boundary Spanner

While much of this book focuses on advice for those in titled leadership positions, it is also important to remember that employees should always practice self-leadership. Enacting self-leadership means committing to intentional and inclusive language and behaviors. In addition to being mindful of your influence on others, engaging in self-leadership can also allow you to become a boundary spanner. Boundary spanners are individuals who can link disparate groups within or outside of the organization. This function not only helps to centralize information and build an appreciation of other groups, but it can also enhance an employee's intrinsic value and social capital because of the linking function they serve and the scope of relationships they develop.

So, what does boundary spanning look like? Let us start with a focal employee, Elizabeth, who works in a large metropolitan hospital's marketing department. As a member of the marketing department, Elizabeth already interacts with a wide variety of employees at all levels. For example, she is charged with leading marketing efforts for the hospital's orthopedics, obstetrics and gynecology, and palliative care units. Additionally, when the hospital forms a project group for emergency preparedness and needs a marketing representative, Elizabeth joins. Also, as someone who is dedicated to employee engagement, Elizabeth volunteers for the employee recognition group. She also learned of a weekly yoga group that meets on-site and signed up for that as well. Aside from living a full life, Elizabeth is also serving essential roles in her organization above and beyond those for which she was hired. Besides fulfilling her marketing duties, she serves as a liaison formally and informally between the various groups she is a part of and the stakeholders she serves. When the marketing department has to make decisions about the emergency group or create fliers for an upcoming employee recognition event, they can defer to Elizabeth. As a member of these other groups, it is also likely that she will get a quicker response than if the inquiry were to come from a non-member. Boundary spanners can act as the glue in the connecting functions that they play in organizations and, as such, have been referred to as unofficial PR ambassadors (Omilion-Hodges & Baker, 2014). Serving in boundary spanner roles or other groups where no formal leader is appointed presents the opportunity to emerge as the leader.

Leadership Emergence

While leadership emergence can be incredibly complex, Borman (1975) and colleagues offer an accessible model to clarify the process. They talk about leadership emergence as a "method of residues." What the researchers mean by this is that initially, all group members have the opportunity to emerge as the leader. That is until they intentionally or inadvertently remove themselves from contention. Members who either fail to contribute to the group or offer outlandish suggestions or who use exclusionary behavior or language are tacitly removed from the running. After initial members become non-contenders, two (or more) camps tend to emerge. These usually include two leadership candidates and their trusted lieutenants—a group member who endorses their ideas and their approach. Once one of the two candidates proves him/her/themselves as the clear leader, all other members look to them for guidance and influence.

If you want to emerge as the leader, being engaged in discussions, helping to moderate conversation, and practicing active listening will help you be viewed as an early contender. There may also be instances when you do not want or do not have the time to serve as the leader. In these cases, it is always best to be honest about your availability and your intentions. If members do not directly express their desire or inability to lead, some common passive behaviors individuals often engage in include (Ellis & Fisher, 1994):

- Missing group meetings or coming late or leaving early
- Contributing very little or not at all to group discussion
- Indicating that you are not an "idea person" but could help to carry out the group's plan
- Physically attending meetings, but paying more attention to your screens (i.e., phone, tablet, computer) than to the group discussion

Leadership Moments: Takeaways for Leaders & Members

- **High-quality team relationships can counteract a low-LMX relationship:** While it is typically in an employee's best interest to develop a high-quality leader–member exchange, sometimes it is just not in the cards. However, recent research (Wang & Hollenbeck, 2019) has found that in instances where members have highly developed expertise and are not easily replaceable, TMX may provide a shield against low-LMX consequences. Authority differentiation, or the degree to which the leader is the sole decision-maker or if power is distributed, also plays a vital role. In teams with low authority differentiation, high TMX not only counteracts low-LMX relationships but also minimizes the otherwise positive impact of LMX. This finding bodes well for team cohesion and functioning and alleviates some of the stress placed on both leader and member in developing a high-quality exchange relationship.
- **Communication is critical:** The research is unanimous; communication is the vehicle through which relationships are developed and maintained. Communication is also the means through which goals are set, people aligned, and conflict navigated. The bottom line is that if teams are to function, members must communicate intentionally and frequently. If teams want to harness the group's collective power, members should establish group communication guidelines. Shared communication guidelines can include specific group roles that should be fulfilled and rotated through, norms for handling conflict, and regularly scheduled check-ins that can be

used to discuss group functioning. Time should also be set aside for members to develop a rapport over a sip or a bite.

- **Leadership functions and needs differ based on the team:** Work teams are morphing away from the traditional face to face model that has ruled organizations for decades. This change means that leaders need to adapt and consider how best to approach collaborative work and foster cohesion in whatever context the team exists. Regardless of format, the leader should survey members to ensure that they have access to the communication tools and resources they need to be successful. When employees have the resources they need to be successful, the leader should hold meetings to enlist members' help in deciding best practices for collaboration and feedback. Team buy-in often looks like bi-monthly individual one-on-one check-in meetings and bi-monthly team meetings. In virtual teams, leaders should designate time for banter, such as a group morning coffee or a weekly lunch date. If ideas stem from these meetings, great, but the goal is to give members opportunities to develop trusting interpersonal relationships and fulfill members' interpersonal needs.

Mini Case Study: "Functional Group Roles"

After reading this chapter, you realize that your team has developed some bad habits in terms of group roles. For example, not only do you not have enough members routinely enacting the positive task and relational roles, but you can think of a specific member in your group who is the "monopolizer" and another who drains members' energy because they embody the "self-confessor" role. You also realize that you have a "central negative," which helps explain why it can be so challenging to get everyone on the same page.

1. How can you use your new knowledge of group roles to improve collective group functioning?
2. Thinking about routine meetings in particular, how can your knowledge of these roles begin to reshape the group's dynamic?
3. Now that you have a name for some of the negative and or unproductive group roles, how can you engage with individual members to encourage them to enact more positive roles?

4. Considering the favorable outcomes that positive group roles have on team output, what can formal leaders do to encourage these behaviors and roles?

References

Bakar, H., & Sheer, V. C. (2013). The mediating role of perceived cooperative communication in the relationship between interpersonal exchange relationships and perceived group cohesion. *Management Communication Quarterly, 27*(3), 443–465. https://doi.org/10.1177/0893318913492564.

Banks, G. C., Batchelor, J. H., Seers, A., O'boyle, E. H., Pollack, J. M., & Gower, K. (2013). What does team-member exchange bring to the party? A meta-analytic review of team and leader social exchange. *Journal of Organizational Behavior, 35*(2), 273–295. https://doi.org/10.1002/job.1885.

Borman, W. C. (1975). Effects of instructions to avoid halo error on reliability and validity of performance evaluation ratings. *Journal of Applied Psychology, 60*(5), 556–560. https://psycnet.apa.org/doi/10.1037/0021-9010.60.5.556.

Chen, Z., & Liu, Y. (2020). The effects of leadership and reward policy on employees' electricity saving behaviors: An empirical study in China. *International Journal of Environmental Research and Public Health, 17*(6), 2019. https://doi.org/10.3390/ijerph17062019.

Chen, Z., Takeuchi, R., & Shum, C. (2013). A social information processing perspective of coworker influence on a focal employee. *Organization Science, 24*(6), 1618–1639. https://doi.org/10.1287/orsc.2013.0820.

Chiaburu, D. S., & Harrison, D. A. (2008). Do peers make the place? Conceptual synthesis and meta-analysis of coworker effects on perceptions, attitudes, OCBs, and performance. *Journal of Applied Psychology, 93*(5), 1082–1103. https://doi.org/10.1037/0021-9010.93.5.1082.

Cragan, J. F., Wright, D. W., & Kasch, C. R. (2009). *Communication in small groups: Theory, process, skills* (7th ed.). Wadsworth Cengage Learning.

Communication in the real world: An introduction to communication studies. (n.d.). https://open.lib.umn.edu/communication/.

Ellis, D. G., & Fisher, B. A. (1994). *Small group decision making: Communication and the group process* (4th ed.). McGraw-Hill.

Farmer, S. M., Barton, F. W., Van Dyne, L., & Kamdar, D. (2015). The contextualized self: How team-member exchange leads to coworker identification and helping OCB. *Journal of Applied Psychology, 100*(2), 583–595. https://doi.org/10.1037/a0037660.

Golden, T. D. (2006). The role of relationships in understanding telecommuter satisfaction. *Journal of Organizational Behavior, 27*(3), 319–340. https://doi.org/10.1002/job.369.

Hooper, D. T., & Martin, R. (2008). Beyond personal leader-member exchange (LMX) quality: The effects of perceived LMX variability on employee reactions. *Leadership Quarterly, 19*(1), 20–30. https://doi.org/10.1016/j.leaqua.2007.12.002.

International Workplace Group. (2019, March). *The IWG global workspace survey: Welcome to Generation Flex—The employee power shift*. https://assets.regus.com/pdfs/iwg-workplace-survey/iwg-workplace-survey-2019.pdf.

Janis, I. (1972). *Victims of groupthink*. Houghton Mifflin.

Larson, C., & LaFasto, F. (1989). *Teamwork: What must go right/what can go wrong*. Sage.

Lee, K. (2020). The joint effects of leader-member exchange and team-member exchange in predicting job crafting. *Sustainability (Switzerland), 12*(8), 3283. https://doi.org/10.3390/SU12083283.

Li, A. N., & Liao, H. (2014). How do leader–member exchange quality and differentiation affect performance in teams? An integrated multilevel dual process model. *Journal of Applied Psychology, 99*(5), 847–866. https://psycnet.apa.org/doi/10.1037/a0037233.

Li, H., Feng, Z., Liu, C., Cheng, D., & Province, J. (2014). The impact of relative leader-member exchange on employees' work behaviors as mediated by psychological contract fulfillment. *Social Behavior and Personality, 42*(1), 79–88. https://doi.org/10.2224/sbp.2014.42.1.79.

Liao, F. Y., Yang, L. Q., Wang, M., Drown, D., & Shi, J. (2013). Team-member exchange and work engagement: Does personality make a difference? *Journal of Business and Psychology, 28*, 63–77. https://doi.org/10.1007/s10869-012-9266-5.

Liao, H., Liu, D., & Loi, R. (2010). Looking at both sides of the social exchange coin: A social cognitive perspective on the joint effects of relationship quality and differentiation on creativity. *Academy of Management Journal, 53*(5), 1090–1109. https://doi.org/10.5465/amj.2010.54533207.

Liden, R. C., & Maslyn, J. M. (1998). Multidimensionafity of leader-member exchange: An empirical assessment through scale development. *Journal of Management, 24*, 43–72. https://doi.org/10.1177/014920639802400105.

Liden, R. C., Wayne, S. J., & Sparrowe, R. T. (2000). An examination of the mediating role of psychological empowerment on the relations between the job, interpersonal relationships, and work outcomes. *Journal of Applied Psychology, 85*(3), 407–416. https://psycnet.apa.org/doi/10.1037/0021-9010.85.3.407.

Mann, A., & Adkins, A. (2017, March). *America's coming workplace: Home alone*. Gallup. https://news.gallup.com/businessjournal/206033/america-coming-workplace-home-alone.aspx.

Martins, L. L., & Shalley, C. E. (2011). Creativity in virtual work: Effects of demographic differences. *Small Group Research, 42*, 536–561. https://doi.org/10.1177/1046496410397382.

Muñoz-Doyague, M. F., & Nieto, M. (2012). Individual creativity performance and the quality of interpersonal relationships. *Industrial Management & Data Systems, 112*, 125–145. https://doi.org/10.1108/02635571211193671.

Newton, R. (2015, July 14). How to co-lead a team. *Harvard Business Review*. https://hbr.org/2015/07/how-to-co-lead-a-team.

Omilion-Hodges, L. M., & Ackerman, C. D. (2017). From the technical know-how to the free flow of ideas: Exploring the effects of leader, peer, and team communication on employee creativity. *Communication Quarterly, 66*(1), 38–57. https://doi.org/10.1080/01463373.2017.1325385.

Omilion-Hodges, L. M., & Baker, C. R. (2013). Contextualizing LMX within the workgroup: The effects of LMX and justice on relationship quality and resource sharing among peers. *The Leadership Quarterly, 24*, 935–951. https://doi.org/10.1016/j.leaqua.2013.10.004.

Omilion-Hodges, L. M., & Baker, C. R. (2014). Everyday talk and convincing conversations: Utilizing strategic internal communication. *Business Horizons, 57*(3), 435–445. https://doi.org/10.1016/j.bushor.2014.02.002.

Omilion-Hodges, L. M., & Baker, C. R. (2017). Communicating leader-member relationship quality: The development of leader communication exchange scales to measure relationship building and maintenance through the exchange of communication-based goods. *International Journal of Business Communication, 54*(2), 115–145. https://doi.org/10.1177/2329488416687052.

Omilion-Hodges, L. M., Ptacek, J. K., & Zerilli, D. H. (2016). A comprehensive review and communication research agenda of the contextualized workgroup: The evolution and future of leader-member exchange, coworker exchange, and team-member exchange. *Annals of the International Communication Association, 40*(1), 343–377. https://doi.org/10.1080/23808985.2015.11735265.

Prykucki, B. (2012, November 30). *Self-directed work teams allow employee leadership to shine*. Michigan State University, MSU Extension. https://www.canr.msu.edu/news/self_directed_work_teams_allow_employee_leadership_to_shine.

Schermuly, C. C., & Meyer, B. (2015). Good relationships at work: The effects of leader-member exchange and team-member exchange on psychological empowerment, emotional exhaustion, and depression. *Journal of Organizational Behavior, 37*(5), 673–691. https://doi.org/10.1002/job.2060.

Seers, A. (1989). Team-member exchange quality: A new construct for role-making research. *Organizational Behavior and Human Decision Processes, 43,* 118–135. https://doi.org/10.1016/0749-5978(89)90060-5.

Seers, A., Petty, M. M., & Cashman, J. F. (1995). Team-member exchange under team and traditional management: A naturally occurring quasi-experiment. *Group and Organization Management, 20*(1), 18–38. https://doi.org/10.1177/1059601195201003.

Seers, A., Wilkerson, J. M., & Grubb, W. L. (2006). Toward measurement of social exchange resources: Reciprocal contributions and receipts. *Psychological Reports, 98,* 508–510.

Seo, J., Nahrgang, J. D., Carter, M. Z., & Hom, P. W. (2018). Not all differentiation is the same: Examining the moderating effects of leader-member exchange (LMX) configurations. *Journal of Applied Psychology, 103*(5), 478–495. https://doi.org/10.1037/apl0000262.

Sheer, V. C. (2015). "Exchange lost" in leader-member exchange theory and research: A critique and a reconceptualization. *Leadership, 11*(2), 213–229. https://doi.org/10.1177/1742715014530935.

Sherony, K. M., & Green, S. G. (2002). Coworker exchange: Relationships between coworkers, leader-member exchange, and work attitudes. *Journal of Applied Psychology, 87*(3), 542–548. https://doi.org/10.1037/0021-9010.87.3.542.

Sias, P., & Jablin, F. M. (1995). Differential superior-subordinate relations, perceptions of fairness, and coworker communication. *Human Communication Research, 22*(1), 5–38. https://doi.org/10.1111/j.1468-2958.1995.tb00360.x.

Stayer, R. (1990). How I learned to let my workers lead. *Harvard Business Review, 68*(6), 66–83.

Terpstra-Tong, J., Ralston, D. A., Treviño, L. J., Naoumova, I., de la Garza Carranza, M. T., Furrer, O., Li, Y., & Darder, F. L. (2020). The quality of leader-member exchange (LMX): A multilevel analysis of individual-level, organizational-level and societal-level antecedents. *Journal of International Management, 26*(3), 100760. https://doi.org/10.1016/j.intman.2020.100760.

Tse, H. H. M. (2014). Linking leader-member exchange differentiation to work team performance. *Leadership & Organization Development Journal, 35*(8), 710–724. https://doi.org/10.1108/LODJ-09-2012-0119.

Tse, H. H. M., Dasborough, M. T., & Ashkanasy, N. M. (2008). A multi-level analysis of team climate and interpersonal exchange relationships at work. *Leadership Quarterly, 19,* 195–211. https://doi.org/10.1016/j.leaqua.2008.01.005.

Vinarski-Peretz, H., Binyamin, G., & Carmeli, A. (2010). Subjective relational experiences and employee innovative behaviors in the workplace. *Journal of*

Vocational Behavior, 78(2), 290–304. https://doi.org/10.1016/j.jvb.2010.09.005.

Wang, L. C., & Hollenbeck, J. R. (2019). LMX in team-based contexts: TMX, authority differentiation, and skill differentiation as boundary conditions for leader reciprocation. *Personnel Psychology, 72*(2), 271–290. https://doi.org/10.1111/peps.12306.

Weick, K. E., Sutcliffe, K. M., & Obstfeld, D. (2005). Organizing and the process of sensemaking. *Organization Science, 16*(4), 409–421. https://doi.org/10.1287/orsc.1050.0133.

Xu, A. J., Loi, R., & Lam, L. W. (2015). The bad boss takes it all: How abusive supervision and leader-member exchange interact to influence employee silence. *Leadership Quarterly, 26*(5), 763–774. https://doi.org/10.1016/j.leaqua.2015.03.002.

PART II

Exploring the Various Intersections of Communication and Leadership

CHAPTER 5

Leadership in Different Organizations and Sectors

Abstract Just as leaders should tailor their communication based on their audience (which you will read more about in Chapter 7), it is necessary to consider how leadership differs in various organizations and sectors. For example, do leaders communicate and "lead" differently whether they work for a for-profit or non-profit organization? Are there differences between leadership styles in Fortune 500 companies versus small startup businesses? The research literature is rife with findings linking certain leadership characteristics and styles to different organizational types and sectors. For example, task-oriented leadership behaviors have been linked to staff- and patient relative-assessed quality of care in healthcare (Havig et al., 2011), and charismatic and transformational leaders are most effective in the military, but special consideration should be taken concerning the type of task, people involved, and resources and time available in each situation (Hamad, 2015). This chapter approaches many types of organizations and sectors—such as non-profit, healthcare, education, military, startups, telework, and employee-owned—and explores how leadership differs in each. Research and expertise within each organization are summarized and translated into practical suggestions for effective leadership.

Keywords Non-profits · Healthcare · Military · Startups · Telework

L. M. Omilion-Hodges and J. K. Ptacek, *Leader-Member Exchange and Organizational Communication*, New Perspectives in Organizational Communication, https://doi.org/10.1007/978-3-030-68756-4_5

Just as leaders should tailor their communication based on their audience (which you will read more about in Chapter 7), it is necessary to consider how leadership differs in various organizations and sectors. For example, do leaders communicate and "lead" differently whether they work for a for-profit or non-profit organization? Are there differences between leadership styles in Fortune 500 companies versus small startup businesses? The research literature is rife with findings linking specific leadership characteristics and styles to different organizational types and sectors, as discussed in this chapter.

Leader–member exchange plays a vital role in each type of organization. In fact, the relationships leaders build with employees are critical to many key organizational outcomes, no matter the type of organization. However, LMX likely looks different in each organization type. For example, leaders in non-profit organizations might focus on inspiring vision within each employee to build dedication toward their work that is crucial for retaining non-profit employees. In contrast, a leader in a healthcare organization may be able to build relationships with employees based on their mutual interests in caring for others. Different organizational goals shape how leaders communicate with members. This chapter describes several organizations and industries and explores some of their unique benefits and challenges and how leadership differs in each. Research within each type of organization is summarized and translated into practical suggestions for effective leadership.

Organization Types

Factors such as employee needs, organizational goals, and leadership styles vary depending on the organization's type. Below we explore various organizations, including non-profits, healthcare, education, military, startups, telework, and employee-owned. Leadership styles are introduced as they apply to different organizational contexts but are discussed in greater detail in Chapter 9.

Non-profits

Non-profit organizations face different challenges than for-profit organizations. For example, research (Hoekstra & Peterson, 2005; McClean, 2005) has identified that while leaders in for-profit organizations experience challenges related to investor relations, recruiting, and adopting a marketing orientation, among others, leaders in non-profit organizations focus more on balancing efficiency and effectiveness while keeping mission and passion at the forefront (Bear & Fitzgibbon, 2005; McMurray et al., 2010). *Mission* is at the core of the creation of a non-profit organization, and leaders must not only focus on professionally managing and maintaining performance objectives and financial pressures to keep the organization running, but doing so with a base that may be primarily composed of volunteers or underpaid employees (Bear & Fitzgibbon, 2005). That being said, the LMX relationship may look different in this type of organization, as leaders and members may spend more time communicating about the organizational mission and why it matters personally to them. Additionally, the reward systems for non-profit organizations may differ considerably from for-profits. Non-profits' rewards are closely tied to reaching a social mission, whereas for-profit organizations are linked with profit-related accomplishments (McMurray et al., 2010). Considering this focus, leaders of non-profits must be passionate, organized, and excellent at articulating and inspiring a vision (Bear & Fitzgibbon, 2005). With these challenges and differences in mind, just as we know that leaders cannot communicate with each member in an organization in the same way, we cannot expect the same leadership style to work successfully in organizations that have different goals and varied employee motivations.

Although the number of non-profit organizational contexts is too numerous to pinpoint just one best communication practice or effective leadership style (Lord et al., 2001), some styles have been found to work well in specific contexts. For example, research (McMurray et al., 2010) in a religious/church-based non-profit organization found transformational leadership behaviors to consistently promote positive emotions, well-being, and commitment in members. In a study with church members, others (Allen et al., 2013) also found that transformational leadership (which focuses on followers' values and motives to work toward change) encouraged a psychological climate for both organizational creativity and organizational change readiness, whereas laissez-faire leadership (in which the leader overall avoids decisions and action) was negatively associated with these outcomes and transactional leadership had no relationship with either outcome. Transformational leadership has also been linked to creating strong cultural consensus on organizational values that bolster innovation within non-profit human service organizations (Jaskyte, 2004). Other research of employees across various non-profit organizations (Yasir et al., 2016) has found that transformational leadership is positively related to employee trust, whereas laissez-faire leadership is negatively related to employee trust; furthermore, transformational and transactional leadership (i.e., a quid pro quo approach to the leader–member relationship) is positively related to employee trust toward organizational change capacity. Taken together, findings suggest that while a transformational style of leadership is effective in addressing the needs of various non-profit organizations, a laissez-faire leadership style should be avoided. Being just a competent leader is often not sufficient to encourage the change and creativity that is integral to managing a successful non-profit organization. Instead, leaders must adopt more transformational behaviors (Allen et al., 2013).

If you want to be a successful leader in a non-profit organization, it is all about balancing and being aware of the competing challenges that can shift over time. Bear and Fitzgibbon (2005) forward several pragmatic communication strategies, stemming from the leadership attributes of *context*, *preparation*, and *persuasion*, for how to lead in a non-profit organization successfully:

- Continuously develop professional leaders who understand non-profit organizations
- Create clear roles, responsibilities, and expectations for members
- Include board and staff members in decision-making
- Seek and utilize staff and board members' strengths
- Invest in good people and evaluate their performance
- Share best practices with other non-profit organizations
- Develop a strong organizational culture
- Persuade others of your mission and work

In addition to these suggestions, Table 5.1 includes some tips on igniting passion among employees, not only in non-profits but also across organizational contexts.

Table 5.1 Sharpening your communication skills: igniting passion across organizational contexts

As a leader, inspiring passion among members is not just for non-profit organizations. In every type of company, leaders are expected to inspire and motivate employees to work toward the organizational mission and overcome today's work challenges. Bilimoria and Godwin (2005) address five elements of engaging employees' passion:

- **A positive vision of the future:** A leader should communicate an ideal image that the organization aims to achieve and a clear path in which to obtain and sustain it. This provides a goal and steps for organizational members to work toward. Good vision statements are inspirational, positive, and look to the future.
- **Inspiring core values:** A good vision should be built from an organization's values. Values show what is important to the organization and serve as guidelines for their decisions. Good leaders inspire these values through leading by example.
- **An engaging and inclusive leadership style:** It is important for a leader to recognize which leadership style(s) are most effective in a given context and how the style(s) impact the organization so they can adjust when needed. They must lead in an engaging and inclusive way to inspire enthusiasm and empower others.
- **Emotional intelligence competencies:** Emotional intelligence involves understanding your own and others' emotions and managing these emotions within your relationships with others. A strong leader-member relationship involves an emotionally intelligent leader who can establish positive emotional connections.
- **Leadership courage:** Courage is not only required in making risky decisions that could be greatly rewarding, but it is also integral to inspiring passion. Courage shows that a leader has more than just technical know-how, and it is exemplified through making difficult decisions, confronting issues, and doing what is right.

Source Bilimoria and Godwin (2005)

Healthcare

Leader–member exchange is integral to many healthcare organizations' outcomes, not just for organizational members but for patients. For example, leadership style has been recognized as one of the most important patient satisfaction indicators, reducing adverse effects, patient safety, and other quality of care components (Sfantou et al., 2017). The Institute of Medicine (IOM, 2001) has identified six aims for healthcare quality, which include:

- **Safe:** provide care to patients safely and avoid harm
- **Effective:** services are necessary and have been proven to benefit patients
- **Patient-centered:** consider individual patient needs, wants, and values
- **Timely:** care is given in a timely manner with minimal waiting

- **Efficient:** using only necessary equipment, supplies, ideas, and energy
- **Equitable:** each individual is provided the same quality of care regardless of personal characteristics

Successful leaders in healthcare organizations prioritize quality care and strive to lead others to do the same. Research (Sfantou et al., 2017) has found relationships among various leadership styles and effectively upholding quality care standards and related employee outcomes. For example, consensus leaders (i.e., those who solicit and apply input from their members) improved quality of certain healthcare services and decreased employee turnover levels (Castle & Decker, 2011). Consensus leaders strive to build LMX relationships based on open and frequent communication with employees. Resonant leadership (i.e., leaders with high emotional intelligence and empathy) has been linked to high-quality LMX relationships, which influence work environment quality and safety climate, ultimately decreasing medication errors as well as nurse turnover and emotional exhaustion (Squires et al., 2010). Communication in these relationships is focused on listening and understanding employees' feelings and needs. A task-oriented leadership style (i.e., particularly focusing on structure, coordination, and communicating clear roles and expectations) has been positively related to staff- and patient relative-assessed quality of care (Havig et al., 2011). Transformational leadership, focused on communicating a clear vision and connecting employees to that vision has also been linked to several positive outcomes, such as lower patient mortality, effective organizational culture, and increased patient satisfaction and safety, among others (Casida & Pinto-Zipp, 2008; Sfantou et al., 2017).

Leaders in healthcare organizations face several challenges, including recruiting the best providers, keeping turnover low, and reducing stress and burnout. Hargett and colleagues (2017) identified five core communication-based healthcare leadership competencies based on the core principle of patient-centeredness. These include:

- **Integrity:** having personal integrity and communicating effectively
- **Teamwork:** building and maintaining relationships and motivating people

- **Critical thinking**: having a strong knowledge base and pursuing excellence
- **Emotional intelligence**: developing self-awareness and continuing personal development
- **Selfless service:** maintaining patient-centeredness

Education

Although many healthcare and education organizations are non-profit, we cannot assume that the same leadership styles are effective across these contexts (McMurray et al., 2010). Leadership roles in academic organizations also look different from other organizations. For example, traditional organizational senior leadership roles might include President, Vice-President, and Chief Executive, whereas academic leadership roles include Deans and Heads of School (Black, 2015). Furthermore, teacher, faculty, and researcher roles also include some form of leadership responsibility. Current challenges in higher education include globalization and internationalization of universities, the growth of for-profit private universities, shifting to virtual environments, changing technologies, and cuts to public funding (Black, 2015; Tipple, 2010). Public education in the United States also faces many challenges, such as growing classroom size, a technology gap between students and teachers, parent involvement, pushing back against privatization, and lack of funding (Alvarez et al., 2018; Chen, 2020).

Research has found certain leadership styles to be useful in various educational contexts. For example, Pepper (2010) has found that a balance of transformational and transactional leadership styles allows educational members to combine expertise in decision-making to work toward change and a shared vision. Similarly, Voon and colleagues (2009) found a preference toward transformational and transactional leadership styles in higher education leadership, with less preference toward a laissez-faire leadership style. Others (Alonderiene & Majauskaite, 2016) have found that transformational, servant (or serving others through leading), and coach styles of leadership are positively related to job satisfaction in higher education employees and are preferred over transactional and autocratic styles. This means that LMX relationships in many educational contexts are strengthened through open and transparent communication, involvement in decision-making, and communicating a clear vision for the organization.

The myriad issues facing the education sector require leaders to have a clear understanding of the complexities of educational organizations and the skills necessary to lead others and effectively handle these issues while prioritizing student learning. Jones and colleagues (2012) argue for a more distributed leadership approach (which has many transformational leadership qualities), which embraces all organizational members, both in direct and indirect roles related to students' teaching and learning. This more inclusive and collaborative leadership model is considered necessary in the education sector and highlights the value of informal leadership (Ramsden, 1998). Others (Tipple, 2010) promote transformational leadership to motivate and inspire faculty to uphold their institutional vision and bolster job commitment and situational leadership to adapt to the continually changing educational environment. Drawing from the above suggestions and others, if you want to be an effective educational leader and build high-quality LMX relationships which lead to positive outcomes, you can focus on these ten traits (Lathan, n.d.):

- Understand the importance of building community
- Empower teachers and cultivate leadership skills
- Utilize data and resources to drive improvement
- Articulate a vision and a plan that members will support
- Create collaborative, inclusive learning environments
- Be passionate about your work
- Encourage risk-taking
- Lead by example
- Persevere and stay with a school for at least five years
- Be a lifelong learner

Military

Working in the military is a drastically different type of work than most other types of organizations. Many of its members must risk their own lives and welfare for those of others, and they can experience various adverse psychological effects while doing so (Taylor, 2005). The military is also one of the largest organizational sectors. Over 1.4 million people are on active duty within the multiple departments in the US military, and another 1.1 million are serving in the National Guard and Reserves (U.S. Department of Defense, n.d.). Considering the unique nature of military work and the number of members within its organizations, it is important to think about how leadership and LMX work within the military sector.

Military leaders face distinct challenges including the fact that commanders get no say in which service members work in their units, members are under contract so they cannot be fired, military commanders have a very high turnover rate, and service members are given responsibility at a much younger age than employees in business. Military commanders have more power than civilian leaders, and military commanders' workdays never end as they are responsible for their troops 24 hours a day (Taylor, 2005). These are in addition to the challenges facing modern military leadership, such as recruitment and retention, adapting to technology changes, using innovative evaluation methods for members, and motivating and developing other leaders, to name a few (Taylor, 2005).

Given the military organization's challenges, it is no wonder that leadership is at the core of the military's vision (Wong et al., 2003). It may also not be surprising that situational leadership may be necessary as leaders must adapt to the current circumstances and the organizational culture (Sousa et al., 2015). Hamad (2015) argues that charismatic and transformational leaders are most effective in the military, with the caveat that special consideration should be taken concerning the type of task, people involved, and resources and time available in each situation. This highlights the importance of LMX in that each leader–member relationship may vary depending on the person and the particular context of the work. Laurence (2011) urges us to consider incorporating authentic leadership with transformational, charismatic, and individualized leadership styles to highlight self-awareness, relational transparency, and other authentic behaviors that can lead to member trust and engagement. Communication skills that are especially important for military leaders include encouragement, inspiring motivation, listening to members' needs, and articulating a clear vision. Additionally, assertive leadership communication has been found to have a positive correlation with extraordinary effort, group effectiveness, and satisfaction (Sousa et al., 2015).

Being an effective leader in the military sector requires adapting to the unique challenges that the military faces. However, some leadership skills common in many types of organizations are also necessary for successful military leadership. For example, the United States Army

Field Manual (FM 22-100; Army, 1990) states the following fundamental communication expectations for Army leaders:

- Demonstrate tactical and technical competence
- Teach subordinates
- Be a good listener
- Treat soldiers with dignity and respect
- Stress basics (demonstrate and teach fundamental soldiering skills)
- Set the example
- Set and enforce standards

Start-Ups

Start-up organizations are quite different from all other organization types because "start-up" is a temporary term for an organization. A start-up is a new organization created based on a perceived market need for a product, service, or platform (McGowan, 2018). Start-ups begin small with the goal to grow tremendously, sometimes being acquired by larger existing companies. Starting an organization like this is often risky and uncertain because of its innovative nature. It forces the organization to effectively find its niche in the market and effective ways of running (McGowan, 2018). That being said, it can also lead to great rewards, as is evidenced in successful start-ups such as Amazon, Facebook, and Uber. Leadership is a vital component of a successful start-up, as there are no existing structures or procedures set in place in a brand new organization (Bryant, 2004). Start-up organizations face their own set of challenges that can either make or break the business. Some of these challenges (Salamzadeh & Kesim, 2015) include:

- **Financial:** all businesses need funds to begin, and for many new businesses they must find sources for this funding
- **Human resources**: as a start-up business grows, it may need additional employees
- **Support mechanisms:** a start-up often needs additional resources, such as venture capital or small business development centers to continue to grow and succeed

- **Environmental elements:** start-ups must pay attention to current trends, legal issues, and market limitations to avoid making critical mistakes

Hoekstra and Peterson (2005) add that start-up organizations face a potential challenge of leadership personality. An entrepreneur and leader of a start-up organization may have the skills needed to build the business early on but may have difficulty shifting once the business grows and changes. This suggests that using a situational leadership style and being flexible and adaptive are critical for a startup to succeed. Frequent communication with members and listening and responding to their needs as the organization grows and changes are important to building high-quality LMX relationships in startup organizations. Furthermore, in a study consisting of over 200 startups, researchers (Ensley et al., 2006) have found that using a shared leadership style within a startup team—including using directive, transactional, transformational, and empowering leader–member communication—led to more growth and performance in the organization. Researchers (Ensley et al., 2006) also explored a more traditional, top-down vertical leadership style in start-up organizations and have found that while directive and transactional communication behaviors were positively related to organizational growth, transformational and empowering communication styles were not. This is surprising given what we know about transformational leadership. Still, it also highlights the unique context of start-up organizations, in that transformational and empowering communication from the top-down may be perceived as unnecessary or even manipulative (Ensley et al., 2006).

If you want to build a start-up company, you likely already have the passion and creativity to put your ideas in place. However, you must consider what it takes to lead your organization to survive the difficult startup phase successfully. Drawing from the above findings and others (Isaacs, 2020; Raichur, 2018), here are some pragmatic communication considerations for effective leadership in a startup:

- Be confident, passionate, and positive to inspire followers to be that way too
- Be organized and have a clear vision
- Be humble and show genuine concern for others

- Understand your team and welcome challenges
- Embrace workers of all ages and diverse backgrounds
- Ask the right questions to hire the best people with a diversity of thought
- Provide the resources that your members need
- Communicate at all levels and be transparent
- Foster an open company culture where everyone feels important and included

Telework

Any of the above-mentioned types of organizations can have employees who work remotely, but can we lead in the same way in both in-person and virtual work environments? Virtual teams experience unique leadership challenges such as greater and more diverse conflict, time differences that hinder synchronous communication, difficulty achieving shared objectives and accountability, and limited relationship-development among leaders and team members (De Paoli & Ropo, 2015). Because telework is so different from a traditional work environment, we need to consider how leader–member exchange is impacted and how to best address these issues through virtual modalities. Furthermore, working remotely has increased 115% in the United States over the last ten years. Over half of working people indicate they would prefer a job that provided the option to telework (Remoters, 2020). Between this trend and the COVID-19 pandemic, organizations have been forced to find ways to make working remotely more easily accessible and possible. This has also forced leaders to consider ways in which they must adapt to maintain strong leader–member relationships.

Leadership is essential in virtual teams' success as relationship building, task coordination, and information dissemination are critical and often more challenging to accomplish remotely (Liao, 2017). Given the unique challenges of virtual leadership alone combined with those already present in all of the above traditional organizations, it is wise to consider that a situational mindset is necessary for telework. Research has also found several other effective leadership styles in various teleworking contexts, such as emergent, shared, and transformational leadership (De Paoli & Ropo, 2015). For example, encouraging self-management abilities within teams and adopting a shared leadership approach can help address the challenges of influence and motivation in virtual teams by team members helping to guide each other (Liao, 2017). Research (Hoch & Kozlowski, 2014) has found that shared leadership can strengthen team performance both in virtual and in-person teams. Additionally, transformational leadership has been connected to global virtual team success in motivating members, leader effectiveness, and team members' satisfaction with their leader (Zayani, 2008). Furthermore, research (Gajendran & Joshi, 2012) has found that LMX and communication frequency influence team decisions in virtual organizations, so it is critical to maintain frequent leader–member communication.

In addition to frequent communication from leaders to effectively run a virtual team, we want to highlight some practical steps for enabling shared leadership in virtual organizations. Leadership and organizational experts Hoegl and Muethel (2016) offer five research-based pragmatic communication leadership strategies:

- **Accept the new rules of the game:** accept that a leader's role may be different from in a co-located team, where it is easier to oversee members' work.
- **Respect team members' competencies:** understand that team members can also possess useful leadership abilities to help the team.
- **Encourage leadership behaviors:** actively find and encourage members to lead their work and help others.
- **Loosen the reins and avoid the "responsibility trap":** trust that you can provide team members autonomy and include them in decision making.
- **Becoming a true team member:** actively participate in the team's shared leadership and support team task accomplishments.

Employee-Owned

An employee-owned organization, also called an employee stock ownership plan (ESOP), is one in which employees are shareholders in the company (Casselbury, 2019). They are based on the principle that if employees have rights of participation and control, they focus on organizational productivity and success (Sauser, 2009). Employee-owned organizations are increasingly emerging and becoming more common in the United States and countries worldwide (see Table 5.2 for an orga-

Table 5.2 Leadership in action—organizational profile: Publix

As the world's largest employee-owned company and one of *Fortune's* "100 Best Companies to Work For," the Publix grocery chain exemplifies some notable qualities of a successful employee-owned organization (Clark, 2017).
Founded in 1930, the company has never laid off a single employee, or as they're called at Publix, "associates." Associates get frequent raises and receive and give feedback often. They also have a tuition reimbursement plan for employees who work there for over six months (Clark, 2017).
Here are some lessons related to supporting the Publix mission from founder, George Jenkins (Publix, n.d.):
1. Invest in others
2. Prepare for opportunity
3. Be there
4. Respect the dignity of the individual
How did Publix become one of the best companies to work for? They recognized the importance of building relationships and working together, providing opportunities to grow, being involved and listening to others, and giving everyone a voice and mutual respect.
These strategies have worked for Publix, as they now have over 1200 stores across seven states (Clark, 2017).

Source Clark (2017) and Publix (n.d.)

nizational example). As of 2020, there are an estimated 6600 employee-owned organizations in the U.S. with over 14 million members (NCEO, 2020). Generally, ESOP members do well financially, making more in wages and retirement assets than employees in non-ESOP organizations (NCEO, 2020). However, employee-owned organizations also face unique challenges. They experience greater risks of degeneration (they may not be able to maintain their democratic structure) and the abuse of power (having power can lead to corruption and selfishness) (Sauser, 2009). Furthermore, transitioning leadership from business founders can be difficult and result in business failure (Stranahan, 2019).

So what types of leadership styles work best when everyone owns the company? One obvious answer is shared leadership. Many employee-owned organizations have replaced traditional management with self-managed work teams, where leadership is shared (Sauser, 2009). Self-managed work teams, or autonomous workgroups, use participative decision making and share tasks and work responsibilities (Schermerhorn, 2005). Communication skills, especially important for leaders in this context, include frequent and open discussions and clear expectations of what needs to be done. Another leadership style that is effective in employee-owned companies is servant leadership. Outcomes of servant leadership—such as job satisfaction, organizational citizenship behavior, and organizational commitment—align with those pursued by employee-owned companies, so it would make sense to not only be a servant leader, but also lead in ways which manifests servant leadership among members (Sauser, 2009). LMX relationships can be successful by putting others' needs ahead of one's own, listening, and communicating empathy and understanding.

Considering the unique nature of leading in an employee-owned organization requires one to think in ways that can address all the possible challenges in this type of organization. Those (Sauser, 2009; Vanderslice, 2014) who have experienced and/or researched these challenges offer some practical communication-specific recommendations for leading and sustaining an employee-owned company:

- **Participation:** Have a participatory mindset and involve employees in strategic decisions.
- **Fairness:** Include employees in decisions by involving engagement, explanation, and clarity of expectations so that they are less likely to perceive a decision as unfair.
- **Development opportunities:** Offer employees opportunities to learn new skills, build knowledge, and take on new responsibilities.
- **Clarity about power and authority:** Understand the shift in power while still ensuring that decisions are made and employees are empowered.
- **Establish common foundational values:** Explicitly adopt a set of common foundational values that all employees know and practice.
- **Encourage servant leadership:** The success of an employee-owned organization rests on everyone helping each other.
- **Self-managed work teams**: All members participate and hold responsibility and help each other to grow.

Leadership Moments: Takeaways for Leaders and Members

- **Leadership challenges and demands vary by organization:** Because organizations have different goals and needs, it is not surprising that they hold additional opportunities for leaders. For example, a military or healthcare organization where individual lives are on the line would demand that leaders prioritize certain tasks before others every single time. However, a retail organization may have a series of tasks in a day that can be done in any order. How a leader communicates this information also depends on the demands of the situation. Recognizing and adapting to the current situation and organizational context is an important skill for an effective leader.

- **There is no one "perfect" leadership style:** Research shows that some aspects of various leadership styles are more or less effective for different types of organizations. For example, while transformational leadership and empowering communication has found to be effective in many types of organizations, it can be interpreted as more manipulative in start-up companies (Ensley et al., 2006). Furthermore, even switching from a co-located organization to telework within the same position and organization can demand a different leadership style as people work differently remotely. Understanding what types of behaviors members respond well to, instead of using one leadership style all the time, can improve work outcomes, including leader–member exchange relationships.
- **There are opportunities for members to engage in informal leadership in every organization:** As a leader, it may be challenging to let go of the idea that you must be in charge of what everyone is doing all the time. However, researchers (Hoegl & Muethel, 2016) argue that sharing responsibility and providing opportunities, and allowing employees to lead in certain situations can help make teams more effective. Encouraging an employee to help others can give them a sense of empowerment and build a connection with the organization.

Mini Case Study: "Going Virtual"

As an office manager of a manufacturing company, you are used to managing your team in person. You have daily meetings with your team in the conference room, and you are easily able to walk around to check on employees' progress throughout the day. The open office layout also allows team members to communicate throughout the day, bouncing ideas off each other and problem solving together. Although your company allows some employees to work from home, those individuals are on their own virtual team, and your team members specifically chose to come to the office every day because of the benefits of in-person work. However, recently your company has decided to shift to 100% telework, meaning that you and your employees now work from home. While the work you do is still the same, everything feels like it has changed. Overall productivity numbers have gone down, team cohesion seems to have declined, and some employees have even reached out to you and said they are struggling to stay on top of their workload in this new environment.

1. What are some of the other challenges you anticipate having now that your team is working remotely?
2. What can you do to help your employees struggling to stay on track?
3. How can you use what you know about shared leadership and virtual leadership to improve team communication and effectiveness?

References

Allen, S. L., Smith, J. E., & Da Silva, N. (2013). Leadership style in relation to organizational change and organizational creativity: Perceptions from nonprofit organizational members. *Nonprofit Management and Leadership, 24*(1), 23–42. https://doi.org/10.1002/nml.21078.

Alonderiene, R., & Majauskaite, M. (2016). Leadership style and job satisfaction in higher education institutions. *International Journal of Educational Management, 30*(1), 140–163. https://www.doi.org/10.1108/IJEM-08-2014-0106.

Alvarez, B., Walker, T., Long, C., & Litvinov, A. (2018, August 3). *10 challenges facing public education today.* National Education Association. https://www.nea.org/advocating-for-change/new-from-nea/10-challenges-facing-public-education-today.

Army, U. S. (1990). *Field manual 22-100, military leadership.* Washington, DC: US Government Printing Office. https://armyoe.files.wordpress.com/2018/03/1990-fm-22-100.pdf.

Bear, A. B., & Fitzgibbon, M. A. (2005), Leadership in a not-for-profit world: A mixed toolbox. In R. R. Sims & S. A. Quatro (Eds.), *Leadership: Succeeding in the private, public, and not-for-profit sectors* (pp. 87–104). M. E. Sharpe. https://citeseerx.ist.psu.edu/viewdoc/download?doi=10.1.1.457.9326&rep=rep1&type=pdf#page=107.

Bilimoria, D., & Godwin, L. (2005). Engaging people's passion: Leadership for the new century. In R. R. Sims & S. A. Quatro (Eds.), *Leadership: Succeeding in the private, public, and not-for-profit sectors* (pp. 260–279). M. E. Sharpe.

Black, S. A. (2015). Qualities of effective leadership in higher education. *Open Journal of Leadership, 4*(02), 54. https://doi.org/10.4236/ojl.2015.42006.

Bryant, T. A. (2004). Entrepreneurship. In G. R. Goethals, G. J. Sorenson, & J. M. Burns (Eds.), *Encyclopedia of leadership* (Vol. 1, pp. 442–448). Sage. http://dx.doi.org.libproxy.library.wmich.edu/10.4135/9781412952392.

Casida, J. J., & Pinto-Zipp, G. (2008). Leadership-organizational culture relationship in nursing units of acute care hospitals. *Nursing Economics, 26*(1), 7–15. Retrieved from https://pubmed.ncbi.nlm.nih.gov/18389837/.

Casselbury, K. (2019, April 5). *How does an employee-owned company work?* Chron. https://smallbusiness.chron.com/employeeowned-company-work-44184.html.

Castle, N. G., & Decker, F. H. (2011). Top management leadership style and quality of care in nursing homes. *The Gerontologist, 51*(5), 630–642. https://doi.org/10.1093/geront/gnr064.

Chen, G. (2020, July 9). *10 major challenges facing public schools.* Public School Review. https://www.publicschoolreview.com/blog/10-major-challenges-facing-public-schools.

Clark. (2017, September, 27). *10 things you probably didn't know about Publix.* https://clark.com/shopping-retail/surprises-you-probably-didnt-know-about-publix/.

De Paoli, D., & Ropo, A. (2015). Open plan offices—The response to leadership challenges of virtual project work? *Journal of Corporate Real Estate, 17*(1), 63–74. https://doi.org/10.1108/JCRE-08-2014-0020.

Ensley, M. D., Hmieleski, K. M., & Pearce, C. L. (2006). The importance of vertical and shared leadership within new venture top management teams: Implications for the performance of startups. *The Leadership Quarterly, 17*(3), 217–231. https://doi.org/10.1016/j.leaqua.2006.02.002.

Gajendran, R. S., & Joshi, A. (2012). Innovation in globally distributed teams: The role of LMX, communication frequency, and member influence on team decisions. *Journal of Applied Psychology, 97*(6), 1252–1261. https://doi.org/10.1037/a0028958.

Hamad, H. (2015). Transformational leadership theory: Why military leaders are more charismatic and transformational? *International Journal on Leadership, 3,* 1–8.

Hargett, C. W., Doty, J. P., Hauck, J. N., Webb, A. M., Cook, S. H., Tsipis, N. E., Neumann, J. A., Andolsek, K. M., & Taylor, D. C. (2017). Developing a model for effective leadership in healthcare: A concept mapping approach. *Journal of Healthcare Leadership, 9,* 69. https://doi.org/10.2147/JHL.S141664.

Havig, A. K., Skogstad, A., Kjekshus, L. E., & Romøren, T. I. (2011). Leadership, staffing and quality of care in nursing homes. *BMC Health Services Research, 11*(1), 327. https://doi.org/10.1186/1472-6963-11-327.

Hoch, J. E., & Kozlowski, S. W. (2014). Leading virtual teams: Hierarchical leadership, structural supports, and shared team leadership. *Journal of Applied Psychology, 99*(3), 390. https://doi.apa.org/doi/10.1037/a0030264.

Hoegl, M., & Muethel, M. (2016). Enabling shared leadership in virtual project teams: A practitioners' guide. *Project Management Journal, 47*(1), 7–12. https://doi.org/10.1002/pmj.21564.

Hoekstra, E., & Peterson, S. R. (2005), Beyond Wall Street: Leadership challenges unique to small private companies and entrepreneurial firms. In R. R. Sims & S. A. Quatro (Eds.), *Leadership: Succeeding in the private, public, and not-for-profit sectors* (pp. 46–64). M. E. Sharpe.

Institute of Medicine (IOM). (2001). *Crossing the quality chasm: A new health system for the 21st century*. The National Academies Press. https://www.nap.edu/read/10027/chapter/1.

Isaacs, O. (2020, April 12). *8 tips for running a startup like a true leader*. Entrepreneur. https://www.entrepreneur.com/article/346876.

Jaskyte, K. (2004). Transformational leadership, organizational culture, and innovativeness in nonprofit organizations. *Nonprofit Management and Leadership, 15*(2), 153–168. https://doi.org/10.1002/nml.59.

Jones, S., Lefoe, G., Harvey, M., & Ryland, K. (2012). Distributed leadership: A collaborative framework for academics, executives and professionals in higher education. *Journal of Higher Education Policy and Management, 34*(1), 67–78. https://doi.org/10.1080/1360080X.2012.642334.

Lathan, J. (n.d.) *10 traits of successful school leaders*. University of San Diego. https://onlinedegrees.sandiego.edu/effective-educational-leadership/.

Laurence, J. H. (2011). Military leadership and the complexity of combat and culture. *Military Psychology, 23*(5), 489–501. https://doi.org/10.1080/08995605.2011.600143.

Liao, C. (2017). Leadership in virtual teams: A multilevel perspective. *Human Resource Management Review, 27*(4), 648–659. https://doi.org/10.1016/j.hrmr.2016.12.010.

Lord, R. G., Brown, D. J., Harvey, J. L., & Hall, R. J. (2001). Contextual constraints on prototype generation and their multilevel consequences for leadership perceptions. *Leadership Quarterly, 12*(3), 311–338. https://doi.org/10.1016/S1048-9843(01)00081-9.

McClean, R. K. (2005). From monopoly to competition: Challenges for leaders in the deregulated investor-owned utility industry. In R. R. Sims & S. A. Quatro (Eds.), *Leadership: Succeeding in the private, public, and not-for-profit sectors* (pp. 3–24). M. E. Sharpe. https://citeseerx.ist.psu.edu/viewdoc/download?doi=10.1.1.457.9326&rep=rep1&type=pdf#page=23.

McGowan, E. (2018, March 1). *What is a startup company, anyway?* Startups.com. https://www.startups.com/library/expert-advice/what-is-a-startup-company.

McMurray, A. J., Pirola-Merlo, A., Sarros, J. C., & Islam, M. M. (2010). Leadership, climate, psychological capital, commitment, and wellbeing in a non-profit organization. *Leadership & Organization Development Journal, 31*(5), 436–457. https://doi.org/10.1108/01437731011056452.

National Center for Employee Ownership. (2020). *Employee stock ownership plan (ESOP) facts*. https://www.esop.org.

Pepper, K. (2010). Effective principals skillfully balance leadership styles to facilitate student success: A focus for the reauthorization of ESEA. *Planning and Changing, 41,* 42–56. Retrieved from https://www.proquest.com.libproxy.library.wmich.edu/docview/909493024/fulltext/29C5026D0F604BD9PQ/1?accountid=15099.

Publix. (n.d.). *Lessons from our founder*. http://corporate.publix.com/about-publix/culture/lessons-from-our-founder.

Raichur, A. (2018, February 18). *4 tips for leading a startup to success*. Startup Nation. https://startupnation.com/manage-your-business/leading-startup-success/.

Ramsden, P. (1998). *Learning to lead in higher education*. Routledge.

Remoters. (2020, June 13). *Remote work trends for 2020: The present & future of remote work [updated]*. https://remoters.net/remote-work-trends-future-insights/.

Salamzadeh, A., & Kesim, H. K. (2015). *Startup companies: Life cycle and challenges*. 4th International conference on employment, education and entrepreneurship (EEE), Belgrade, Serbia. https://doi.org/10.2139/ssrn.2628861.

Sauser, W. I. (2009). Sustaining employee owned companies: Seven recommendations. *Journal of Business Ethics, 84*(2), 151–164. https://doi.org/10.1007/s10551-008-9679-2.

Schermerhorn, J. R., Jr. (2005). *Management* (8th ed.). Wiley.

Sfantou, D. F., Laliotis, A., Patelarou, A. E., Sifaki-Pistolla, D., Matalliotakis, M., & Patelarou, E. (2017). Importance of leadership style towards quality of care measures in healthcare settings: A systematic review. *Healthcare, 5*(4), 73. https://doi.org/10.3390/healthcare5040073.

Sousa, P., Rouco, C., Nogueira, F., Carvalho, A., & Dias, D. (2015). *The impact of leadership behaviors and communication styles of military leaders on the performance of followers*. Proceedings of the 11th European Conference on Management Leadership and Governance (pp. 429–436). Retrieved from https://repositorio.ipv.pt/bitstream/10400.19/4409/1/11ECMLG15_PS_CR_FN_AC_DD_Final(1).pdf.

Squires, M., Tourangeau, A., Spence Laschinger, H. K., & Doran, D. (2010). The link between leadership and safety outcomes in hospitals. *Journal of Nursing Management, 18*(8), 914–925. https://doi.org/10.1111/j.1365-2834.2010.01181.x.

Stranahan, S. (2019, January 2). *Transitioning leadership at an employee-owned firm*. Medium. https://medium.com/fifty-by-fifty/transitioning-leadership-at-an-employee-owned-firm-992f183c217c.

Taylor, C. (2005). The achievements and challenges of military leadership. In R. R. Sims & S. A. Quatro (Eds.), *Leadership: Succeeding in the private, public, and not-for-profit sectors* (pp. 177–194). M. E. Sharpe.

Tipple, R. (2010). Effective leadership of online adjunct faculty. *Online Journal of Distance Learning Administration, 13*(1). Retrieved from https://www.westga.edu/~distance/ojdla/spring131/tipple131.html.

U.S. Department of Defense. (n.d.). *About the Department of Defense (DOD)*. https://archive.defense.gov/about/.

Vanderslice, G. (2014, September). *Leadership challenges in ESOP companies*. Praxis Consulting Group. https://praxiscg.com/wp-content/uploads/2016/07/Sep201420ESOP20Report20Leadership20Challenges20in20EO20Companies.pdf.

Voon, M. L., Lo, M. C., Ngui, S. K., & Peter, S. (2009). *Leadership styles in context of institution of higher education in Malaysia*. Retrieved from bai2009.org/file/Papers/1657.doc.

Wong, K. C., Yuen, A. H., & Law, N. (2003). ICT implementation and school leadership: Case studies of ICT integration in teaching and learning. *Journal of Education Administration, 41*(2), 158–170. https://doi.org/10.1108/09578230310464666.

Yasir, M., Imran, R., Irshad, M. K., Mohamad, N. A., & Khan, M. M. (2016). Leadership styles in relation to employees' trust and organizational change capacity: Evidence from non-profit organizations. *Sage Open, 6*(4), 1–12. https://doi.org/10.1177/2158244016675396.

Zayani, F. A. (2008). *The impact of transformational leadership on the success of global virtual teams: An investigation based on the Multifactor Leadership Questionnaire* (Doctoral dissertation). Capella University. ProQuest Dissertations Publishing. https://search.proquest.com/openview/466509e1baccc8174ad121aed24e0609/1?pq-origsite=gscholar&cbl=18750&diss=y.

CHAPTER 6

Diversity and Ethics in LMX

Abstract Most organizations are diverse and growing more varied over time in terms of employee makeup. Although having a diverse workforce is beneficial in many ways, issues of gender, race, ethnicity, age, and generation, among others, can hinder organizational effectiveness. Good leaders must be able to understand the differing needs of each employee and how this influences communication. Employees' various identities influence their leadership needs in many ways, stressing the importance of contingent perspectives of leadership communication. It is also important to acknowledge the ethical nature of leader-member exchange. It is human nature to form preferences toward certain groups of people, such as those who look similar to us and share things in common. This becomes an ethical concern when these preferred groups of people are given more advantages over others, especially when a leader does not recognize they are forming these preferences. This chapter explores research on how these implicit biases can lead to unintentional unethical behavior, challenges the assumption that leaders are always "correct" and "moral" in their actions, and offers practical ways to recognize one's own implicit biases to level the playing field for all members of the diverse workforce.

Keywords Diversity · Ethical leadership · Implicit bias · Inclusion

L. M. Omilion-Hodges and J. K. Ptacek, *Leader-Member Exchange and Organizational Communication*, New Perspectives in Organizational Communication, https://doi.org/10.1007/978-3-030-68756-4_6

Most organizations are diverse and growing more diverse over time in terms of employee makeup. The United States Census Bureau estimates that the country will reach a demographic turning point in the year 2030, with major changes in the population's makeup in terms of race and ethnicity and retirement-aged people (Vespa et al., 2020). Although having a diverse workforce is beneficial in many ways, issues of gender, race, ethnicity, age and generation, among others can hinder organizational effectiveness. Good leaders must be able to understand the differing needs of each employee and how this influences communication. Furthermore, how a leader practices inclusion within their organization affects diversity related to outcomes such as employee turnover (Nishii & Mayer, 2009). Employees' various identities influence their leadership needs in many ways, stressing the importance of contingent perspectives of leadership communication.

In addition to considering the diverse workgroup, it is also important to acknowledge ethical concerns related to LMX. It is human nature to form preferences toward particular groups of people, such as those who look similar to us and share things in common. This becomes an ethical concern when these preferred groups of people are given advantages over others, especially when a leader does not recognize they are forming these preferences. LMX is an essential consideration in organizational ethics in that leader and member communication shapes how ethics are understood and made sense of within an organization. This chapter explores research on how these implicit biases can lead to unintentional unethical behavior, challenges the assumption that leaders are always "correct" and "moral" in their actions, and offers practical ways to recognize one's own implicit biases to level the playing field for all members.

Diversity and Inclusion

Diversity and inclusion, while often go hand in hand and are used interchangeably, are conceptually different. Through an analysis of various definitions, Mor Barak (2013) has defined diversity globally as:

> the division of the workforce into distinct categories that (a) have a perceived commonality within a given cultural or national context, and that (b) impact potentially harmful or beneficial employment outcomes such as job opportunities, treatment in the workplace, and promotion prospects—irrespective of job-related skills and qualifications. (p. 129)

Others have acknowledged that diversity is explicitly considered in terms of differences between demographic characteristics such as age, gender, and race (Acquavita et al., 2009) and could refer to any personal attribute which influences how individuals perceive one another (Gonzalez & Denisi, 2009). Inclusion can be thought of as the degree to which individuals feel they are part of an organization and its processes, such as decision-making, access to information, and connectedness to others in the organization (Mor Barak, 2013).

Research has found some outcomes related to diversity and inclusion in the workplace. Positive perceptions of diversity climate—in which there are fair employment practices, employees' diverse characteristics are respected, and equal opportunities are provided—can increase job satisfaction. Similarly, a climate of inclusion has been associated with job satisfaction (Brimhall et al., 2014). In addition to job satisfaction, perceptions of a positive diversity climate can lead to increased employee well-being, organizational commitment, and lower intention to leave the organization (Brimhall et al., 2014; Gonzalez & Denisi, 2009). Furthermore, inclusion has been positively connected to outcomes such as employee well-being and career advancement (Mor Barak, 2013; Mor Barak & Levin, 2002). Climates of diversity and inclusion also work together to influence other work outcomes. For example, positive perceptions of diversity climate are also related to positive feelings of inclusion and have been found to increase job satisfaction and reduce employee turnover intentions (Brimhall et al., 2014).

Diversity and inclusion have also been explored concerning LMX. For example, research (Nishii & Mayer, 2009) has found less of a relationship between demographic diversity (in terms of age, race, and gender) and turnover when LMX is high. In other words, high-quality LMX can reduce the likelihood of turnover in diverse groups. However, Nishii and Mayer (2009) suggest that if a leader cannot develop high-quality relationships with each member in a demographically diverse group, it is better not to develop these high-quality relationships with anyone in the group. Additionally, perceptions of LMX have been found to influence members' perceptions of organizational climate for diversity, and perceptions of inclusion influence perceptions that high-quality LMX increases job satisfaction (Brimhall et al., 2014).

Scholars have differing viewpoints on the impact of diversity. On the one hand, diversity is argued to offer a number of benefits to an organization. For example, research has found organizational diversity to be related to innovativeness, creativity, enhanced problem-solving, and improved reputation (Brimhall et al., 2014; Richard et al., 2004; Shore et al., 2009). Furthermore, having a diverse workforce can expose organizational members to different worldviews, experiences, and ways of thinking (Shore et al., 2009). By taking advantage of diverse contributions of ideas, an organization can perform better and make higher-quality decisions (Choi & Rainey, 2010). However, in some cases, diverse workgroups have been found to lead to adverse outcomes such as turnover, loss of profit, intergroup conflict, and withdrawal from organizational citizenship behaviors (Brimhall et al., 2014; Mamman et al., 2012; Sacco & Schmitt, 2005). Additionally, Brimhall et al. (2014) found that the longer someone has spent in an organization, the less favorable perceptions they had of diversity climate.

Regardless of the potential negative impacts of diversity, organizational climate is becoming increasingly diverse. It is up to leaders to determine if they can leverage the benefits of diversity in their organization or let it negatively affect their success (see Table 6.1 for a leader example). Furthermore, understanding the potential issues with diversity can help leaders to overcome them effectively. Researchers have argued that LMX can dramatically impact how diversity is perceived in workgroups and organizations. For example, whereas racial diversity has been found to

Table 6.1 Leadership in action—leader profile: Mellody Hobson

As the president and co-CEO of Chicago-based investment company Ariel Investments, Mellody Hobson is an expert in both leadership and how to diversify an organization. She has not only served on boards of companies such as Starbucks and JPMorgan Chase, among others, but she has won numerous awards, four honorary doctorates, and has been named in Time Magazine's "100 Most Influential People" in the world (Executive Leadership, n.d.).
In her 2014 TED Talk, Hobson called for the need "for us to be comfortable with the uncomfortable conversation about race" (Hobson, 2014). She described how they view diversity at Ariel Investments as a competitive advantage, how smart businesses deal with the issue of race head on instead of avoiding it.
Hobson explained, "our businesses and our products and our science, our research, all of that will be better with greater diversity" (Hobson, 2014). Indeed, groundbreaking ideas and inventions can be more easily discovered through diverse groups of people.
Even if you don't run you own company, Hobson argues that you can still be "color brave," by observing your environment purposely and inviting people in who are different from yourself. It may just help you to solve a really difficult problem.

Source Executive Leadership (n.d.) and Hobson (2014)

negatively impact organizational performance in some cases, when diversity management practices and team processes moderate it, racial diversity leads to positive organizational performance (Choi & Rainey, 2010). Understanding different types of diversity, such as those described in this chapter, can help leaders embrace their organization's differences.

Types of Diversity

Next, we address some of the different types of diversity that influence LMX communication, including gender and sex, race and ethnicity, and age and generation.

Gender and Sex

Gender refers to "socially constructed characteristics of women and men—such as the norms, roles, and relationships that exist between them" (WHO, n.d.-b). Although sometimes used interchangeably with sex, which refers to biological differences between males and females, the two terms are distinct and should be conceptualized differently (Newman, 2018). Conceptualizations of gender vary between societies and can also change over time (WHO, n.d.-b). Discrimination on the basis of sex is evidenced through the disparity between men and women who hold leadership positions, wage gap, and differential treatment in the workplace (Parker & Funk, 2017; Yukl, 2013). Most of our understanding of leadership and organizations has been based on fairly homogeneous groups, namely, white men, in the United States (Ayman & Korabik, 2010). Furthermore, ideas of what made an "effective" leader were based on communication styles and behaviors that were primarily masculine, suggesting that men were more qualified for leadership roles than women (Yukl, 2013). The "glass ceiling" is a term that has been used to describe a barrier that prevents women and other minorities in the workplace from achieving advancement (Casini, 2016). Recognizing this issue and how it pertained to workplace discrimination in the United States, the Civil Rights Act of 1964 prohibited employment discrimination based on sex, race, religion, or national origin (History.com Editors, 2020). However, gender discrimination and inequality still occur, and gender discrimination can also intersect with other personal factors such as age, race, and sexual orientation (WHO, n.d.-b). For example, women of color experiencing heightened discrimination and difficulties in workplace advancement sometimes use the term "concrete ceiling" (Sanchez-Hucles & Davis, 2010), emphasizing feelings of powerlessness.

Considering how communication and leadership can be gendered can help leaders better recognize and manage gender-based preferential treatment in organizations. A cultural preference for masculine traits places preference on values such as assertiveness, performance, success, and competition, which tend to be associated with men (Hofstede, 1994). Alternatively, values such as quality of life, having close interpersonal relationships, service, and solidarity are considered more feminine and are associated with women (Hofstede, 1994). Recent claims suggest that organizations are changing in ways which acknowledge the need for more feminine-related traits, such as inclusiveness, empathy, and shared power to increase organizational effectiveness (Yukl, 2013). Cultures with high gender egalitarianism consider both masculine and feminine attributes essential and necessary in organizations and leadership. These cultures tend to value a more transformational leadership style, emphasizing participation, support, and relation-oriented communication (Yukl, 2013).

Race and Ethnicity

Race can be defined as "any one of the groups that humans are often divided into based on physical traits regarded as common among people of shared ancestry" (Merriam-Webster, n.d.).

The United States Census Bureau (2020) classifies race into categories of White, Black or African American, American Indian or Alaska Native, Asian, and Native Hawaiian or Other Pacific Islander, and acknowledges that people can indicate more than one race. Furthermore, race is measured by self-identification and not biology (U.S. Census Bureau, 2020). Ethnicity is defined as "a social group that shares a common and distinctive culture, religion, language, or the like" (Dictionary.com, n.d.). Race and ethnicity are considered social constructs used to categorize people (Yudell et al., 2016). Race and ethnicity are at the core of considering diversity, based on several psychology theories on how humans categorize and identify themselves. For example, people tend to immediately judge one another based on observable characteristics, such as race, when they have no additional information. People tend to group themselves with others they perceive to be similar; when people form in-groups with those who are similar to them, in-group members are privileged and out-group members tend to face negative outcomes (Shore et al., 2009). Despite legislation such as the Civil Rights Act, employees still face differential treatment based on race and ethnicity in the workforce today.

Later in this chapter, we will discuss ways to identify your own racial biases and how to manage racial or ethnic diversity in the workplace. Along with this, it is important to consider how culture can influence perceptions of leadership communication. It is estimated that by the year 2030, international migration will play a greater role than natural increase (or births) in growing the population of the United States (Vespa et al., 2020). This means that organizations are becoming increasingly diverse in terms of race and ethnicity and cultural norms that may differ from the United States. This means it is essential to consider, especially for those in leadership positions, cultural value dimensions—or different approaches to social norms (Hofstede, 1994).

Individualism and Collectivism

Cultures vary on the extent to which they value the collective needs of others. Members of individualistic cultures tend to behave more autonomously and value personal goals and independence (Triandis, 2018). Alternatively, members of collectivistic cultures tend to think of themselves more as part of a collective and value the group's goals over their own (Triandis, 2018). This is not to say that all people do not have individualistic or collectivistic tendencies, or that a culture is solely individualistic or collectivistic. However, countries such as the United States, Australia, England, and the Netherlands tend to have strong individualistic values, whereas countries with stronger collectivistic values include China, Argentina, Mexico, and Sweden (Yukl, 2013). Studies have found that these values also influence how organizational members can behave or respond to leadership communication. For example, research (Welbourne et al., 2015) has found that organizational members with strong collectivism values were more resilient against experiencing burnout due to incivility, and those with stronger individualism values experienced more burnout and dissatisfaction after encountering incivility. In an analysis of LMX dimensions and diversity in terms of individualism and collectivism, researchers (Duncan & Herrera, 2014) found that the more collectivistic employees perceived the organizational culture to be, the more positively they perceived their leader's LMX. Concerning leadership styles, Jung and Avolio (1999) found that more collectivistic employees tended to generate more ideas with a transformational leader. In contrast, individualistic employees generated more ideas with a transactional leader. Another consideration for leaders is that individual emphasis on achievement can make fostering a culture of shared values or cooperation more difficult (Yukl, 2013).

Power Distance

Power distance considers how power is distributed in organizations. In high power distance cultures, leaders are regarded with more power and authority and subordinates tend to follow a leader's orders without challenging them (Yukl, 2013). This also means employees are less likely to be consulted in decision-making and organizations will have stricter policies (Smith et al., 2002). In low power distance cultures, employees are more likely to challenge a leader's decision and see less inequality due to position or status. Cultures such as Western Europe, New Zealand, and the United States are considered to have a low power distance, and cultures such as Russia, China, Taiwan, Mexico, and Venezuela are considered as having a high power distance (Yukl, 2013). It is important to consider ways in which LMX relationships are influenced by power distance cultural values. For example, research (Anand et al., 2018) has found that the relationship between LMX and organizational citizenship behaviors is smaller in high power distance contexts. It is not surprising that authoritarian leadership styles emphasize a high power distance relationship, but research (Siddique et al., 2020) has found that power distance can moderate the relationship between authoritarian leadership and LMX and outcomes such as employee embeddedness. Furthermore, in high power distance cultures where employees may experience lower job satisfaction and performance under an authoritarian leader, high-quality LMX relationships can reduce the negative effects of this leadership style (Siddique et al., 2020). In other words, leaders in high power distance contexts can positively impact employee outcomes (such as satisfaction) by building high-quality LMX relationships.

Uncertainty Avoidance

Uncertainty avoidance refers to the degree to which people prefer structure (Hofstede, 1994). In high uncertainty avoidance cultures, people are less comfortable with ambiguity and the unknown. They tend to value social norms and clear rules because it helps them avoid uncertainty (Yukl, 2013). People in low uncertainty avoidance cultures tend to be more easygoing and flexible (Hofstede, 1994). Countries considered to have high uncertainty avoidance values include France, Spain, Germany, Switzerland, Russia, and India, and countries considered to be low in uncertainty avoidance include the United States, United Kingdom, Canada, Denmark, and Sweden (Yukl, 2013). Sullivan et al. (2003) suggest that members of high uncertainty avoidance cultures tend to be more concerned about the immediacy of communicating with and receiving feedback from leaders, may value contributions more in work relationships, and may place more value on professional respect in an LMX relationship because they tend to focus more strongly on expert knowledge. It may also be more acceptable as a leader to provide less detailed direction, introduce more change, and encourage risk-taking in lower uncertainty avoidance cultures (Selvarajah et al., 2018).

Age and Generation

Age is another important demographic factor to consider in organizational diversity in part because different age generations may have different workplace needs. For example, recent research (Omilion-Hodges & Ptacek, 2019) has suggested that young people currently entering the workforce may prefer more relational behaviors from their manager. In contrast, older generations may value more task-related behaviors. We will address some of these various behaviors and needs by generation below. However, another reason why it is important to consider age and generation in LMX relationships is that individuals can experience workplace discrimination based on their age or perceived age. A number of research studies identify age discrimination in older employees, with preferential treatment given to younger employees in terms of performance ratings, hiring decisions, and salary (Shore et al., 2009). The term "ageism" is used to describe stereotyping, prejudice, and discrimination against people based on age, and it often tends to impact older people more negatively (WHO, n.d.-a.). Understanding and overcoming these negative stereotypes is necessary for building effective LMX relationships. For example, Shore et al. (2009) suggest that positive workgroup relationships can prevent negative effects of age discrimination and capitalize upon the knowledge and experience of all employees.

Organizational research has often looked to generational differences in the workplace. There are many findings that distinguish generations of workers on organizational variables such as work values, attitudes, leadership, teamwork, and others (Lyons & Kuron, 2014). Generations are believed to think and behave differently based on technology, historical events, and other cultural and societal influences (Lyons & Kuron, 2014). The four most prominent generations in the United States workforce today are now considered.

Baby Boomers (Born 1946–1964)
Baby Boomers are considered the oldest group of individuals in the workforce, ranging in age from about 57 to 75 years old, with many members having already retired (Dimock, 2019). Having experienced the Vietnam War, economic prosperity, and social change, this generation has been described as loyal and competitive in the workforce, having feelings of entitlement, and flexible in terms of change and growth (Gibson et al., 2009). Leaders may be successful in motivating Baby Boomers through money and praise (Gibson et al., 2009). Leaders are also encouraged to meets this generation's needs in the workplace so they will feel engaged, and find and play up their strengths and passions (Nelson, 2019).

Generation X (Born 1965–1980)
Generation X—sometimes called the "Sandwich Generation" being sandwiched between the two larger generations—are between about 41 and 56 years old (Parker & Patten, 2013). This generation is also currently experiencing the stress and financial burdens of being "sandwiched" between caring for young children and their aging parents (Parker & Patten, 2013). Having witnessed a number of economic uncertainties, corporate downsizing, and high levels of divorce, this generation has been characterized as being independent, less trusting, and less loyal than Baby Boomers (Gibson et al., 2009). In considering what they may desire in terms of workplace behaviors, Generation X members are considered more individualistic than collectivistic, value mentors and immediate feedback. They are good at multitasking and competition (Sessa et al., 2007). Additionally, leaders are encouraged to take a hands-on approach, acknowledge work-life balance, and provide continuous skills training (Mulvanity, 2001).

Generation Y (Born 1981–1996)
Generation Y—or more commonly called "Millennials"—are around 25 to 40 years old now (Dimock, 2019). This is currently the largest generation at over 72 million people, surpassing Baby Boomers, as many Millennials are offspring of the Baby Boomer generation (Fry, 2020). This generation has been influenced by various technologies and exposed to more of the world through social networking and the ability to communicate instantly. Millennials have been described as being realistic, globally aware, answer-seeking, and more accepting of diversity than previous generations (Gibson et al., 2009). In the workplace, this generation is incredibly tech-savvy, values meaningful work, and has a willingness to learn (Sessa et al., 2007). Leaders should offer quick feedback, emphasize the importance of the work, and provide additional development opportunities to Millennial members (Gibson et al., 2009).

Generation Z (1997–2012)
Generation Z—sometimes referred to as "post-Millennials" or the "iGeneration"—is the latest generation to begin entering the workforce, with members ranging from about 9 to 24 years old (Dimock, 2019). The oldest of its members are only now graduating college or newly out into the workforce, so we know less about this generation's needs and working trends. However, research (Omilion-Hodges & Ptacek, 2019) has found that this new generation of workers will prefer more relationship-oriented leaders over task-oriented leaders. Similarly, others (Matos, n.d.) suggest they will prefer coaching over managing and will expect leaders to trust them and let them solve problems.

Ethical Leadership

In addition to thinking about how workgroups can be diverse and how to meet those challenges, it is necessary to consider the ethical nature of LMX. Ethical leadership can be defined as "the demonstration of normatively appropriate conduct through personal actions and interpersonal relationships, and the promotion of such conduct to followers through two-way communication, reinforcement, and decision-making" (Brown et al., 2005, p. 120). Considering this, LMX communication can shape how ethics are understood and enacted in an organization. For example, research (Hansen et al., 2013) has found that LMX relationships play a role in the relationship between ethical leadership and outcomes such as employee commitment to their organization and supervisor. Ethical leadership has also been predictive of followers' job satisfaction, dedication, and willingness to report problems (Brown et al., 2005), and negatively related to workgroup relationship conflict (Mayer et al., 2012). It is suggested that an organization's ethical leadership is influential to employees through a "trickle down" effect from immediate supervisors, emphasizing the importance for all organizational leaders to demonstrate ethical leadership (Hansen et al., 2013). Ethical leaders encourage followers to uphold ethical standards, but they also influence this behavior by doing it themselves. Ethical leadership also influences follower job satisfaction and commitment directly and indirectly by shaping perceptions of the ethical workplace climate (Neubert et al., 2009).

So how does someone lead ethically? First, an ethical leader leads by example. Ethical leadership has significant positive associations with both leader moral identity symbolization (demonstrating moral traits through their actions) as well as leader moral identity internalization (moral traits embedded into one's self-concept) (Mayer et al., 2012). Leaders would do well to role model ethical behavior and commit to honest, ethical, and accountable communication with followers (Bakar & Omilion-Hodges, 2019). Furthermore, Brown et al. (2005) developed a measure of ethical leadership, using 10 specific criteria of an ethical leader. These traits are summarized as follows:

- Listens to what employees have to say
- Disciplines employees who violate ethical standards
- Conducts his/her personal life in an ethical manner
- Has the best interests of employees in mind
- Makes fair and balanced decisions
- Can be trusted
- Discusses business ethics or values with employees
- Sets an example of how to do things the right way in terms of ethics
- Defines success not just by results but also the way that they are obtained
- When making decisions, asks "what is the right thing to do?"

Implicit Bias

In addition to engaging in the behaviors mentioned above, ethical leaders must also recognize the human nature of forming preferences toward certain groups of people (a free test is discussed below). Even the most ethical leader can have biases that they are not even aware of, called implicit bias. Implicit, or unconscious, bias refers to attitudes or stereotypes we may have toward people without our knowledge (Perception Institute, n.d.). Examples of this include avoiding promoting an older employee because you think they do not have a recent college graduate's skills, not hiring someone because their name sounds "different," or taking advice from a man because you perceive him to be more credible than a woman. Studies have found that these scenarios still take place in organizations today (Reiners, 2019). Implicit biases can be dangerous because they can affect our judgments and behaviors (Perception Institute, n.d.). This can lead to individual workplace members making more money, having increased access to opportunities, and being treated better or being listened to more than others. Even if we believe we are completely aware of these biases, an ethical leader must challenge the assumption that they are always "correct" and "moral" in their actions.

Recognizing and Challenging Your Own Biases

So how can you recognize and challenge your own biases? One way is through taking implicit biases tests. A widely used example is the Implicit Association Test (IAT) which can be accessed online through Project Implicit (https://implicit.harvard.edu/implicit/). The website has various tests that include images and questions developed to identify biases that you might not otherwise know you had in terms of someone's race, age, weight, disability, gender, and others. Once you identify some of your implicit biases, you should frequently check yourself to make sure you are not letting those biases slip into the decisions you make and how you communicate with others. Although each LMX relationship is different, they should not be different because of biases. Furthermore, Holder (2016) suggests three questions to ask yourself to uncover hidden biases for individual team members.

- Is there a team member who would view my feedback as negative if I give them any feedback at all?

- Who on the team do I dislike working with? Why do I dislike working with them?
- Which person on the team do I have a difficult time getting to know?

Recognizing and Challenging Organizational Biases

In addition to recognizing and challenging one's own biases, the next step is for leaders to address these biases in their organization (see Table 6.2 for suggestions on starting conversations to address workplace bias). Many organizations have diversity and inclusion training or implicit bias training programs that can help members work toward being more inclusive and recognizing their own implicit prejudices. However, some of these programs fail to resolve these issues as intended, especially mandatory diversity training that can contain negative messages and easily forgotten information (Dobbin & Kalev, 2016). One study (Dobbin & Kalev, 2016) found that successful diversity programs that *actually* increase diversity succeed in sparking engagement in ways such

Table 6.2 Sharpening your communication skills: starting conversations to address workplace bias

Recognizing your own implicit biases as a leader is a good start in working toward a more diverse and inclusive organization and in building quality relationships with all of your followers. However, if others in your organization don't do the same, unfair practices can still be common. As a leader, you can and should start conversations with others to address these issues and encourage them to understand their own biases and their effects. Drawing from various sources on this topic (Boudreau, 2020; Heal Our Communities, n.d.) there are some specific steps you can take to begin these conversations:

- Start by recognizing your own biases
- Begin conversations by establishing common ground and getting to know each other
- Allow yourself and followers to make mistakes and learn from them
- Discuss different ways that biases affect everyone, instead of pretending they aren't there
- Have the conversations even if they are uncomfortable and understand they impact people differently
- Focus on exploring, listening, and learning instead of blaming or belittling
- Agree to have mutual respect
- Allow others to share feelings and experiences without interrupting
- When closing the conversation, extend gratitude to everyone and ask others to share how it impacted them

Source Boudreau (2020) and Heal Our Communities (n.d.)

as mentoring, increasing contact among different groups, and promoting social accountability. Furthermore, some programs may fail if they neglect to consider systemic bias. In addition to evaluating one's own implicit biases, it is essential to consider how systemic and structural issues exist that perpetuate workplace bias. Asare (2019) identified four ways in which this can occur:

- **Exclusive and hostile work environments:** In addition to recognizing individual biases and changing behavior, the organization itself must handle inequitable treatment reasonably. When frequent complaints of specific issues occur, the organization needs to establish specific actions and policies to prevent further occurrences.
- **Affinity bias:** Even if a leader has been able to identify their biases, if there are existing structures that allow preferential treatment to happen, it can persist. For example, a diverse search and evaluation committee could help prevent a manager from continuously hiring individuals with whom they share similarities.
- **Network gap:** Professional networking plays a huge role in helping someone to get a job. However, "who you know" can be closely tied to the area where someone grew up and the college they attended, which automatically privileges someone who can afford to live in a more expensive area and go to a more expensive college (or attend college at all). Organizations could combat this by evaluating job candidates with objective measures and blind systems to avoid bias based on name and gender.
- **Structural racism:** Understanding issues such as white privilege can help organizations dismantle systemic oppression. Organizations should assess any policies they may have that could enable racial inequities, such as grooming and appearance policies that prohibit certain hairstyles.

Leadership Moments: Takeaways for Leaders and Members

- **Consider the intersections of organizational members' characteristics and needs:** Leaders and members alike come from different backgrounds. LMX suggests that each workplace relationship is different because each individual is different. Considering how sex and gender, race and ethnicity, age, and various cultural influences can influence each person's values, beliefs, and ways of working can help workplace members better understand and work with one another.

- **Diversity can be the key to organizational success if understood:** Just as understanding each other's differences can help build organizational harmony, having a diverse workforce can be a leader's greatest tool for success if fostered properly. Benefits of a diverse workgroup include enhanced innovation, creativity, problem-solving, reputation, and greater worldviews.
- **Consider how your implicit biases shape your workplace behavior:** Even if we think we are objective in our decisions and communication, we are all influenced by implicit or unconscious biases that we are not aware of. Taking an Implicit Association Test can help uncover some of these biases, but then it is up to you to consistently keep these biases in check.

Mini Case Study: "These New Hires Seem Very…Similar"

You are one of several managers in charge of hiring at your advertising firm. You and three other managers usually rotate taking the lead in hiring rounds. During the latest round of hiring, Steve—a young, white male—was in charge of interviewing and hiring. When you looked through the new hires' paperwork, you noticed something interesting—they were all young, white males. You commented to Steve, "These new hires seem very…similar." Steve laughed and said, "Oh, I guess so. They seemed like the most qualified and best fit for the company out of all the applicants." However, as you looked through the stack of applications, you noticed that some applicants with the same experience and skills as those hired didn't even get an invitation for an interview. After learning about diversity, ethical leadership, and implicit bias, you realize some changes need to be made in your company's hiring practices.

1. What are some specific things you can personally do to make sure you are as unbiased as possible next time it's your turn to choose candidates to interview and hire?

2. What are some suggestions you would make to change your workplace policies on hiring to address issues of diversity and implicit bias?
3. How can you talk to the other hiring managers at your organization to help them recognize their own implicit biases?

References

Acquavita, S. P., Pittman, J., Gibbons, M., & Castellanos-Brown, K. (2009). Personal and organizational diversity factors' impact on social workers' job satisfaction: Results from a national internet-based survey. *Administration in Social Work, 33*(2), 151–166. https://doi.org/10.1080/03643100902768824.

Anand, S., Vidyarthi, P., & Rolnicki, S. (2018). Leader-member exchange and organizational citizenship behaviors: Contextual effects of leader power distance and group task interdependence. *The Leadership Quarterly, 29*(4), 489–500. https://doi.org/10.1016/j.leaqua.2017.11.002.

Asare, J. G. (2019, December 29). Your unconscious bias trainings keep failing because you're not addressing systemic bias. *Forbes*. https://www.forbes.com/sites/janicegassam/2020/12/29/your-unconscious-bias-trainings-keep-failing-because-youre-not-addressing-systemic-bias/#98da9051e9d3.

Ayman, R., & Korabik, K. (2010). Leadership: Why gender and culture matter. *American Psychologist*, *65*(3), 157–170. https://psycnet.apa.org/doi/10.1037/a0018806.

Bakar, H. A., & Omilion-Hodges, L. (2019). The mediating role of relative communicative behavior on the relationship between ethical leadership and organizational identification. *Leadership & Organization Development Journal, 41*(1), 52–72. https://doi.org/10.1108/LODJ-04-2019-0190.

Boudreau, E. (2020, August 3). *A leader's guide to talking about bias*. Harvard Graduate School of Education. https://www.gse.harvard.edu/news/uk/20/08/leaders-guide-talking-about-bias.

Brimhall, K. C., Lizano, E. L., & Barak, M. E. M. (2014). The mediating role of inclusion: A longitudinal study of the effects of leader–member exchange and diversity climate on job satisfaction and intention to leave among child welfare workers. *Children and Youth Services Review, 40,* 79–88. https://doi.org/10.1016/j.childyouth.2014.03.003.

Brown, M. E., Treviño, L. K., & Harrison, D. A. (2005). Ethical leadership: A social learning perspective for construct development and testing. *Organizational Behavior and Human Decision Processes, 97*(2), 117–134. https://doi.org/10.1016/j.obhdp.2005.03.002.

Casini, A. (2016). Glass ceiling and glass elevator. *The Wiley Blackwell Encyclopedia of Gender and Sexuality Studies*, 1–2. https://doi.org/10.1002/9781118663219.wbegss262.

Choi, S., & Rainey, H. G. (2010). Managing diversity in US federal agencies: Effects of diversity and diversity management on employee perceptions of organizational performance. *Public Administration Review, 70*(1), 109–121. https://doi.org/10.1111/j.1540-6210.2009.02115.x.

Dictionary.com. (n.d.). Ethnicity. *Dictionary.com*. Retrieved November 21, 2020, from https://www.dictionary.com/browse/ethnicity.

Dimock, M. (2019, January 17). *Defining generations: Where Millennials end and Generation Z begins*. Pew Research Center. https://www.pewresearch.org/fact-tank/2019/01/17/where-millennials-end-and-generation-z-begins/.

Dobbin, F., & Kalev, A. (2016, August). Why diversity programs fail. *Harvard Business Review*. https://hbr.org/2016/07/why-diversity-programs-fail.

Duncan, P., & Herrera, R. (2014). The relationship between diversity and the multidimensional measure of leader-member exchange (LMX-MDM). *Journal of Management Policy and Practice, 15*(1), 11–24.

Executive Leadership. (n.d.). *Ariel Investments*. https://www.arielinvestments.com/our-executive-team/.

Fry, R. (2020, April 28). *Millennials overtake Baby Boomers as American's largest generation*. Pew Research Center. https://www.pewresearch.org/fact-tank/2020/04/28/millennials-overtake-baby-boomers-as-americas-largest-generation/.

Gibson, J. W., Greenwood, R. A., & Murphy, E. F., Jr. (2009). Generational differences in the workplace: Personal values, behaviors, and popular beliefs. *Journal of Diversity Management (JDM), 4(*3), 1–8. https://doi.org/10.19030/jdm.v4i3.4959.

Gonzalez, J. A., & Denisi, A. S. (2009). Cross-level effects of demography and diversity climate on organizational attachment and firm effectiveness. *Journal of Organizational Behavior: The International Journal of Industrial, Occupational and Organizational Psychology and Behavior, 30*(1), 21–40. https://doi.org/10.1002/job.498.

Hansen, S. D., Alge, B. J., Brown, M. E., Jackson, C. L., & Dunford, B. B. (2013). Ethical leadership: Assessing the value of a multifoci social exchange perspective. *Journal of Business Ethics, 115*(3), 435–449. https://doi.org/10.1007/s10551-012-1408-1.

Heal Our Communities. (n.d.). *Talking about racism, racial equity and racial healing with friends, family, colleagues and neighbors*. https://healourcommunities.org/wp-content/uploads/2018/12/NDORH_ConversationGuide_2019_V6_12-10-18-FINAL_proofed.pdf.

History.com Editors. (2020, February 10). *Civil Rights Act of 1964*. https://www.history.com/topics/black-history/civil-rights-act.

Hobson, M. (2014, March). *Color blind or color brave?* [Video]. TED. https://www.ted.com/talks/mellody_hobson_color_blind_or_color_brave#t-548576.
Hofstede, G. (1994). Management scientists are human. *Management Science, 40*(1), 4–13. https://doi.org/10.1287/mnsc.40.1.4.
Holder, N. (2016, January 5). *Three crucial questions for uncovering unconscious bias in the workplace*. Lab Manager. https://www.labmanager.com/business-management/three-crucial-questions-for-uncovering-unconscious-bias-in-the-workplace-10727.
Jung, D. I., & Avolio, B. J. (1999). Effects of leadership style and followers' cultural orientation on performance in group and individual task conditions. *The Academy of Management Journal, 42*(2), 208–218. https://doi.org/10.5465/257093.
Lyons, S., & Kuron, L. (2014). Generational differences in the workplace: A review of the evidence and directions for future research. *Journal of Organizational Behavior, 35*(S1), S139–S157. https://doi.org/10.1002/job.1913.
Mamman, A., Kamoche, K., & Bakuwa, R. (2012). Diversity, organizational commitment and organizational citizenship behavior: An organizing framework. *Human Resource Management Review, 22*(4), 285–302. https://doi.org/10.1016/j.hrmr.2011.12.003.
Matos, K. (n.d.). *How to prepare your workplace for Generation Z*. Culture Amp. https://www.cultureamp.com/blog/how-to-prepare-your-workplace-for-generation-z/.
Mayer, D. M., Aquino, K., Greenbaum, R. L., & Kuenzi, M. (2012). Who displays ethical leadership, and why does it matter? An examination of antecedents and consequences of ethical leadership. *Academy of Management Journal, 55*(1), 151–171. https://doi.org/10.5465/amj.2008.0276.
Merriam-Webster. (n.d.). Race. *Merriam-Webster.com dictionary*. Retrieved November 21, 2020, from https://www.merriam-webster.com/dictionary/race.
Mor Barak, M. E. (2013). *Managing diversity towards a globally inclusive workplace* (3rd ed.). Sage.
Mor Barak, M. E., & Levin, A. (2002). Outside of the corporate mainstream and excluded from the work community: A study of diversity, job satisfaction and well-being. *Community, Work & Family, 5*(2), 133–157. https://doi.org/10.1080/13668800220146346.
Mulvanity, E. W. (2001, November 1). *Generation X in the workplace: Age diversity issues in project teams*. Project Management Institute. https://www.pmi.org/learning/library/generation-x-workplace-age-diversity-style-7904.
Nelson, B. (2019, February 5). *How to get the best out of Baby Boomers*. Gallup. https://www.gallup.com/workplace/246443/best-baby-boomers.aspx.

Neubert, M. J., Carlson, D. S., Kacmar, K. M., Roberts, J. A., & Chonko, L. B. (2009). The virtuous influence of ethical leadership behavior: Evidence from the field. *Journal of Business Ethics, 90*(2), 157–170. https://doi.org/10.1007/s10551-009-0037-9.

Newman, T. (2018, February 7). *Sex and gender: What is the difference?* Medical News Today. https://www.medicalnewstoday.com/articles/232363.

Nishii, L. H., & Mayer, D. M. (2009). Do inclusive leaders help to reduce turnover in diverse groups? The moderating role of leader–member exchange in the diversity to turnover relationship. *Journal of Applied Psychology, 94*(6), 1412–1426. https://doi.org/10.1037/a0017190.

Omilion-Hodges, L. M., & Ptacek, J. K. (2019). Personal factors, wants, and needs: Exploring vocational anticipatory socialization through young adults' preferences for managerial communication behaviors. *International Journal of Business Communication*, 1–20. https://doi.org/10.1177/2329488419893745.

Parker, K., & Funk, C. (2017, December 14). *Gender discrimination comes in many forms for today's working women.* Pew Research Center. https://www.pewresearch.org/fact-tank/2017/12/14/gender-discrimination-comes-in-many-forms-for-todays-working-women/.

Parker, K., & Patten, E. (2013, January 30). *The Sandwich Generation.* Pew Research Center. https://www.pewsocialtrends.org/2013/01/30/the-sandwich-generation/.

Perception Institute. (n.d.). *Implicit bias.* https://perception.org/research/implicit-bias/.

Reiners, B. (2019, August 12). *12 unconscious bias examples and how to avoid them in the workplace.* Built In. https://builtin.com/diversity-inclusion/unconscious-bias-examples.

Richard, O. C., Barnett, T., Dwyer, S., & Chadwick, K. (2004). Cultural diversity in management, firm performance, and the moderating role of entrepreneurial orientation dimensions. *Academy of Management Journal, 47*(2), 255–266. https://doi.org/10.5465/20159576.

Sacco, J. M., & Schmitt, N. (2005). A dynamic multilevel model of demographic diversity and misfit effects. *Journal of Applied Psychology, 90*(2), 203–231. https://psycnet.apa.org/doi/10.1037/0021-9010.90.2.203.

Sanchez-Hucles, J. V., & Davis, D. D. (2010). Women and women of color in leadership: Complexity, identity, and intersectionality. *American Psychologist, 65*(3), 171–181. https://psycnet.apa.org/doi/10.1037/a0017459.

Selvarajah, C., Meyer, D., Waal, A. D., & van der Heijden, B. I. J. M. (2018). Dutch managerial leadership strategies: Managing uncertainty avoidance, feminine-related social roles, organisation prosperity focus, and work orientation within a Polder Framework. *Contemporary Management Research, 14*(2), 87–120. https://doi.org/10.7903/cmr.18279.

Sessa, V. I., Kabacoff, R. I., Deal, J., & Brown, H. (2007). Generational differences in leader values and leadership behaviors. *The Psychologist-Manager Journal, 10*(1), 47–74. https://doi.org/10.1080/10887150709336612.

Shore, L. M., Chung-Herrera, B. G., Dean, M. A., Ehrhart, K. H., Jung, D. I., Randel, A. E., & Singh, G. (2009). Diversity in organizations: Where are we now and where are we going? *Human Resource Management Review, 19*(2), 117–133. https://doi.org/10.1016/j.hrmr.2008.10.004.

Siddique, C. M., Siddique, H. F., & Siddique, S. U. (2020). Linking authoritarian leadership to employee organizational embeddedness, LMX and performance in a high-power distance culture: A mediation-moderated analysis. *Journal of Strategy and Management, 13*(3), 393–411. https://doi.org/10.1108/JSMA-10-2019-0185.

Smith, P. B., Peterson, M. F., & Schwartz, S. H. (2002). Cultural values, sources of guidance, and their relevance to managerial behavior: A 47-nation study. *Journal of Cross-Cultural Psychology, 33*(2), 188–208. https://doi.org/10.1177/0022022102033002005.

Sullivan, D. M., Mitchell, M. S., & Uhl-Bien, M. (2003). The new conduct of business: How LMX can help capitalize on cultural diversity. In G. B. Graen (Ed.), *Dealing with diversity* (pp. 183–218). Information Age Publishing. https://ecommons.udayton.edu/mgt_fac_pub/13.

Triandis, H. C. (2018). *Individualism & collectivism*. Taylor & Francis.

U.S. Census Bureau. (2020, April 21). *About race*. https://www.census.gov/topics/population/race/about.html.

Vespa, J., Medina, L., & Armstrong, D. M. (2020, February). *Demographic turning points for the United States: Population projections for 2020 to 2060*. Census.gov. https://www.census.gov/content/dam/Census/library/publications/2020/demo/p25-1144.pdf.

Welbourne, J. L., Gangadharan, A., & Sariol, A. M. (2015). Ethnicity and cultural values as predictors of the occurrence and impact of experienced workplace incivility. *Journal of Occupational Health Psychology, 20*(2), 205–217. https://psycnet.apa.org/doi/10.1037/a0038277.

World Health Organization (WHO). (n.d.-a). *Ageism*. https://www.who.int/ageing/ageism/en/.

World Health Organization (WHO). (n.d.-b). *Gender and health*. https://www.who.int/health-topics/gender#tab=tab_1.

Yudell, M., Roberts, D., DeSalle, R., & Tishkoff, S. (2016). Taking race out of human genetics. *Science, 351*(6273), 564–565. https://doi.org/10.1126/science.aac4951.

Yukl, G. (2013). *Leadership in organizations* (8th ed.). Pearson.

CHAPTER 7

Leadership and Context: Reading the Room

Abstract Leadership effectiveness is highly dependent upon each situation that takes place—in other words, there is no "one size fits all" for leadership. Although there are various perspectives on the subject, a large body of research suggests that complex relationships exist between multiple organizational factors and leadership. Contingency theories identify influential factors such as the task being completed, the leader's personality, and the makeup of the work team, among other factors. In sum, we must recognize that leader communication must be tailored to address a plethora of contextual factors. This chapter also provides practical suggestions for tailoring effective leadership communication to various individuals/groups and contexts. This includes information on tailored communication and how to engage in-group and out-group members. Another critical contextual consideration is choosing the right channel of communication, in addition to the right time, message, and response. This chapter also draws from message design logic in explaining how leaders effectively craft messages in situations that vary in complexity. In considering context, we will also consider how elements of LMX may change when applied across different cultural settings.

Keywords Contingency theory · Context · Tailored communication · Communication channels · Message design logics

L. M. Omilion-Hodges and J. K. Ptacek, *Leader-Member Exchange and Organizational Communication*, New Perspectives in Organizational Communication, https://doi.org/10.1007/978-3-030-68756-4_7

Leadership effectiveness is highly dependent upon each situation that takes place—in other words, there is no "one-size-fits-all" for leadership. Although there are various perspectives on the subject, a large body of research suggests that complex relationships exist between multiple organizational factors and leadership. Contingency theories identify influential factors such as the task being completed, the leader's personality, and the work team's makeup, among other factors. Fiedler's (1967) contingency theory, for example, emphasizes the match of leader style to the situation. Some scholars argue that individual employee characteristics influence how organizational situations are perceived, which in turn, impact employee attitudes and behaviors. Others stress the importance of organizational structure and techniques on organizational effectiveness. In sum, we must recognize that leader communication must be tailored to address a plethora of contextual factors.

This chapter also provides practical suggestions for tailoring effective leadership communication to various individuals/groups and contexts. This includes information on tailored communication and how to engage in-group and out-group members. Another crucial contextual consideration is choosing the right channel of communication, in addition to the right time, message, and response. This chapter also draws from message design logic in explaining how leaders effectively craft messages in situations that vary in complexity. In considering context, we will also consider how elements of LMX may change when applied across different cultural settings.

Contingency Theory: No One-Size-Fits-All

Certainly, we can argue that certain leadership traits and behaviors are more effective than others regarding positive employee outcomes. In fact, Chapter 9 and other chapters in this book identify some of these traits and behaviors. However, the fact that we must consider how the success of these leadership components depends on factors such as type of workplace, work objectives, individual LMX relationships, and others, suggests that there is no one "perfect" leadership style. In other words, "effective" leadership at any moment depends on how well a leader's qualities and communication meet the demands of the current situation (Amanchukwu et al., 2015). This understanding has led researchers to develop contingency theories to explain why leadership traits and behaviors vary depending on the situation (Yukl, 2013).

Fiedler developed one such contingency theory in the 1960s. According to this model, the leader characteristic that is most relevant to the situation is measured by the Least Preferred Coworker (LPC) scale (Strube & Garcia, 1981). This scale suggests that a leader's style can be determined by describing the employee they would least like to work with. A high LPC score indicates that a leader is more relationship-oriented and motivated by close, interpersonal relationships. In contrast, a low LPC score suggests the leader is more task-oriented and will focus on achieving task objectives first and put relationship building with followers second (Yukl, 2013). Therefore, contingency theory can help a leader understand how they should tailor their communication with employees based on their LPC score. Fiedler's contingency theory centers on the idea that situational control determines the relationship between LPC score and group performance (Yukl, 2013). Situational control consists of three distinct factors (Strube & Garcia, 1981):

- **Group atmosphere:** Quality of the leader's relationships with other employees
- **Task structure:** How structured work tasks are
- **Leader position power:** The extent of the leader's formal authority

The situation is considered to be most effective when relationships with employees are good, tasks are highly structured, and the leader has a high level of power (Yukl, 2013). While this is just one theory that considers factors that are most important in determining effective leadership, they all agree that context and situation matter.

Tailored Communication

In considering that effective leadership and building strong individual LMX relationships are contingent upon a variety of contexts and individual member wants and needs, it is necessary to think about the role of communication. Effective leadership relies on the ability of the leader to tailor their communication for each follower. However, this is not always easy, and it is a skill that can take time to develop. Drawing from information-processing theory (Hackman & Johnson, 2013), which describes how leaders can choose effective styles for each situation based on how they process and categorize information, Hackman and Johnson

(2013) identify some implications for why leaders need to develop their contextual communication skills:

- **Develop your knowledge and experience base:** As a leader learns more about and practices leadership, they enhance their ability to understand a variety of situations and build-related skills.
- **Acknowledge the power of categorization:** Being able to accurately "categorize" employees (such as if they are in-group or out-group) and understand followers individually can help a leader to more readily respond to them in a way that best suits their needs.
- **Know your audience:** Understanding how each individual and group responds to various leadership styles is important. A leader should know what followers expect from them depending on relationship history, organizational culture, and the situational context.
- **Performance counts:** Being an effective leader depends on how well followers perceive the leader to contribute to group outcomes.
- **Be flexible:** Being able to adjust based on the situation, and understanding that a response in one situation may not be effective in another, is critical. Asking for feedback and noticing how followers react to a leader's behaviors can help make these adjustments.
- **Focus attention on the "we" and not the "me":** Encourage collective identification, focusing on shared values, and working toward organizational goals as a group. One way to do this is to be mindful of using inclusive language such as "we" and "us."

Important considerations in tailoring one's leadership communication include learning the right channel, the right time, the right message, and the right response to communicate with members based on the situation (Table 7.1).

Choosing the Right Channel

We have heard jokes about "meetings that should have been emails." If you have experienced this yourself, you know the importance of using the right communication channel to match the message. Building on contingency theory and information-processing theory, media richness theory looks at the channels in which organizational communication occurs. The theory suggests that various communication media offer different levels

Table 7.1 Sharpening your communication skills: engaging out-group members

Having out-group members in an organization is natural and in fact, inevitable. These employees may choose to exclude themselves from others in the workgroup or they may be excluded for various reasons. No matter what the reason, out-group members are still valuable team members because they can offer different perspectives, help combat groupthink, and serve other important functions. However, it can be more difficult for a leader to engage with out-group members because they may not align with in-group members who may share the same values, characteristics, and ways of communicating that a leader is used to. Northouse (2021) offers several strategies on how to communicate with out-group members:

- **Listen:** Out-group members could feel left out or alienated from the group, and may feel like their ideas and opinions are heard less than in-group members'. Listening is a key communication behavior for leaders to engage out-group members. This includes being attentive, open-minded, and patient
- **Show empathy:** Not only is it important to listen to out-group members, but a leader should also try to understand their perspective and feelings. This includes restating or paraphrasing what the member has said, reflecting on the dialogue, and showing support.
- **Recognize unique contributions:** Acknowledging that someone is competent and well-able to do their job is an important motivational mechanism. Taking the time as a leader to recognize an out-group member's abilities and unique contributions can not only show the member that they are valued, but also inspire them to recognize their own strengths.
- **Foster inclusion:** Even if out-group members choose to not be part of the in-group, they may still want to feel connected in other ways. Some ways a leader can encourage inclusion is by inviting an out-group member to join in an activity and ask for their thoughts.
- **Create a special relationship:** LMX centers around the unique relationships that a leader has with each follower, and this means out-group members too. Building a special relationship with an out-group member based on trust, respect, and clear communication can help the member to feel more connected and be more willing to contribute and take on responsibilities.
- **Give out-group members a voice and empower them:** Providing space for an out-group member to share their thoughts with the group can help them to feel just as valued as the other members. Additionally, a leader should empower them to be involved and responsible in decision making and other activities.
- **Understand their needs:** Although a leader should continuously work toward building a strong relationship with out-group and in-group members alike, they should keep in mind that someone may choose to be in the out-group. For example, someone who is working part-time or has a high desire to separate their work- and home-life may not want to be as involved as some in-group members. Understanding these members' wants and needs can help a leader to communicate with them more effectively.

Source Northouse (2021)

of understanding, with "rich" media offering the most cues to clarify ambiguous communication and frames of reference (Daft & Lengel, 1986). Common channels of communication, in order from high to low levels of richness, include:

- Face-to-face
- Video conferencing (with audio and visual components)
- Telephone
- Two-way radio
- Written, addressed documents (letters, email, text messages)
- Written, unaddressed documents (bulk mail, fliers, posters, websites)

Media with high richness, such as face-to-face communication, provides an increased number of cues to process and understand the message, such as body language and tone of voice, and allows for the synchronous exchange of feedback (Daft & Lengel, 1986). Media that are lean in richness, such as a written document, provide fewer cues and restrict input. Media with low richness are most effective when communicating easily understood messages or include standard information (Daft & Lengel, 1986). Rich media are more effective in building relationships with employees, as a leader can gain understanding about the employee's communication style, answer questions, and get more feedback on how the employee responds to the leader's messages. Lean media are more impersonal and can hinder a quality LMX relationship.

Electronic media can offer several opportunities as well as challenges in communication between leaders and members. As organizations are becoming more dispersed and implementing telework, the use of electronic media is increasing. While video conferencing software enables a synchronous communication experience close to face-to-face communication, issues such as a slight lag in connection and feeling less collaborative cause many people to still prefer face-to-face over video conferencing channels (Sklar, 2020). However, the use of tools such as emoticons, images, and videos in computer-mediated-communication channels can provide more cues to reduce message ambiguity.

Leaders should consider the type of message they are wanting to communicate when choosing a communication channel. For example, if there are equivocal issues involved that may require clarification or demonstration on how to perform a task, a media-rich channel should be chosen. When discussing a topic that involves decision-making or a sensitive issue where employees may want to share their opinions or ask questions, it would be appropriate to hold a meeting where members can communicate face-to-face. However, if the message is a brief reminder or involves clear steps, an email could be more appropriate and considerate of employees' time.

Choosing the Right Time

In addition to deciding which channel is most appropriate for communicating with employees, considering the right time also matters. Several factors play into effective timing of a message, including urgency, intent, and requirements of the message, work schedules, when employees are most productive, and when other work activities are taking place, to name a few. For example, it has been suggested that Monday mornings are the worst time to hold meetings because that is when most employees are most productive or may have the day off (Burnison, 2019). Some research argues that mid-afternoon and mid-week meetings are the best times, and more specifically, Tuesdays around 2:30 to 3:00 PM because employees have time to prepare and are also less likely to have competing deadlines (Burnison, 2019; Rubin, 2010). Alternatively, if there is an issue that requires important decision-making, research (Danziger et al., 2011) has found that it is best to do so either first thing in the morning or after lunchtime when hunger will be least distracting. Furthermore, research (Kouchaki & Smith, 2014) has also found that people tend to have more moral awareness and self-control—and engage in fewer unethical behaviors—in the morning compared to the afternoon, a phenomenon called the "morning morality effect."

When considering the timing of email communication, research (Sims, 2017) has found that while most work emails are sent in the middle of the week during the late morning, they have a slightly higher rate of being opened by everyone if sent earlier in the week or even after work hours. Other research (Ng, 2018) has found that emails are more likely to be opened on the weekends because they have less competition from other work emails. However, the most crucial factor to consider here is context. Understanding your workgroup and organization's specific dynamics can provide the most information about when the best time is to communicate. Specifically, when deciding the best time to send an email, Sims (2017) suggests thinking about the following factors:

- **Your audience and workspace:** Are employees working at desks where they have constant access to email and will be able to check them immediately? Are employees used to receiving frequent emails? You might also consider if people are working in different time zones and when most people will be available to check the email.
- **Your goals and message intent:** Is the email meant to get a quick response, or does it require in-depth reading? Is it intended to communicate information that employees can read at any time, or is it meant to engage them in conversation? This is important in choosing a time when employees may all be available to engage, if necessary.
- **Your organizational culture:** Is work-life balance an important consideration, or are employees accustomed to receiving emails after work hours? Is it common in your company to send multiple emails a day, or should they be sent sparingly?

Choosing the Right Message

Another critical contextual consideration is how a leader can choose the right message to followers. As this book emphasizes, the message a leader chooses can depend on the type of relationship they have with each follower and the leader's communication strengths. Put simply, everyone—leader and workgroup members—work from different assumptions regarding their interpretations and production of messages. One way to think about this is through message design logics, which is defined as "the kind of communication-constituting belief system the message producer relies on in reasoning from the goals sought to the message design used" (O'Keefe, 1988, p. 92). O'Keefe argues that there are three main message design logics which individuals use to communicate. These include:

- **Expressive:** Expressive design logic views language as a way for expressing one's thoughts and feelings and is the most straightforward of the three. This logic assumes that communication serves the primary goal of expression and generally overlooks or disregards the situation's context.
- **Conventional:** Conventional design logic views communication as a cooperative, two-way exchange that follows social rules. This relies

on mutual conventional understandings of interaction, and although the language is still considered as a means of expression, these expressions are made with the goal to achieve a desired effect. This logic strongly considers the context of the situation and which responses are most appropriate in the given context.

- **Rhetorical:** Rhetorical design logic views communication as the production and negotiation of our social selves and situations. This is the most sophisticated style of logic in that it views context as being created by the message itself, and meaning is enacted through coordination and negotiation.

These three types of message design logics can help explain why people communicate in different ways. Furthermore, this model argues that someone's message style can vary based on the specific situation and tasks involved (O'Keefe & McCornack, 1987). However, these logics are presented in a progression. Each one builds on the previous, meaning that one cannot effectively employ a conventional message design without understanding that communication can first be used to make an expression. Further, a rhetorical message design cannot be used without understanding the rules of conventional messaging (O'Keefe & McCornack, 1987). An effective leader should consider the various ways in which they can craft a message to a follower and the impact in which can have. For example, consider a situation in which you want to remind employees to submit their timesheets on time.

- An expressive message may say, "**Submit your timesheet by Friday**"—This is simple and to the point. This may work for straightforward situations in which not much interpretation or conversation is needed.
- A conventional message would consider communication rules such as politeness. It may say, "**Please submit your timesheet by Friday. Thank you!**"
- A rhetorical message may also consider context and what might persuade people to adhere to the policy. It may say, "**Please help us to achieve 100% timesheet submissions this week by turning in your timesheet by Friday. Thank you!**" It would follow previous expressive and conventional rules but also consider multiple goals.

It is important also to consider how different cultural settings can influence how someone might interpret a message. Some components of culture were described in more detail in Chapter 6. For example, in individualistic cultures, an employee may appreciate a one-on-one conversation with a manager about a difficult situation. In contrast, in more collectivistic cultures, an employee may appreciate support from the group. Additionally, considering the organizational culture and how leaders and members usually communicate about and handle various situations can influence the degree to which some messages are more or less acceptable.

Choosing the Right Response

Effective leaders don't just craft effective messages to employees, but they effectively respond to employees as well. This includes replying to electronic messages in a timely order, following up with employee concerns, and responding in ways that enhance the leader–member relationship. One important part of choosing the right response is to enact active listening skills. As discussed in previous chapters, active listening includes asking questions, paraphrasing, and maintaining eye contact and positive body language to show that you are paying attention and engaged in the conversation. Message design logics can also help leaders to determine appropriate responses to follower messages. For example, consider a situation in which an employee needs an extension on a project because they are dealing with a stressful family issue at home.

- An expressive design logic often disregards context and is straightforward. It may completely avoid any acknowledgment of the employee's issue. An example response might be, "**You can have an extension until Friday**."
- A conventional design logic would be considered a normative behavior, and many leaders are considered to be conventional. This type of message would likely include a comforting message or even an offer for assistance. An example response might be, "**I am sorry that you are going through this. How about an extension until Friday? Please reach out if you need any help**."
- A rhetorical design logic would further contextualize the situation and realize there are multiple goals here. An example message may begin by taking some time to make sure that first the employee has

been heard and is cared about, such as saying "**I am sorry you are going through this. How are you feeling?**" followed by offering support and statements such as, "**We will figure out a solution to get your project finished. We care about you and want to make sure you are doing alright**" while emphasizing "we" statements to signal connection.

Another vital consideration in communicating appropriate responses to employees that help to build and maintain high-quality LMX relationships is emotional intelligence. Emotional intelligence (EI; also known as emotional quotient or EQ) is defined as "the ability to monitor one's own and others' feelings and emotions, to discriminate among them and to use this information to guide one's thinking and actions" (Salovey & Mayer, 1990, p. 189). This relates to leadership and LMX because a leader's emotional intelligence can help them manage how they communicate with others and how they understand the feelings of others and respond appropriately, which can also strengthen LMX relationships. Research (Goleman, 1998) has found that emotional intelligence accounts for two-thirds of necessary leadership abilities, pointing out that EI matters more than cognitive intelligence or technical knowledge. Goleman (2004) has identified five components of emotional intelligence, including:

- **Self-awareness:** Understanding your own emotions, strengths/weaknesses, motivations, and values, and how they affect others.
- **Self-regulation:** Being able to control your emotions or impulses effectively and thinking before acting.
- **Social skill:** Building rapport and quality relationships with other people.
- **Empathy:** Being able to consider and understand other people's feelings, and treating others according to their emotional reactions.
- **Motivation:** Valuing achievement for the sake of achievement itself, instead of primarily for money or status.

Although these processes exist in everyone, people differ in their ability to understand and express their emotions; however, these skills can be learned and improved upon (Salovey & Mayer, 1990). Seeking feedback from others, practicing these capabilities, and being persistent in

Table 7.2 Leadership in action—leader profile: Indra Nooyi

Indra Nooyi, former CEO of PepsiCo, is a leader that many would consider to have high emotional intelligence and high-quality LMX relationships with her employees. One example of this is when she wrote letters to the parents of all of her executive team members, thanking them for what their child had contributed to the company (Morey, 2018).

Nooyi understands the importance of emotional intelligence, including components of social skill and empathy. She has said, "You need to look at the employee and say, 'I value you as a person. I know that you have a life beyond PepsiCo, and I'm going to respect you for your entire life, not just treat you as employee number 4,567'" (Morey, 2018).

Nooyi has also worked to instil strong values in her employees. Upon stepping down from her role of CEO with PepsiCo and the 24 years she spent with the company, she wrote a letter to her employees, sharing some lessons she has learned along the way in hopes to inspire them one last time (Nooyi, 2018):

- Have a clear, compelling vision for what you want to accomplish
- Focus on the short-term and the long-term
- Bring people along with you
- Be good listeners
- Be lifelong students
- Think hard about time, make the most of your days, and be mindful of your choices

Ranked as Forbes' second most powerful women in business in 2017 (Howard, 2017), Nooyi is a strong example of how to exhibit emotional intelligence and authentic leadership while leading a successful organization.

Source Howard (2017), Morey (2018), and Nooyi (2018)

improving upon them can help you become more emotionally intelligent (Goleman, 2004). Table 7.2 provides one such leadership example.

Leadership Moments: Takeaways for Leaders and Members

1. **There is no "one-size-fits-all" to leadership:** The most effective leadership varies in each situation. Contingency theory (Fiedler, 1967) argues that factors such as group atmosphere, task structure, and leader position power all play an influential role in determining the effectiveness between leadership style and group performance. A leader should also keep in mind that they cannot enact the same style with each employee and certainly not in every situation. For example, sometimes a more task-oriented style is preferred, whereas other situations demand a more relationship-oriented leadership style.

2. **Communication varies by situation and needs:** Remember that while not everything needs to be communicated in a meeting, not everything should be sent in an email either. Assessing the complexity of a message to determine the level of processing it requires can help an individual choose the appropriate communication channel. For example, an ambiguous message or an issue that requires lengthy discussion or decision-making would require more media richness, such as a face-to-face conversation. However, a quick reminder to do something that employees already know-how to do could be communicated in a convenient email.
3. **It's not just what you say, it's how you say it:** In addition to considering the best channel and time to communicate with others, the message content is essential in relationship building. A leader or coworker who consistently overlooks the context of an emotional or stressful situation can create a sense of disconnection from others. Determining and evaluating your own level of emotional intelligence can help you be more cognizant of each situation's unique context and help you respond appropriately.

Mini Case Study: "Trouble Connecting"

You have recently hired a new employee, Deanna, but you have been having trouble connecting with her. You want to figure out a way to build a better relationship with her because you have fairly strong relationships with all of your other employees. Deanna is a good worker, but she doesn't seem interested in joining in personal conversations with the rest of the group so you don't know much about her. Additionally, a couple days ago you overheard her saying that she doesn't feel like her opinions matter. You pride yourself on your ability to come up with creative plans and most members of your work team willingly contribute to the conversation, but Deanna usually stays quiet. You know you need to do something soon before your relationship with her worsens and she alienates herself from the group even more.

1. Considering the context of this situation, what might be the best channel of communicating with Deanna about this issue?
2. How can you apply what you know about engaging out-group members to make Deanna feel more included?

3. What are some other considerations that you should keep in mind when approaching Deanna to try to build your relationship with her?

References

Amanchukwu, R. N., Stanley, G. J., & Ololube, N. P. (2015). A review of leadership theories, principles and styles and their relevance to educational management. *Management, 5*(1), 6–14. https://doi.org/10.5923/j.mm.20150501.02.

Burnison, G. (2019, April 2). *Monday is the worst day to schedule your meetings. Science says this is the best time (and way) to do it.* CNBC. https://www.cnbc.com/2019/04/01/science-says-this-is-the-best-time-and-day-to-schedule-a-meeting-if-you-want-to-be-productive.html.

Daft, R. L., & Lengel, R. H. (1986). Organizational information requirements, media richness and structural design. *Management Science, 32*(5), 554–571. https://doi.org/10.1287/mnsc.32.5.554.

Danziger, S., Levav, J., & Avnaim-Pesso, L. (2011). Extraneous factors in judicial decisions. *Proceedings of the National Academy of Sciences, 108*(17), 6889–6892. https://doi.org/10.1073/pnas.1018033108.

Fiedler, F. E. (1967). *A theory of leadership effectiveness*. McGraw-Hill.

Goleman, D. (1998). *Working with emotional intelligence*. Bantam.

Goleman, D. (2004). What makes a leader? *Harvard Business Review, 82*(1), 82–91. Retrieved from: https://www.knoxeducation.com/sites/main/files/file-attachments/6_leadership.pdf.

Hackman, M. Z., & Johnson, C. E. (2013). *Leadership: A communication perspective* (6th ed.). Waveland.

Howard, C. (2017, November 1). The 19 most powerful women in business 2017: CEOs and more with ambitious goals. *Forbes*. https://www.forbes.com/sites/carolinehoward/2017/11/01/the-19-most-powerful-women-in-business-2017-ceos-and-more-with-ambitious-goals/#2d4525de5b89.

Kouchaki, M., & Smith, I. H. (2014). The morning morality effect: The influence of time of day on unethical behavior. *Psychological Science, 25*(1), 95–102. https://doi.org/10.1177/0956797613498099.

Morey, R. (2018, July 16). *How 5 emotionally intelligent CEOs handle their power*. Pagely. https://pagely.com/blog/emotionally-intelligent-ceos/.

Ng, R. (2018, November 18). *Best time to send email: A matter of when and where*. Yesware. https://www.yesware.com/blog/best-time-to-send-email/.

Nooyi, I. (2018, October 2). *Parting words as I step down as CEO.* LinkedIn. https://www.linkedin.com/pulse/parting-words-i-step-down-ceo-indra-nooyi/.

Northouse, P. G. (2021). *Introduction to leadership: Concepts and practice* (5th ed.). Sage.

O'Keefe, B. J. (1988). The logic of message design: Individual differences in reasoning about communication. *Communications Monographs, 55*(1), 80–103. https://doi.org/10.1080/03637758809376159.

O'Keefe, B. J., & McCornack, S. A. (1987). Message design logic and message goal structure. *Human Communication Research, 14*(1), 68–92. https://doi.org/10.1111/j.1468-2958.1987.tb00122.x.

Rubin, C. (2010, June 4). *When is the best time for a meeting?* Inc. https://www.inc.com/news/articles/2010/06/best-time-for-meetings.html?_ga=2.117469257.1753319746.1602537305-868160349.1602133376.

Salovey, P., & Mayer, J. D. (1990). Emotional intelligence. *Imagination, Cognition and Personality, 9*(3), 185–211. https://doi.org/10.2190/DUGG-P24E-52WK-6CDG.

Sims, K. (2017, October 27). *When is the best time to send internal emails?* Bananatag. https://blog.bananatag.com/internal-comms/when-is-the-best-time-to-send-internal-emails.

Sklar, J. (2020, April 24). *'Zoom fatigue' is taxing the brain. Here's why that happens*. National Geographic. https://www.nationalgeographic.com/science/2020/04/coronavirus-zoom-fatigue-is-taxing-the-brain-here-is-why-that-happens/.

Strube, M. J., & Garcia, J. E. (1981). A meta-analytic investigation of Fiedler's contingency model of leadership effectiveness. *Psychological Bulletin, 90*(2), 307–321. https://doi.org/10.1037/0033-2909.90.2.307.

Yukl, G. A. (2013). *Leadership in organizations* (8th ed.). Pearson.

CHAPTER 8

When Good People Are Bad Leaders: When and Why Leadership Fails

Abstract It is easy to lead people with easy interpersonal relationships, but what happens when we do not get along with our followers? Sometimes leadership is hard—it is difficult to relate to people when we differ in various ways, such as politics, family obligations, work ethics, and other personal differences. This chapter offers practical suggestions for communicating and connecting with people we struggle to get along with. These suggestions also draw from quotations from well-respected leaders throughout history. Furthermore, this chapter explores what experts have to say on using language to frame your ideas using strategic communication effectively. This chapter also addresses how conflict style can influence a leader's relationship with their followers. Research shows that while one conflict style may be effective for certain situations, it may not be the best in others, and when considered in conjunction with leadership styles, it can have a large impact on organizational outcomes (e.g., Richmond et al., 1983). This chapter explores each of the five conflict styles (competing, collaborating, compromising, avoiding, and accommodating), provides examples of when each may be used and includes a quiz for determining one's conflict style.

Keywords Bad leadership · Employee differences · Framing and strategic language · Conflict styles

L. M. Omilion-Hodges and J. K. Ptacek, *Leader-Member Exchange and Organizational Communication*, New Perspectives in Organizational Communication, https://doi.org/10.1007/978-3-030-68756-4_8

It is easy to lead people with whom we have easy interpersonal relationships, but what happens when we do not get along with our followers? Sometimes leadership is hard—it is difficult to relate to people when we differ in various ways, such as politics, family obligations, work ethics, and other personal differences. This chapter offers practical suggestions for communicating and connecting with people we struggle to get along with. These suggestions include quotations from well-respected leaders throughout history. Another issue that leaders often face is effectively framing their ideas using strategic communication. We will explore what experts such as Fairhurst and Sarr (1996) and others have to say on using language to be intentional leaders.

This chapter also addresses how conflict style can influence a leader's relationship with their followers. Research shows that while one conflict style may be useful for certain situations, it may not be the best in others. When considered in conjunction with leadership styles, conflict management can significantly impact organizational outcomes (e.g., Richmond et al., 1983). We will explore each of the five conflict styles (competing, collaborating, compromising, avoiding, and accommodating) and provide examples of when each may be effective. This chapter also features a quiz for helping you to determine your conflict style.

When Leadership Is Hard

Although we often equate the word "leadership" with "good leadership," this idea is very limiting. It can also make someone believe that if they lack a particular skill or have failed as a leader in the past that they should not be a leader or are not meant to be a leader. This, fortunately, is not the case. All leaders have faced challenges many times throughout their lives. In fact, leaders face challenges every day, whether in solving a problem, making a decision, managing conflict, motivating followers, etc. However, one sign of "good leadership" is perseverance to keep going and learn from mistakes when faced with difficulties. Consider the following quotes from respected leaders (Economy, 2015; Searcy & DeVries, 2012; Walter, 2013):

- "Successful leaders see the opportunities in every difficulty rather than the difficulty in every opportunity"—Reed Markham, author, professor, and consultant

- "Leadership and learning are indispensable to each other"—John F. Kennedy, former US President
- "Don't be intimidated by what you don't know. That can be your greatest strength and ensure that you do things differently from everyone else"—Sara Blakely, founder of Spanx
- "I make plenty of mistakes and I'll make plenty more mistakes, too. That's part of the game. You've just got to make sure that the right things overcome the wrong ones"—Warren Buffett, CEO of Berkshire Hathaway

Among the challenges for leaders is building and maintaining high-quality leader–member relationships. Building strong relationships with followers may be easy when you share similarities because similarity breeds liking. As mentioned in Chapter 6, diversity in teams can be beneficial in many ways, but this can pose challenges if differences between leaders and members prevent them from connecting. Some contexts in which it may be difficult for leaders and members to connect are differences in politics, family obligations, work ethics, and other personal differences. We will explore each of these and provide some practical suggestions on overcoming these differences and making a connection.

Political Differences

Political differences can create tension between even close family members and friends, and individuals in the workplace are not exempt from this. A study (American Psychological Association, 2016) conducted leading up to the 2016 United States presidential election found that 17% of employees reported feeling stressed out because of political discussions at work, and 20% of employees avoided some coworkers altogether because of their political views. Other effects of political discussions at work have led to employees feeling less productive and more negative while at work (APA, 2016). Indeed, politics can be a sensitive subject in the workplace because coworkers can be extremely polarized on topics they feel passionate about. Considering this, there are several things that leaders can do to connect with members despite political differences (Ballard, 2017). Some ideas include:

- Establish a clear policy limiting political activity at work
- Emphasize a culture of respect and civil communication

- Actively lead by example by showing respect and civility to all employees
- Recognize that employees may feel more stressed during high political seasons, such as during election years
- Focus on shared goals, values, and teamwork—find some common ground and similarities

Family Obligation Differences

It may be difficult for a leader to understand an employee's family needs if they differ from their own. For example, suppose someone is not caring for a sick relative, a disabled relative, an elderly parent, or children. In that case, they may not understand the demands on someone experiencing one or a combination of these situations. Furthermore, each organizational member has a different family situation, all of which come with unique challenges. Even two coworkers who have the same number of children, for example, can experience very different family structures, time commitments, and needs. It is also essential to consider that employees do not have to disclose their family obligations to their employers and may hesitate to do so out of fear that they will miss out on opportunities or be treated differently than other employees. Avni Patel Thompson, CEO, and founder of Modern Village, says, "There are some managers who are unsympathetic to the challenges their employees face at home and some who intentionally turn a blind eye" (Knight, 2020, n.p.). Thompson adds that while managers may have good intentions, they may lack empathy or the know-how to support employees in these situations. As a leader, there are some specific things to do when connecting with employees with different family obligations (Knight, 2020; U.S. Equal Employment Opportunity Commission, n.d.), such as:

- Create an open and trusting environment where employees feel comfortable sharing information about their personal lives, as well as an inclusive culture which recognizes the contributions of all members
- If someone shares personal information with you, show concern and empathy, genuinely listen to and remember what they say, and ask appropriate questions to build your understanding of their situation
- Check-in on each employee often and follow up with an employee if they are going through a challenging family situation

- Post work schedules as early as possible to allow for employees to have time to schedule their responsibilities
- Provide training and development opportunities to all employees regardless of their obligations so that everyone has the information needed to perform their jobs best
- Provide reasonable personal or sick leave for employees to handle caregiving responsibilities, make overtime requirements as family-friendly as possible, and reassign job duties that employees cannot perform due to personal responsibilities

Work Ethics Differences

Another way in which a leader and employees can feel disconnected from one another is if they share differences in work ethics. This can go both ways, as leaders can have poor work ethics, likely losing trust and respect from followers. However, effective leaders must set and demonstrate ethical standards in their organization. Sometimes ethics are apparent, such as in situations when stealing or harming someone is involved. But regarding work ethics, which can be thought of as values that guide someone's workplace behavior or how they feel about the importance of work (Cambridge Dictionary, n.d.), the lines can be more blurry. It can be frustrating if an employee does not have the same work ethics or standards of working, but it is important to remember that everyone has learned these values in different ways. For example, while you might think someone being late daily is rude and demonstrates a poor work ethic, that person may not believe timeliness is a big deal if they still get all of their work done. They may also come from a culture where time is considered polychronic rather than monochronic, as is the case in the United States. Furthermore, as mentioned in family obligations, individuals could have personal schedule conflicts that prevent them from getting to work early. Concepts such as timeliness are also cultural, so it is helpful to consider how various cultural differences can influence someone's idea of good work ethics. If a leader finds that it is challenging to connect with an employee because of differences in work ethics, it may help to consider the following suggestions (Meyer, 2019; Roy, 2020):

- As a leader, set clear guidelines and policies on expectations, such as deadlines to complete work and what behaviors are unacceptable.

There is a difference between an employee just doing something differently and outright violating an established policy.

- Be a mentor and set a good example through your behaviors. Consistency on the leader's part can motivate others to develop the same work ethics.
- Make space for constant and mutual feedback—set one-on-one time with each employee to give them feedback on how they are doing and ask them how they think you are doing and how you can better help them.
- Recognize and emphasize someone's contributions and things they are doing well, instead of just picking out and focusing on their downfalls. Each employee can offer distinct benefits to the team.
- Consider if your expectations are realistic, and do not judge someone if they don't have the same dedication. For example, if you stay late to complete extra work, but someone else does not, do not assume that they don't care about their job.
- Be cognizant of employees' needs. Meeting employee needs can motivate them to be more engaged in their work.

Personal Differences

In addition to differences in political views, family obligations, and work ethics, a leader may have difficulty connecting with an employee due to a number of other personal differences. Again, it is often easier to build relationships when you can find similarities with someone else, so, understandably, it may be harder to connect with those who we perceive to share no similarities. However, you will certainly work with many people throughout your career who you perceive to be very different from yourself, whether in communication style, prioritizing tasks or relationships, personal interests, or other factors. In addition to the suggestions provided above, it may be helpful to try these general suggestions for connecting with employees (Economy, 2014).

- Show that you value each employee and respect their time, culture, and opinions
- Create a work environment where everyone feels safe to try new things and share their ideas
- Be transparent and share information with everyone

- Give every employee opportunities for more responsibility and growth
- Trust every employee to do their job instead of strictly guiding them with an excess of policies and procedures
- Engage with each employee frequently, checking in on them and asking for their ideas and thoughts
- Take time to recognize and reward every employee (even in small ways such as a verbal or written thank you) for their excellent contributions, and publicly celebrate team efforts

Additionally, it's important to remember that building high-quality LMX relationships takes work and time. Thankfully, leaders can improve their skills through practice, dedication to their followers, and emulating the values they want to instill in others. Consider these related quotes from famous leaders (Newell, 2016; Tichy & Charan, 2020; Walter, 2013):

- "Leaders are made, they are not born. They are made by hard effort, which is the price which all of us must pay to achieve any goal that is worthwhile"—Vince Lombardi, former American football coach
- "You have to look at leadership through the eyes of the followers and you have to live the message. What I have learned is that people become motivated when you guide them to the source of their own power and when you make heroes out of employees who personify what you want to see in the organization"—Anita Roddick, founder of The Body Shop
- "Good business leaders create a vision, articulate the vision, passionately own the vision, and relentlessly drive it to completion. Above all else, though, good leaders are open. They go up, down, and around their organization to reach people. They don't stick to the established channels. They're informal. They're straight with people. They make a religion out of being accessible"—Jack Welch, former CEO of General Electric

Framing Ideas Using Strategic Language

Part of building good LMX relationships and getting others on board with your ideas in the language you use. Language is, after all, the "critical link between vision and the leader's ability to powerfully communicate its essence" (Conger, 1991, p. 31). One way in which language is used effectively among leaders is in the art of framing. Framing can be defined as:

> the ability to shape the meaning of a subject, to judge its character and significance. To hold the frame of a subject is to choose one particular meaning (or set of meanings) over another. When we share our frames with others (the process of framing), we manage meaning because we assert that our interpretations should be taken as real over other possible interpretations. (Fairhurst & Sarr, 1996, p. 3)

Language plays a part in framing as it helps us focus and make sense of abstract situations, categorize things, and remember and understand information (Fairhurst, 2005). Leaders can help manage meaning through language to help create a frame in the listener's mind (Fairhurst & Sarr, 1996). Fairhurst and Sarr (1996) identify five specific tools or language forms that leaders use to design memorable frames for followers. These include:

- **Metaphors:** These compare one thing to something else. Use this when you want something to take on a new meaning. An example of this would be, "When we put our heads together, we're like an unstoppable freight train."
- **Jargon:** Using jargon or catchphrases helps to put something into familiar terms. Use this when you want to enhance meaning. An example of this includes, "We need to put our noses to the grindstone and get this project done."
- **Contrast:** This explains the subject in terms of its opposite, as sometimes it is easier to describe something by identifying what it is not. An example of this is, "This week will not be like last week; we have different tasks to accomplish."
- **Spin:** This can cast the subject in a positive or negative light. Use this when you want to identify either the strengths or weaknesses of something. An example of this would be, "This brilliant new computer system is going to be well worth the cost by saving us time and making it easier to help customers."
- **Stories:** This includes explaining the subject by providing examples. Use this when you want to draw attention or build rapport, as people

Table 8.1 Leadership in action—organizational profile: Zappos

If you are wondering how an organization can use storytelling to build their culture, Zappos can provide some insight. As CEO Tony Hsieh says, "a great brand is a story that never stops unfolding" (Emerson, 2019). Zappos emphasizes the importance of storytelling through various initiatives: • The Zappos Insights company was created by Zappos to share stories about the company's culture and their customer service approach (Zappos Insights, n.d.). • Every year, Zappos puts out a "culture book" and asks every employee to write something about their company (BIF, 2014). • They even have a YouTube channel called "Zappos Stories" which includes stories about employees, culture, community service, and more. Through these initiatives and others, Zappos shares stories about its culture, which includes an array of incredible customer service stories, to further strengthen their culture (Klotz-Guest, 2017). The company started as an online shoe store in 1999 and has since grown in product assortment and popularity, priding themselves on their customer service (Zappos, n.d.). But even before customer service, their main priority is company culture (BIF, 2014). Hsieh argues that if the culture is good, everything else falls into place.

Source Business Innovation Factory (2014), Emerson (2019), Klotz-Guest (2017), Zappos (n.d.), and Zappos Insights (n.d.)

like hearing stories. An example of this would be, "I remember when I first started with this company..."

Of course, these framing tools should be used strategically and thoughtfully, as there are times when they would not be appropriate to use. For example, you should avoid using a metaphor or story if they mask alternative meanings, or you should avoid using jargon if it risks being overused (Fairhurst & Sarr, 1996). Jargon can also exclude individuals who are unfamiliar with it and even diminish shared meaning between people. But when used well, framing tools and vivid language can inspire and build commitment among followers (Conger, 1991), as exemplified in Table 8.1.

Conflict Style and Leadership

Conflict is a normal part of organizational life. There will inevitably be some kind of conflict when a group of people works together because no one is similar in every way. It is also important to remember that conflict is not always a bad thing; in fact, conflict can be conducive to developing good ideas, creative solutions to problems, relationships, and other outcomes. Conflict is also a way to show that members care and are invested in organizational decisions. However, people also differ in how they handle conflict, making it difficult for leaders to connect with some employees (or employees to connect with their leader). People generally fall into one of five general conflict styles described below. Each of these styles varies in terms of how cooperative or concerned you are for others' concerns and how assertive or concerned you are for your ideas (Blake & Mouton, 1964; Kilmann & Thomas, 1975). We also identify situations in which each conflict style may be effectively used (Northouse, 2021).

- **Competing (high assertive—low cooperative):** This style puts one's desires first and often involves using control over the other party to get what you want. This style can be disadvantageous because it does not consider the other person's feelings. Still, sometimes competition can help challenge others and can be useful in situations where immediate action is needed.
- **Collaborating (high assertive—high cooperative):** This style is the most preferred because it fully considers both party's feelings and works toward getting maximum rewards for everyone involved. Although this style is the most difficult because it requires the most effort and time from both parties, it is the one which we should strive for in most situations.
- **Compromising (mid assertive—mid cooperative):** This style often happens when collaboration cannot be reached. It requires some give and take from both parties without entirely ignoring or fully tending to either party's full needs. Compromising is often viewed positively because it considers both parties' needs and can reach a quicker resolution than a collaborating style. This style would most often be used when there is not enough time or resources to work toward full collaboration.
- **Avoiding (low assertive—low cooperative):** This style is passive and usually ignores the conflict altogether; instead, organizational members may just change the subject or pretend the conflict does not exist. Although this style can be detrimental to relationships and lead to anxiety associated with avoiding resolving an issue, it can help in trivial situations where there is no need to address it. This style can also be used initially to provide conflicting parties to calm down before engaging with each other.
- **Accommodating (low assertive—high cooperative):** This style is the opposite of the competing conflict style because it puts other's

needs before one's own. This style can be disadvantageous because the accommodating party is making all of the sacrifices. Still, it can help lessen conflict, especially when the issue is more important to the other party.

As mentioned above, although collaboration is the most preferred conflict style, there are situations in which other styles may be best, perhaps due to time or resource constraints, or the situation does not call for the effort required for collaboration. Understanding how to communicate effectively to manage conflict as a leader can positively influence your relationships with followers. Table 8.2 includes a short quiz you can take to determine which conflict style you most often align with. After determining your typical conflict style, you may consider how this can shape your relationships as a leader and practice conflict resolution suggestions from Chapter 2 and Table 8.3 in this chapter.

Leadership Moments: Takeaways for Leaders & Members

- **Leadership is not always easy:** Even if a leader is well-liked by nearly everyone and seems to do all the "right" things, there are times when it may be challenging to connect with a follower. This can be due to a number of reasons, but often it can stem from leader–member differences such as political viewpoints, family obligations, work ethics, or other personal differences. Recognizing these differences and making efforts to listen to, value, and respect the other person can bridge the disconnection and strengthen the LMX relationship.
- **Using the right language can go far:** How a leader uses language can make all the difference in whether people listen to and get on board with ideas. The ability to frame a situation and help it make sense to others requires developing skills and practice. Using tools appropriately, such as metaphors, jargon, contrast, spin, and stories can inspire followers and build commitment toward goals (Fairhurst & Sarr, 1996).
- **Conflict style can influence LMX relationships:** Conflict is inevitable in organizational life, and the way a leader handles conflict can play a significant role in LMX relationships. Although a collaborating style is most preferred, there are situations where other

Table 8.2 Identifying your conflict style

This chapter has discussed the five main conflict styles. Although you can differ in your conflict style depending on the context, you may defer to one style more often than others. Below, circle the choice which best describes the degree to which you agree with each statement. Then, add up the numbers in each category to determine which conflict style you most align with. This can help you to reflect on some of the strengths and limitations of your primary conflict style. To access a full version of a similar conflict style inventory, see https://www.riverhouseepress.com/style-matters-inventory.

	Never	*Sometimes*	*Often*	*Always*
Competing				
When in an argument I pull all the stops; I'm determined to win.	0	1	2	3
If someone upsets me, I have no problem confronting them.	0	1	2	3
I am usually right in arguments.	0	1	2	3
It's okay if I have to lose some friends in order to achieve my goals.	0	1	2	3
Collaborating				
When there is an issue I try to figure out the best solution that makes all of us happy.	0	1	2	3
During a disagreement I make sure to share my feelings and also fully listen to others' feelings.	0	1	2	3
Before making a decision I make sure that I have as much information as possible from everyone involved.	0	1	2	3
I view conflict as a good thing because it allows me to work with others toward solutions and learn more about them to build our relationship.	0	1	2	3
Compromising				
I am willing to give something in order to get something else when negotiating with someone.	0	1	2	3
I prefer to resolve issues quickly, even if I don't get absolutely everything I want.	0	1	2	3
I am happy with some give and take for the common good.	0	1	2	3
It's better to be somewhat happy in a conflict resolution than to have one person happy and the other miserable.	0	1	2	3
Avoiding				
I don't like arguments so I try to avoid them as much as possible.	0	1	2	3

(continued)

Table 8.2 (continued)

If someone confronts me about something I tend to back down in order to not deal with the confrontation.	0	1	2	3
If I'm upset with someone I will keep it to myself so I don't upset them.	0	1	2	3
If I ignore an issue it usually just resolves itself.	0	1	2	3
Accommodating				
I work hard to make others happy.	0	1	2	3
I tend to put others' needs first over my own needs.	0	1	2	3
I would rather give up a goal of mine in order to preserve my relationship with someone.	0	1	2	3
Even if I'm super busy with something, if a friend calls and needs some help, I will drop what I'm doing.	0	1	2	3

Table 8.3 Sharpening your communication skills: resolving conflict in the workplace

This chapter identifies different conflict styles and ways in which we can understand how differences in communication during conflict can create either connection or disconnection between a leader and follower, and Chapter 2 additionally provides some general guidelines for addressing conflict. Here we provide some specific, practical strategies for resolving conflict (Northouse 2021) that have not yet been addressed, but can be helpful in the workplace context:

• **Differentiation:** This occurs early on in a conflict, when both parties clarify their own position on a topic and identify differences in the two sides. Conflict can easily be escalated during this time because it can evoke negative feelings, so it is important to separate the people from the issue by focusing on the conflict itself and isolating the issue. During differentiation both parties give the other side a chance to talk about their feelings and try to understand the differing viewpoints.

• **Fractionation:** This is the process of breaking a conflict into smaller, manageable parts. Breaking a large and complex conflict into smaller pieces is helpful because the parties can work toward resolving each piece instead of trying to resolve several issues at once, which can also reduce the emotional intensity of the conflict and provide small victories along the way. Here both parties can work together to identify components of the issue and devise a plan to attack each aspect.

• **Face saving:** This involves efforts to protect one's self-image during a threat. People can become defensive if they feel that their self-image is being attacked, and this could shift a conflict to become more personal. In order to avoid a conflict escalating, each party should communicate in ways to avoid threatening the other's self-image. To do this, use messages such as "I can see where you're coming from but this is how I see it." This will be much more conducive to resolving the conflict than making personal attacks or trying to make the other person feel unimportant.

Source Northouse (2021)

conflict styles would be easier or more effective. Understanding your conflict style can improve your conflict management skills and build relationships with followers.

Mini Case Study: Building a Connection

You have noticed that one of your employees, Stephen, has often been late for work and his weekly reports are lacking in quality compared to other employees'. When you mentioned this to him during your last monthly check-in, he seemed to get slightly defensive and said he didn't realize it was a problem. His work hasn't improved, and you're beginning to feel that he's a "bad employee." When you mentioned these issues in this month's check-in, Stephen got upset and said he doesn't think that he's being treated fairly, to which you responded, "I don't treat you any differently, and you are held to the same standards as everyone else." You find yourself interacting with him less and less to avoid unpleasant interactions. Still, you know you have to do something to help Stephen develop his skills and build your relationship with him.

1. After learning about how to connect with employees through differences, what are some ways in which you could build your leader–member relationship with Stephen? What are some specific things you can say to him?
2. Which conflict style did you most likely use in your last meeting with Stephen? Which style could you try instead?
3. Using what you learned about conflict resolution strategies, what are some things you can say to address Stephen's work issues in the future?

References

American Psychological Association (APA). (2016, September 16). *1 in 4 employees negatively affected by political talk at work this election season, finds new survey*. https://www.apa.org/news/press/releases/2016/09/employees-political-talk.

Ballard, D. W. (2017, March 2). Navigating political talk at work. *Harvard Business Review*. https://hbr.org/2017/03/navigating-political-talk-at-work.

Blake, R., & Mouton, J. (1964). *The managerial grid: The key to leadership excellence*. Gulf Publishing.

Business Innovation Factory (BIF). (2014, May 23). *BIF-4: Tony Hsieh: For a good time, call Zappos.com* [Video]. Vimeo. https://vimeo.com/96243788.

Cambridge Dictionary. (n.d.). *Work ethic*. Cambridge Dictionary. Retrieved November 21, 2020, from https://dictionary.cambridge.org/us/dictionary/english/work-ethic.

Conger, J. A. (1991). Inspiring others: The language of leadership. *Academy of Management Perspectives, 5*(1), 31–45. https://doi.org/10.5465/ame.1991.4274713.

Economy, P. (2014, August 13). *7 proven ways to genuinely connect with your employees*. Inc. https://www.inc.com/peter-economy/7-proven-ways-to-genuinely-connect-with-your-employees.html.

Economy, P. (2015, March 20). *Sara Blakely's most inspiring quotes for success*. Inc. https://www.inc.com/peter-economy/sara-blakely-19-inspiring-power-quotes-for-success.html.

Emerson, S. (2019, May 5). *7 effective leaders who embrace storytelling and why*. Echo Stories. https://www.echostories.com/7-leaders-who-embrace-storytelling/.

Fairhurst, G. T. (2005). Reframing the art of framing: Problems and prospects for leadership. *Leadership, 1*(2), 165–185. https://doi.org/10.1177/1742715005051857.

Fairhurst, G. T., & Sarr, R. A. (1996). *The art of framing*. Jossey-Bass.

Kilmann, R. H., & Thomas, K. W. (1975). Interpersonal conflict-handling behavior as reflections of Jungian personality dimensions. *Psychological Reports, 37*(3), 971–980. https://doi.org/10.2466/pr0.1975.37.3.971.

Klotz-Guest, K. (2017, October 9).*Building a customer service culture through storytelling*. Keeping It Human. https://www.keepingithuman.com/customer-service-culture-through-storytelling/.

Knight, R. (2020, September 1). When your boss doesn't respect your family commitments. *Harvard Business Review*. https://hbr.org/2020/09/when-your-boss-doesnt-respect-your-family-commitments.

Meyer, T. K. (2019, October 31). *How leaders determine workplace ethics*. Business News Daily. https://www.businessnewsdaily.com/5608-workplace-ethics.html.

Newell, M. (2016, June 10). *What you can learn from Vince Lombardi's timeless leadership wisdom*. Inc. https://www.inc.com/partners-in-leadership/what-you-can-learn-from-vince-lombardis-timeless-leadership-wisdom.html.

Northouse, P. G. (2021). *Introduction to leadership: Concepts and practice* (5th ed.). Sage.

Richmond, V. P., Wagner, J. P., & McCroskey, J. C. (1983). The impact of perceptions of leadership style, use of power, and conflict management style on

organizational outcomes. *Communication Quarterly, 31*(1), 27–36. https://doi.org/10.1080/01463378309369482.
Roy, B. D. (2020, October 9). *10 ways to develop strong work ethics among employees*. Vantage Circle. https://blog.vantagecircle.com/work-ethics/.
Searcy, T., & DeVries, H. (2012). *How to close a deal like Warren Buffett: Lessons from the world's greatest dealmaker*. McGraw Hill Professional.
Tichy, N., & Charan, R. (2020, March 2). Speed, simplicity, self-confidence: An interview with Jack Welch. *Harvard Business Review*. https://hbr.org/1989/09/speed-simplicity-self-confidence-an-interview-with-jack-welch.
U. S. Equal Employment Opportunity Commission. (n.d.). *Employer best practices for workers with caregiving responsibilities*. https://www.eeoc.gov/laws/guidance/employer-best-practices-workers-caregiving-responsibilities.
Walter, E. (2013, September 30). 50 heavyweight leadership quotes. *Forbes*. https://www.forbes.com/sites/ekaterinawalter/2013/09/30/50-heavyweight-leadership-quotes/#5105edf02259.
Zappos. (n.d.). *Who we are*. https://www.zappos.com/about/who-we-are.
Zappos Insights. (n.d.). *About Zappos Insights*. https://www.zapposinsights.com/about.

CHAPTER 9

Self-Reflection: Identifying the Leader in You

Abstract This book emphasizes that there is no "one right style of leadership" and there is no one best way to lead in every situation. That being said, research on leader-member exchange has identified a number of leadership traits that have often been associated with effective leaders. This chapter draws from trait theory exemplified through notable leaders, such as Abraham Lincoln, Eleanor Roosevelt, and Martin Luther King Jr. Trait theory supports the idea that leaders are "born" and have certain qualities or traits that make them great leaders. However, a communicative lens argues that anyone can improve their leadership skills by working on their communication. Some traits covered in this chapter include energy level and stress tolerance, emotional maturity, and personal integrity. Additionally, this chapter explores various leadership styles—such as transformational and servant leaders—with descriptions and straightforward suggestions on how to encapsulate these leadership styles. Readers can also take a quiz to determine what type of leader they are and complete an activity in which readers can create vision statements for one's leadership situated in individual, group, and organizational contexts.

Keywords Leadership traits · Leadership styles · Notable leaders · Vision statements

L. M. Omilion-Hodges and J. K. Ptacek, *Leader-Member Exchange and Organizational Communication*, New Perspectives in Organizational Communication, https://doi.org/10.1007/978-3-030-68756-4_9

This book emphasizes that there is no "one right style of leadership" and there is no one best way to lead in every situation. That being said, research on leader–member exchange has identified several leadership traits that are often associated with effective leaders. Trait theory supports the idea that leaders are "born" and have certain qualities or characteristics that make them great leaders. Such traits include high energy level and tolerance for stress, emotional maturity, and personal integrity (Yukl, 2013). However, the idea that leaders are only as good as the traits they are born with is a historical and now antiquated way to consider leadership ability. A communicative lens emphasizes that anyone can improve their leadership skills by working on their communication. Additionally, effective leaders can identify and strengthen their best traits to become even better leaders.

This chapter draws from notable leaders throughout history, such as Abraham Lincoln, Martin Luther King Jr., and Eleanor Roosevelt to illustrate different yet effective approaches to leadership. Various leadership styles, such as transformational and servant leaders, with descriptions and straightforward suggestions on how to encapsulate these leadership styles, are also explored. In addition to identifying effective leader traits and styles, this chapter further encourages individual leader development by identifying one's strengths and leadership style. This includes a quiz you can take to determine your strongest traits and what type of leadership style you most exemplify. We also discuss how to create a personal vision statement that addresses individual, group, and organizational contexts.

Leadership Traits

The trait theory of leadership suggests that specific traits make some leaders more effective than others. Personality traits can be described as ways in which individuals show patterns of thoughts, feelings, and actions (McCrae & Costa, 1990). Personality traits are relatively stable across someone's life, but needs and motives as a trait can also influence someone's behavior (Yukl, 2013). Widely accepted by researchers, the five-factor model of personality—also referred to as the Big-Five—asserts that someone's personality can be grouped into five major categories (Ackerman, 2020), including:

- Conscientiousness
- Agreeableness

- Neuroticism
- Openness to experience
- Extraversion

These personality traits can be thought of as existing on a spectrum (McCrae, 2002). For example, those who have high neuroticism tend to be more anxious and easily irritated, whereas those with low neuroticism are calmer and more emotionally stable. Research (Judge et al., 2002) has found that four of these traits—extraversion, conscientiousness, emotional stability, and openness—are positively related to effective leadership. In other words, conscientious leaders are often organized and punctual, agreeable leaders are trusting and compassionate, open leaders are curious and imaginative, and extraverted leaders are often also cheerful and sociable (McCrae, 2002). Table 9.1 includes a short quiz to determine your strongest of the five traits.

Furthermore, Yukl (2013) identified nine specific traits, which fall within the five major personality traits, that have consistently related to leadership effectiveness. These include:

- **High energy level and stress tolerance:** Having a high energy level and tolerance for stress can help leaders cope with work demands and solve problems more effectively. It also allows a leader to communicate calmly and confidently with others.
- **Self-confidence:** Self-confidence, which is related to self-esteem and self-efficacy, has been strongly linked to leader effectiveness and advancement in organizations. Self-confident leaders are more influential, likely to set and achieve challenging goals and solve difficult problems. However, it is important not to allow self-confidence to become excessive and perceived as arrogance.
- **Internal locus of control:** Leaders with a high internal locus of control take responsibility for their actions and feel in control of their destiny. They are less likely to believe the things that happen to them are outside of their control, and they take the initiative to plan and solve problems. They are influential but not manipulative or forceful.
- **Emotional stability and maturity:** Emotionally stable and mature leaders are well adjusted, self-aware, and work toward improving themselves. They care about other people, are less impulsive in their

Table 9.1 Identifying your strongest traits

Assessing the Big-Five personality traits is a common way in which people identify their strongest leadership traits. This quick quiz was developed using familiar descriptions of the five major personality traits (Goldberg, 1992; Loehlin et al., 1998) to help you determine which traits are your strongest. Circle the option that best describes you in each statement, and then add up the numbers in each category to estimate your strongest traits.

	Strongly disagree	*Disagree*	*Neutral*	*Agree*	*Strongly agree*
Openness					
I am always willing to listen to new ideas	1	2	3	4	5
I like to think outside the box	1	2	3	4	5
I have a curious mindset	1	2	3	4	5
I appreciate new experiences	1	2	3	4	5
I am imaginative	1	2	3	4	5
Conscientiousness					
I consider myself very responsible	1	2	3	4	5
I am efficient in getting work done	1	2	3	4	5
I consider myself to be organized	1	2	3	4	5
I am practical in most situations	1	2	3	4	5
I am always on time	1	2	3	4	5
Extraversion					
I enjoy meeting new people	1	2	3	4	5
I am talkative when out with friends	1	2	3	4	5
I like to go on new adventures	1	2	3	4	5
I have high energy	1	2	3	4	5
I would not consider myself to be shy	1	2	3	4	5
Agreeableness					
I am always willing to help people out	1	2	3	4	5

(continued)

Table 9.1 (continued)

I get along with pretty much everyone	1	2	3	4	5
I am trusting others	1	2	3	4	5
I am generous to others	1	2	3	4	5
I don't argue much with other people	1	2	3	4	5
Neuroticism					
I tend to worry about a lot of things	1	2	3	4	5
I often feel anxious	1	2	3	4	5
I am quick to get angry	1	2	3	4	5
Things upset me easily	1	2	3	4	5
People tend to irritate me often	1	2	3	4	5
Openness score: _____					
Conscientiousness score: _____					
Extraversion score: _____					
Agreeableness score: _____					
Neuroticism score: _____					
For the first four traits (openness, conscientiousness, extraversion, and agreeableness), your highest score suggests your strongest personality trait that can influence your leadership success. You could consider any score over 20 to be fairly strong in that trait. However, high levels of neuroticism have been negatively associated with effective leadership, so scores below 10 in that category could be considered favorable.					

Source Goldberg (1992) and Loehlin et al. (1998)

actions, and are more receptive to learning and accepting criticism. Leaders with this trait also tend to advance within their organization.

- **Power motivation:** People who work toward positions of authority tend to have a high need for power. They are motivated to influence others and work hard for advancement. However, those with a *personalized* power orientation tend to take advantage of others and use unfavorable tactics to gain power. In contrast, those with a *socialized* power orientation will avoid manipulating others to get ahead and tend to be more emotionally mature and work well with others.

- **Personal integrity:** Leaders with personal integrity will behave in ways that align with their values and are trustworthy and honest. They tend to follow through on their promises, keep people's confidence, and lead by example.
- **Narcissism:** Narcissists tend to have a high personalized power orientation, high need for esteem, and are low in emotional maturity and integrity. Narcissistic leaders may become obsessed with power to the point that they endanger or take advantage of others, with little empathy or concern. Although they can act charismatic to get what they want, they can become defensive when confronted or criticized. Narcissistic leaders may possess positive traits of self-confidence and optimism, which can make them successful, however, they can also often be difficult to work with.
- **Achievement orientation:** Leaders with a high achievement orientation not only have a high need to achieve but are also willing to work hard, accept responsibility, and set task objectives. There tends to be a preferable middle-ground with achievement orientation though, as leaders with moderate achievement orientation are often more effective than those who are either low or high in achievement motivation. Additionally, effective leadership exemplified through achievement orientation includes having a *socialized* power motivation and a leader who works with others instead of solely focusing on their own success.
- **Need for affiliation:** Need for affiliation includes a desire to be liked and accepted by others. Therefore, leaders with a high need for affiliation tend to be less effective overall because they are more concerned with their leader–member relationships than job objectives. They may avoid conflict or confrontation even if it is for the sake of improving work outcomes. On the other hand, leaders with a low need for affiliation can also be ineffective because their leader–member relationships could suffer, leading to low employee engagement.

Leadership Styles

As you consider the type of leader you are and want to be, it may help to think in terms of common leadership styles. However, it is important to note that leaders do not usually encompass just one style of leadership completely, nor do they always use the same style for every situation, as you read about in Chapter 7 about context. As you think about each leadership style, you might also reflect on what aspects are most important to you and how you might develop your leadership style by adopting some of the below characteristics. Although some of these leadership styles share similarities in leader–member communication behaviors, they are distinct in many ways. We review some of the most common leadership styles—including transformational, transactional, charismatic, servant, and laissez-faire—and discuss their effectiveness and ways to exemplify each style. See Table 9.2 for a quiz related to uncovering your predominant managerial communication style.

Transformational

Transformational leadership focuses on followers' values and motives to work toward change (Burns, 1978). Much of a transformational leader's power is built upon mutual trust and understanding (McMurray et al., 2010). Leaders "transform" and inspire followers by emphasizing the importance of the work, encouraging them to look beyond their own needs for the sake of the group or organization, and stimulating their higher-order needs such as self-esteem or self-actualization (Yukl, 2013). Transformational leadership has been promoted consistently in research, encouraging organizations to foster a culture of transformational behaviors (Arnold et al., 2001). Common findings of transformational leadership connect it to effectiveness, productivity, follower satisfaction, and effort (Lo et al., 2010). Furthermore, research (Arnold et al., 2001) has found that transformational leadership increases trust, commitment, and team efficacy, but it does so well above that of a concertive control system that employs high levels of control over members.

Bass and Avolio (1990) identified four main types of transformational behaviors. They are as follows:

- **Idealized influence:** Transformational leaders set positive examples and inspire identification from followers. Followers want to emulate the leader's actions and put others' needs before one's own. This leader does the right thing and has high ethical standards.
- **Individualized consideration:** Transformational leaders support, encourage, and coach others. They care about followers' growth and achievement individually. They provide new and individualize opportunities based on the follower's needs.

Table 9.2 Identifying your managerial communication style

Drawing from existing conceptualizations of various leadership styles and in an effort to understand what types of leadership the newest members of the workforce prefer, Omilion-Hodges and Sugg (2019) have identified several "managerial archetypes" which encapsulate various characteristics of leaders. While there are some overlaps in behaviors between the archetypes, they are each distinct in various ways. In each of the statements below, choose which one best describes how you might behave as a manager (while both may apply in some cases, choose which one you feel strongest about). Then, count the number of A, B, C, and D statements you chose to determine which managerial archetype you most closely align with. The original scale can be located in the Omilion-Hodges and Sugg (2019) article.

Shares as little information as necessary (C)	- or -	Shares an abundance of information (D)
Lots of individual one-on-one time (A)	- or -	Spends very little one-on-one time (C)
Disperses a lot of professional information (B)	- or -	Shares a lot of personal information (D)
Treats employees as equal to yourself (A)	- or -	Clear separation of power and roles (C)
States clear repercussions (B)	- or -	Deadlines are more lax (D)
Spends little time helping train employees (C)	- or -	Actively participates in training employees (B)
Provides role-testing opportunities (B)	- or -	Checks in frequently on progress (A)
Frequent communication focuses on growth (A)	- or -	Frequent interpersonal communication (D)
Models behaviors through demonstrating (B)	- or -	Motivates through inspiring messages (A)
Keeps employees out of decision-making (C)	- or -	Involves employees often in decision-making (D)
A statements: ____ = Mentor Manager		C statements: ____ = Manager Manager
B statements: ____ = Teacher Manager		D statements: ____ = Friend Manager

Which type of manager did you most strongly align with? Thinking about different types of behaviors you would engage in as a manager can help you to understand what your leadership style is like. Recent research (Omilion-Hodges & Ptacek, 2019) has found that college students (who will soon be entering the workforce) tend to prefer mentor managers, followed by teacher managers. However, preferences also depended on individual characteristics. For example, students with higher self-worth prefer a mentor manager over a manager (Omilion-Hodges & Ptacek, 2019). Considering what types of managers each employee prefers can help to strengthen individual LMX relationships.

Source Omilion-Hodges and Ptacek (2019) and Omilion-Hodges and Sugg (2019)

- **Inspirational motivation:** Transformational leaders inspire motivation by articulating a clear shared vision and provide meaning to organizational work. They evoke team spirit by being enthusiastic and optimistic and get others on board with their vision.
- **Intellectual stimulation:** Transformational leaders influence followers to think creatively and outside of the box about problems. They respect others' thoughts and encourage new ideas.

Transformational leadership is often connected to LMX and research (Lee, 2008) has found transformational leadership to be positively and significantly related to all dimensions of LMX. The difference between transformational leadership and LMX is that while transformational leaders aim to *lead* at the individual level, LMX focuses on *relating* (Barbuto & Wheeler, 2006). Furthermore, interpersonally transformational leaders *inspire* followers, whereas the main goal of LMX is to *exchange* with followers, and at the group level transformational leaders focus on uniting the group to meet its goals and LMX leaders work toward developing different exchange relationship with each person (Barbuto & Wheeler, 2006). Despite these differences, transformational leadership and LMX are often considered in conjunction with each other.

Transactional

In addition to transformational leadership, Burns (1978) developed the contrasting idea of transactional leadership. Whereas transformational leadership focuses on the group's togetherness, transactional leadership motivates followers through their self-interests and the exchange or "transaction" of rewards (Yukl. 2013). The leader–follower relationship here is built on reciprocity, and followers are encouraged to work hard to receive incentives such as performance reviews, raises, recognition, and praise (McMurray et al., 2010). Effective transactional leaders can enforce control through a hierarchical structure and are good at planning, organizing, and obtaining results (McMurray et al., 2010). Transactional leadership is positively related to outcomes such as trust in a leader and distributive justice (follower perceptions of fairness about rewards received from their leader) (Ismail et al., 2010). Still, it has been negatively related to outcomes such as innovativeness (Lee, 2008).

Bass and Avolio (1990) argue that transactional leaders engage in three types of behavior:

- **Contingent reward:** Expectations are clearly communicated and incentives are provided once goals are achieved.
- **Active management by exception:** Actively monitoring for mistakes and taking corrective action to avoid further errors.
- **Passive management by exception:** Waiting for mistakes to occur before taking correction action.

Although transformational and transactional leadership styles are positively correlated (Lee, 2008), they differ in some ways. Transactional leadership is positively related to dimensions of LMX such as affect, contribution, and professional respect, although transformational leadership has a stronger relationship with all of these outcomes (Lee, 2008). Furthermore, transformational leadership is more effective in achieving employee commitment than a transactional leadership style (Lo et al., 2010). However, it is not that a leader should "choose" one style over another, but that they can optimize the benefits of both styles *together* to be most successful. In other words, combining the benefits of social exchange with economic exchange can be more useful for the leader–member relationship than using just one leadership style alone (Ismail et al., 2010).

Charismatic

Like transformational leadership, charismatic leadership is often referenced when talking about effective leaders. A primary distinction of charismatic leaders is that they can communicate a vision to their followers and demonstrate their vision through their own actions, inspiring others to follow and believe in the vision as exceptional (Conger et al., 2000). Conger and Kanungo (1987) argue that charisma is attributional, meaning that followers attribute charisma to a leader based on their behaviors. On the other hand, House (1977) argues that a leader does not necessarily have to have exceptional ability attributed to them to be considered charismatic. Charismatic leadership is related to followers' performance and satisfaction (Shamir et al., 1993) and followers' sense of reverence for their leader, collective identity, and perception of group task performance (Conger et al., 2000).

To measure their charismatic leadership model, Conger and Kanungo (1994; Conger et al., 1997) identified five behavioral dimensions of charismatic leadership. The characteristics of a charismatic leader include:

- **Strategic vision and articulation:** Communicates clearly, inspires excitement toward organizational goals, identifies new ideas for the future, takes advantage of new opportunities.
- **Sensitivity to the environment:** Recognizes constraints in the organization's physical and social environment, identifies the abilities and limitations of organizational members.
- **Sensitivity to member needs:** Shows personal concern and sensitivity for others' feelings and needs, create mutual liking and respect.
- **Personal risk:** Makes self-sacrifices for the organization and followers' benefit, builds trust through taking personal risks.
- **Unconventional behavior:** Takes innovative approaches to achieving organizational goals, engages in unconventional behaviors but should be aware of the risk of using novel strategies to succeed.

As suggested above, charismatic and transformational leadership styles are often considered together, and many transformational leaders are thought of as charismatic. In fact, transformational leadership has even been measured using indicators of charismatic leadership (Avolio et al., 1991). In terms of LMX, some (DeGroot et al., 2000) suggest that the charismatic leadership style is more successful when a leader has similar relationships with each member in their group.

Servant

Servant leadership, first emerging in 1970, encapsulates the desire to serve others through leading and is the foundation of ethical leadership (Greenleaf, 1970). Servant leaders reach their primary goal of serving others by helping them to develop, empowering them, and working together to meet shared goals (Yukl, 2013). Servant leadership has been associated with positive outcomes such as lower follower turnover, decreased follower disengagement, organizational citizenship behaviors, follower commitment to leader, and follower self-efficacy (Hunter et al., 2013).

Barbuto and Wheeler (2006) identified five dimensions of servant leadership, including:

- **Altruistic calling:** Desire to positively impact others' lives and put others' interests before one's own.
- **Emotional healing:** Commitment to promoting spiritual healing, communicating empathy, and listening to others.

- **Wisdom:** Being observant and anticipating consequences.
- **Persuasive mapping:** Using sound reasoning and mapping issues to visualize and articulate opportunities to others.
- **Organizational stewardship:** Preparing an organization to care for and make positive contributions to society.

Research (Barbuto & Hayden, 2011) has found that all five servant leadership dimensions are positively related to LMX. Emotional healing was particularly strongly related, meaning that leaders who connect with members emotionally and in a healing context are likely to be good relationship builders (Barbuto & Hayden, 2011). Surely, LMX and servant leadership are similar in some ways such that they both value high-quality communication exchanges and mutual trust (Barbuto & Wheeler, 2006). Servant leadership has also been found effective in many different organizational contexts, as is mentioned in Chapter 5.

Laissez-Faire

Another common leadership style that has been mentioned in this book is laissez-faire. Laissez-faire leadership is instead the absence of leadership in that this type of leader avoid decisions and action (Judge & Piccolo, 2004). This type of leadership is typically considered in two veins: abdicated power and guided freedom. In fact, it has even been called "nonleadership" (Hinkin & Schriesheim, 2008). As the name suggests, an abdication of power approach describes instances when a manager is either unable or unwilling to lead. They may be disgruntled about organizational decisions or policies or may be focused on finding another job. However, a guided freedom approach to laissez-faire can be successful in highly specialized, expert groups. Consider NASA, for example. A manager may not possess the technical know-how of some of their staff, so instead of micromanaging followers' work, the manager focuses on macro-level and administrative concerns. In this sense, the manager is cultivating an environment where employees can focus on enacting their expertise, rather than on typical organizational minutiae.

While there are two primary approaches to this leadership style, most research focuses on the abdication of power aspect. In this sense, laissez-faire leadership is negatively associated with follower job satisfaction, satisfaction with their leader, and leader effectiveness (Judge & Piccolo, 2004). Some argue that laissez-faire leadership is not only ineffective but also destructive. For example, research (Skogstad et al., 2007) has found that this leadership style is positively correlated with role conflict, role ambiguity, and conflicts with coworkers. Although a laissez-faire leader may not be aggressive or actively hostile, their lack of positive behaviors can be detrimental to the organization and its members (Skogstad et al., 2007).

As you could probably tell, laissez-faire leadership has a negative reputation. However, sometimes it can be used effectively, especially if used in combination with other leadership styles. There are some behaviors in which laissez-faire leaders can use to be successful (STU Online, 2018), and these align with the guided freedom approach described above. These communication behaviors include:

- Closely monitor group performance
- Employ highly skilled, well-educated staff
- Treat people as motivated self-starters
- Use the laissez-faire style only with experienced staff
- Give consistent feedback to team members

Although laissez-faire leadership may sound similar to the passive management by exception dimension of transactional leadership, it is considered distinct from transactional leadership in all other ways (Judge & Piccolo, 2004). In fact, laissez-faire leadership has been negatively related to transformational leadership and the contingent reward and active management by exception dimensions of transactional leadership (Judge & Piccolo, 2004). However, research (Lee & Wei, 2008) has found that LMX partially mediates the relationship between laissez-faire leadership and follower effectiveness, extra effort, satisfaction, and organizational commitment. Furthermore, research (Buch et al., 2015) has found that *economic* leader–member exchange (ELMX)—which is a different relationship from LMX and focuses more on obligations and is more impersonal—mediated the negative relationship between laissez-faire leadership and work effort and affective commitment. As mentioned above, these findings suggest that combining laissez-faire leadership with other efforts could be useful in some contexts.

It can be helpful to think of some of these leadership styles as they are exemplified by leaders that we know and may want to emulate. Next, we will identify some notable leaders who have exhibited characteristics of some of these leadership styles.

Notable Leaders

When we think about leadership, we may imagine people who we know or people throughout history who have been good leaders. A good deal of literature is available which emphasizes specific traits and leadership styles exemplified by notable leaders. Since many good leaders lead by example, it can help to analyze some of their behaviors so that we can emulate or draw inspiration from them. Below are a few notable leaders throughout history and some of their most prominent communication and leadership characteristics. Additionally, Table 9.3 includes information on an organization that provides resources on building leadership skills.

Abraham Lincoln

Abraham Lincoln (1809–1865) is often thought of when discussing leadership. As the 16th president of the United States, some of his most

Table 9.3 Leadership in action—organizational profile: Society for Human Resource Management

Founded in 1948, the Society for Human Resource Management (SHRM) literally sells leadership. Rather, they provide resources for individuals to bolster their leadership and human resources skills. As one of the largest associations in the United States (Proctor, 2015), SHRM identifies as "the foremost expert, convener and thought leader on issues impacting today's evolving workplaces" (SHRM, 2020a). As part of their Competency Model on how to be a successful HR professional, they highlight the importance of leadership (SHRM, 2020c). They focus specifically on five main characteristics: • Consensus builder • Influence • Change management • Mission driven • Results- and goal-oriented Their over 300 thousand members have drawn from SHRM's resources to help build their leadership and HR proficiencies, and the organization is supported by a number of successful companies (SHRM, 2020b). For example, their 2020 board of directors include Directors, Presidents, and VPs of companies such as Duke Energy, Google, and Boeing.

Sources Proctor (2015) and SHRM (2020a, 2020b, 2020c)

memorable accomplishments include issuing the Emancipation Proclamation of 1863 which freed people from slavery, secured a victory for the Union in the Civil War, and signed important acts such as the Homestead Acts of 1862, the Revenue Act of 1862, and the Morrill Land-Grant Colleges Act in 1862 (World History EDU, 2019). Lincoln can be considered a transformational leader because of his ability to gain trust and respect from followers, inspire others to make sacrifices for the greater good, and appeal to others' ethical values (Leidner, 2002). He showed genuine concern and respect toward others, often visiting soldiers in hospitals and spending time to speak with them and other constituents (Leidner, 2002).

Bill Gates

Bill Gates (born 1955), cofounder of Microsoft Corporation, is one of the world's wealthiest men and undoubtedly one of the most successful. Several different leadership styles have been associated with Gates. Some identify him as a transformational leader because he can articulate a strong vision, exude passion for his work, and inspire others (Miller, 2018). However, Gates has often been considered an authoritarian or autocratic leader, especially at the beginning of his career. For example, having rarely taken a day off work himself, he was known to monitor the Microsoft parking lot on the weekends to see who was working extra hours (Holley, 2016). Although he did recognize and reward individual and group achievements, he was also known to be demanding and he exercised a lot of control over various aspects of the organization (Thielen, 1999). However, this style was said to work for his team because he chose extraordinarily hardworking and motivated employees who could withstand the intense pressure (Holley, 2016).

Eleanor Roosevelt

Eleanor Roosevelt (1884–1962) was well known as a teacher, writer, activist, humanitarian, and a former First Lady. As the director of the Bureau of Women's Activities of the Democratic Party, she inspired women through her actions and empowered women to work toward change (Lopez, 2013). Later, when she served on the first American Delegation to the United Nations, she worked tirelessly toward human rights worldwide and helped create the Universal Declaration of Human

Rights (Lopez, 2013). In the many different leadership roles she held, Roosevelt has been considered a transformational and charismatic leader (Ismail & Al-Taee, 2012). Indeed, she was inspirational, communicated her goals clearly, and was a positive influence on others. She was also considered a servant leader. Some of her most remarkable traits included showing empathy for others, being aware of others' struggles, and her commitment to helping people and building a global community (Tabors, 2018).

Ella Baker

Ella Baker (1903–1986) is a leader that some may have not heard of because she stayed "behind the scenes," but played a critical role in American civil and human rights (Ella Baker Women's Center, n.d.). In fact, she has been referred to as being "as influential as Dr. [Martin Luther] King in shaping the arc of the US Civil Rights Movement of the 1960's" (Parker, 2020, p. xi). Some of Baker's notable accomplishments include being the national director of the Young Negroes' Cooperation League which helped to develop black economic power, director of branches for the NAACP, and helping Martin Luther King Jr. to organize the Southern Christian Leadership Conference (Ella Baker Women's Center, n.d.). She may be best thought of as both a servant leader and charismatic leader because of her dedication to helping others, ability to listen to others' feelings and address their needs, and commitment to developing others so that they may continue doing important civil rights work, all without seeking (or even receiving in some cases) recognition (Scelfo, 2017).

Martin Luther King Jr.

Martin Luther King Jr. (1929–1968) is another notable leader that we often think about. A Baptist minister and social activist, he played a critical role in the American civil rights movement, helping to bring the Civil Rights Act and Voting Rights Act into legislation (History.com Editors, 2020a). King encompassed several charismatic and transformational leadership traits. His "I have a dream" speech and several others are considered some of the most inspirational speeches of the twentieth century (American Rhetoric, n.d.). Furthermore, King spent a lot of time speaking with citizens and showed a great deal of empathy and concern, putting their needs first; he looked for new ways to integrate change; and he was willing to take risks and speak out for the sake of his mission (Thompson, 2018). King is also considered a prominent example of servant leadership, encompassing all of a servant leader's characteristics, such as listening, empathy, commitment to helping others, and persuasiveness (Gandolfi & Stone, 2018).

Mohandas Karamchand Gandhi

Mohandas Karamchand Gandhi (1869–1948), often called Mahatma, is also thought of as a prime example of servant leadership. He was a lawyer and activist, and played a significant role in India's non-violent movement to gain independence from Great Britain (History.com Editors, 2019). His practices of passive resistance, meditation, and prayer have served as inspirations for other leaders after him, including Martin Luther King Jr. (Little, 2020). Gandhi has also been referred to as both a charismatic and transformational leader, exhibiting characteristics such as appealing to followers' values, emphasizing followers' worth, and being a successful visionary (Bligh & Robinson, 2010; Khatri, 2005). However, his selfless service to others, spirituality, and emphasis on follower needs identify him foremost as a servant leader (Barnabas & Clifford, 2012).

Ruth Bader Ginsburg

Ruth Bader Ginsburg (1933–2020) was a lawyer, professor, social advocate, cofounder of the Women's Rights Project of the American Civil Liberties Union, and the second female justice of the United States Supreme Court. Throughout her career, she fought for gender equality and received the American Bar Association's Thurgood Marshall Award for her dedication to gender equality and civil rights (History.com Editors, 2020b). Some of Ginsburg's notable accomplishments include helping to pass laws against gender discrimination in the workplace, allowing women to apply for bank accounts and mortgages without a male co-signer, and allowing men to receive caregiving and Social Security rights (Rodriguez, 2020). As a leader, Ginsburg was undoubtedly transformational. She inspired women to work toward equality and independence by clearly articulating a vision and inspiring others to emulate her through her actions.

Vision Statements

A common skill of a good leader is the ability to articulate a strong vision for an organization of followers. A vision should help to guide and unite an organization toward a goal, remind followers of what the organization is about and what it wants to become, inspire people to work, keep people on track, and frees organizational members from doing what it has always done but instead provides opportunities to work toward improvement (Lucas, 1998). A vision statement is different from a mission statement because while a mission points to the organization's objectives and how it will reach those objectives, a vision focuses on the organization's desired future (Bain & Company, 2018). Furthermore, a vision statement tells us why an organization is in business, whereas a mission statement tells us its purpose (Kirkpatrick, 2016). For example, Southwest Airlines' (2020) vision is "To be the world's most loved, most efficient, and most profitable airline" and their mission is "...dedication to the highest quality of Customer Service delivered with a sense of warmth, friendliness, individual pride, and Company Spirit."

What a Vision Is and Isn't

Lucas (1998) provides some guidance between what a vision is and what it isn't.

What vision is:

- An organizational charter of core values and principles
- The source for our priorities, plans, and goals
- A puller (not pusher) into the future
- A determination and publication of what makes us unique
- A declaration of independence

What vision isn't:

- A "high concept" statement, a motto or literature
- An advertising slogan
- A strategy or plan
- A view from the top
- A history of our proud past
- A "soft" business issue
- Passionless

Examples of Vision Statements

To provide you with a clearer idea of what real-life vision statements look like, here are some from well-known organizations.

- **Apple:** To make the best products on earth, and to leave the world better than we found it (Rowland, 2020).
- **Disney:** To be one of the world's leading producers and providers of entertainment and information (Williams, 2019).
- **Habitat for Humanity:** A world where everyone has a decent place to live (Habitat for Humanity, 2020).
- **IKEA:** To create a better everyday life for the many people (IKEA, 2019).
- **LinkedIn:** Create economic opportunity for every member of the global workforce (LinkedIn, 2020).
- **Oxfam:** A just world without poverty (Oxfam, 2020).
- **Tesla:** Create the most compelling car company of the twenty-first century by driving the world's transition to electric vehicles (Tesla, 2011).

Table 9.4 includes some specific guidelines on how to write an effective vision statement for your own leadership.

Leadership Moments: Takeaways for Leaders and Members

- **Leaders are made, not born:** Leaders can become more effective by playing up their strongest traits. Trait theory suggests that people are "born" with certain traits that can make them a good leader, so leaders should identify which traits they already possess that make them effective. Identifying the traits that they already have and using those to their advantage while finding ways to overcome those traits that are not strongest can help a leader adjust their behaviors and build stronger LMX relationships with their followers.
- **The most effective leadership style is a combination:** There is no one best leadership style in all situations. In fact, research (Ismail et al., 2010) has found that combining multiple styles can help leaders more effectively communicate in various contexts.

Table 9.4 Sharpening your communication skills: writing an effective vision statement

Now you know that effective vision statements can help inspire and guide followers, but having a vision statement for your own leadership can help you to become the leader you want to be. When writing a good vision statement, here are some guidelines to keep in mind (Peek, 2020; Putter, 2018): • Use clear and succinct language • Think 5–10 years into the future • Don't try to say everything in it, but align it with your values and goals • Use present tense • Communicate your vision to others • Be committed to achieving the vision Now, think about what your personal vision statement might look like. You should also consider how your vision statement impacts the following contexts: • Individual • Group • Organization Which leadership styles and traits do you most want to exemplify? Consider what is most important to you at each level. For example, do you most want to lead, serve, or relate to people at an individual level? Do you want to meet the members' needs, unite the group to achieve goals, or develop different relationships with each individual at the group level? How will you help your organization to be successful? It is important to take into account what your existing strengths are and how you can build upon those as well as refine and improve upon others. Once you have created a vision statement for each of these contexts, you will have a clearer picture of what is most important in driving your success.

Source Peek (2020) and Putter (2018)

For example, mixing the benefits of social exchange from transformational leadership with the economic exchange of transactional leadership can be better than using just one leadership style alone.

Mini Case Study: "We Have Always Done Things This Way"

You have just been hired as the manager of a local grocery store after the former manager was let go. Although the company promotes a "family-focused" culture, it seems that this value has been lost long ago, after the original owner retired and hired a manager to run the store. Employees appear to show up for work begrudgingly and don't have many nice things to say about the former manager or even the organization itself. You notice that many of the policies are outdated, but when you ask employees why they don't try something else, they say "we have always done things this way." You see many opportunities for improvement but know you have a long way to go to build trust and motivation among the employees who have been stuck in a rut for so long.

1. What leadership style(s) might be most effective in this organization?
2. After determining what your strongest leadership traits are, how can you use these to help build strong relationships with employees?
3. How might you write a vision statement for this organization and motivate employees to support the vision?

References

Ackerman, C. (2020, January 9). *Big five personality traits: The OCEAN model explained*. Positive Psychology. https://positivepsychology.com/big-five-personality-theory/.

American Rhetoric. (n.d.). *Top 100 speeches*. https://www.americanrhetoric.com/top100speechesall.html.

Arnold, K. A., Barling, J., & Kelloway, E. K. (2001). Transformational leadership or the iron cage: Which predicts trust, commitment and team efficacy? *Leadership & Organization Development Journal, 22*(7), 315–320. https://doi.org/10.1108/EUM0000000006162.

Avolio, B. J., Waldman, D. A., & Yammarino, F. J. (1991). Leading in the 1990s: The four I's of transformational leadership. *Journal of European Industrial Training, 15*(4). https://doi.org/10.1108/03090599110143366.

Bain & Company. (2018, April 2). *Mission and vision statements*. https://www.bain.com/insights/management-tools-mission-and-vision-statements/.

Barbuto, J. E., & Hayden, R. W. (2011). Testing relationships between servant leadership dimensions and leader member exchange (LMX). *Journal of Leadership Education, 10*(2), 22–37. Retrieved from: https://journalofleadershiped.org/wp-content/uploads/2019/02/10_2_Barbuto-and-Hayden.pdf.

Barbuto, J. E., & Wheeler, D. W. (2006). Scale development and construct clarification of servant leadership. *Group & Organization Management, 31*(3), 300–326. https://doi.org/10.1177/1059601106287091.

Barnabas, A., & Clifford, P. S. (2012). Mahatma Gandhi—An Indian model of servant leadership. *International Journal of Leadership Studies, 7*(2), 132–150. Retrieved from: https://www.regent.edu/acad/global/publications/ijls/new/vol7iss2/IJLS_Vol7Iss2.pdf#page=11.

Bass, B. M., & Avolio, B. J. (1990). Developing transformational leadership: 1992 and beyond. *Journal of European Industrial Training, 14*(5), 21–27. https://doi.org/10.1108/03090599010135122.

Bligh, M. C., & Robinson, J. L. (2010). Was Gandhi "charismatic"? Exploring the rhetorical leadership of Mahatma Gandhi. *The Leadership Quarterly, 21*(5), 844–855. https://doi.org/10.1016/j.leaqua.2010.07.011.

Buch, R., Martinsen, Ø. L., & Kuvaas, B. (2015). The destructiveness of laissez-faire leadership behavior: The mediating role of economic leader–member exchange relationships. *Journal of Leadership & Organizational Studies, 22*(1), 115–124. https://doi.org/10.1177/1548051813515302.

Burns, J. M. (1978). *Leadership*. Harper & Row.

Conger, J. A., & Kanungo, R. N. (1987). Toward a behavioral theory of charismatic leadership in organizational settings. *Academy of Management Review, 12*(4), 637–647. https://doi.org/10.5465/amr.1987.4306715.

Conger, J. A., & Kanungo, R. N. (1994). Charismatic leadership in organizations: Perceived behavioral attributes and their measurement. *Journal of Organizational Behavior, 15*(5), 439–452. https://doi.org/10.1002/job.4030150508.

Conger, J. A., Kanungo, R. N., & Menon, S. T. (2000). Charismatic leadership and follower effects. *Journal of Organizational Behavior, 21*(7), 747–767. https://doi.org/10.1002/1099-1379(200011)21:7%3C747::AID-JOB46%3E3.0.CO;2-J.

Conger, J. A., Kanungo, R. N., Menon, S. T., & Mathur, P. (1997). Measuring charisma: Dimensionality and validity of the Conger-Kanungo scale of charismatic leadership. *Canadian Journal of Administrative Sciences, 14*(3), 290–301. https://doi.org/10.1111/j.1936-4490.1997.tb00136.x.

DeGroot, T., Kiker, D. S., & Cross, T. C. (2000). A meta-analysis to review organizational outcomes related to charismatic leadership. *Canadian Journal of Administrative Sciences, 17*(4), 356–372. https://doi.org/10.1111/j.1936-4490.2000.tb00234.x.

Ella Baker Women's Center. (n.d.). *Ella Baker's story*. https://www.ellabakerwomenscenter.org/ella-bakers-story.html.

Gandolfi, F., & Stone, S. (2018). Leadership, leadership styles, and servant leadership. *Journal of Management Research, 18*(4), 261–269.

Goldberg, L. R. (1992). The development of markers for the Big-Five factor structure. *Psychological Assessment, 4*(1), 26–42.

Greenleaf, R. K. (1970). *The servant as leader*. The Robert Greenleaf Center.

Habitat for Humanity. (2020). *About*. https://www.habitat.org/about/mission-and-vision.

Hinkin, T. R., & Schriesheim, C. A. (2008). An examination of "nonleadership": From laissez-faire leadership to leader reward omission and punishment omission. *Journal of Applied Psychology, 93*(6), 1234–1248. https://psycnet.apa.org/doi/10.1037/a0012875.

History.com Editors. (2019, June 6). *Mahatma Gandhi*. https://www.history.com/topics/india/mahatma-gandhi.

History.com Editors. (2020a, February 21). *Martin Luther King, Jr.* https://www.history.com/topics/black-history/martin-luther-king-jr.

History.com Editors. (2020b, September 21). *Ruth Bader Ginsburg*. https://www.history.com/topics/womens-history/ruth-bader-ginsburg.

Holley, P. (2016, February 3). The crazy thing Bill Gates used to do to monitor workplace productivity. *The Washington Post*. https://www.washingtonpost.com/news/on-leadership/wp/2016/02/03/the-crazy-thing-bill-gates-used-to-do-to-monitor-workplace-productivity/.

House, R. J. (1977). A 1976 theory of charismatic leadership. In J. G. Hunt & L. L. Larson (Eds.), *Leadership: The cutting edge* (pp. 189–207). Southern Illinois University Press.

Hunter, E. M., Neubert, M. J., Perry, S. J., Witt, L. A., Penney, L. M., & Weinberger, E. (2013). Servant leaders inspire servant followers: Antecedents and outcomes for employees and the organization. *The Leadership Quarterly, 24*(2), 316–331. https://doi.org/10.1016/j.leaqua.2012.12.001.

IKEA. (2019). *Our vision and business idea*. https://www.ikea.com/ms/en_JP/about_ikea/the_ikea_way/our_business_idea/index.html.

Ismail, A., Mohamad, M. H., Mohamed, H. A. B., Rafiuddin, N. M., & Zhen, K. W. P. (2010). Transformational and transactional leadership styles as a predictor of individual outcomes. *Theoretical & Applied Economics, 17*(6), 89–104. Retrieved from: https://www.store.ectap.ro/articole/477.pdf.

Ismail, W. K. W., & Al-Taee, F. J. H. (2012). Integrating gender, traits and transformational leadership style as viewed from human resource management strategy. *International Journal of Academic Research, 4*(3), 16–20. Retrieved from: https://www.researchgate.net/profile/Fatima_Habeeb/publication/330262338_INTEGRATING_GENDER_TRAITS_AND_TRANSFORMATIONAL_LEADERSHIP_STYLE_AS_VIEWED_FROM_HUMAN_RESOURCE_MANAGEMENT_STRATEGY/links/5c364478299bf12be3ba6971/INTEGRATING-GENDER-TRAITS-AND-TRANSFORMATIONAL-LEADERSHIP-STYLE-AS-VIEWED-FROM-HUMAN-RESOURCE-MANAGEMENT-STRATEGY.pdf.

Judge, T. A., Bono, J. E., Ilies, R., & Gerhardt, M. (2002). Personality and leadership: A qualitative and quantitative review. *Journal of Applied Psychology, 87*(4), 765–780. https://doi.org/10.1037/0021-9010.87.4.765.

Judge, T. A., & Piccolo, R. F. (2004). Transformational and transactional leadership: A meta-analytic test of their relative validity. *Journal of Applied*

Psychology, 89(5), 755–768. https://psycnet.apa.org/doi/10.1037/0021-9010.89.5.755.

Khatri, N. (2005). An alternative model of transformational leadership. *Vision, 9*(2), 19–26. https://doi.org/10.1177/097226290500900204.

Kirkpatrick, S. A. (2016). *Build a better vision statement: Extending research with practical advice*. Lexington Books.

Lee, J. (2008). Effects of leadership and leader-member exchange on innovativeness. *Journal of Managerial Psychology, 23*(6), 670–687. https://doi.org/10.1108/02683940810894747.

Lee, J., & Wei, F. (2008). Uncover the black-box of leadership effectiveness: Leader-member exchange as the mediator. *Frontiers of Business Research in China, 2*(2), 240–255. https://fbr.springeropen.com/articles/10.1007/s11782-008-0014-7.

Leidner, G. (2002). Lincoln the transformational leader. *Lincoln Herald, 104*(3), 111–118. Retrieved from: https://www.greatamericanhistory.net/transforming_leader.htm.

LinkedIn. (2020). *About LinkedIn*. https://about.linkedin.com.

Little, B. (2020, June 18). *How Martin Luther King Jr. took inspiration from Gandhi on nonviolence*. Biography. https://www.biography.com/news/martin-luther-king-jr-gandhi-nonviolence-inspiration.

Lo, M. C., Ramayah, T., Min, H. W., & Songan, P. (2010). The relationship between leadership styles and organizational commitment in Malaysia: Role of leader–member exchange. *Asia Pacific Business Review, 16*(1–2), 79–103. https://doi.org/10.1080/13602380903355676.

Loehlin, J. C., McCrae, R. R., Costa, P. T., Jr., & John, O. P. (1998). Heritabilities of common and measure-specific components of the Big Five personality factors. *Journal of Research in Personality, 32*(4), 431–453. https://doi.org/10.1006/jrpe.1998.2225.

Lopez, L. (2013, November 10). *Eleanor Roosevelt: World's most admired woman*. Wagner. https://faculty.wagner.edu/lori-weintrob/eleanor-roosevelt-worlds-most-admired-woman/.

Lucas, J. R. (1998). Anatomy of a vision statement. *Management Review, 87*(2), 22–26.

McCrae, R. R. (2002). Cross-cultural research on the five-factor model of personality. *Online Readings in Psychology and Culture, 4*(4), 1–12. https://doi.org/10.9707/2307-0919.1038.

McCrae, R. R., & Costa, P. T. (1990). *Personality in adulthood*. Guilford.

McMurray, A. J., Pirola-Merlo, A., Sarros, J. C., & Islam, M. M. (2010). Leadership, climate, psychological capital, commitment, and wellbeing in a non-profit organization. *Leadership & Organization Development Journal, 31*(5), 436–457. https://doi.org/10.1108/01437731011056452.

Miller, K. (2018, November 18). *9 Bill Gates leadership style traits, skills and qualities*. Future of Working. https://futureofworking.com/9-bill-gates-leadership-style-traits-skills-and-qualities/.

Omilion-Hodges, L. M., & Ptacek, J. K. (2019). Personal factors, wants, and needs: Exploring vocational anticipatory socialization through young adults' preferences for managerial communication behaviors. *International Journal of Business Communication*, 1–20. https://doi.org/10.1177/2329488419893745.

Omilion-Hodges, L. M., & Sugg, C. E. (2019). Millennials' views and expectations regarding the communicative and relational behaviors of leaders: Exploring young adults' talk about work. *Business and Professional Communication Quarterly, 82*(1), 74–100.

Oxfam. (2020). *Vision, mission and beliefs*. https://oxfamapps.org/cymru/vision-mission-and-beliefs/.

Parker, P. S. (2020). *Ella Baker's catalytic leadership: A primer on community engagement and communication for social justice* (Vol. 2). University of California Press.

Peek, S. (2020, May 7). *What is a vision statement?* Business News Daily. https://www.businessnewsdaily.com/3882-vision-statement.html.

Proctor, C. M. (2015). Associations ranked by revenue. *Washington Business Journal*. https://www.bizjournals.com/washington/subscriber-only/2015/10/09/associations.html.

Putter, B. (2018, June 13). *The do's and don'ts of writing effective vision and mission statements*. Medium. https://medium.com/swlh/the-dos-and-donts-of-writing-effective-vision-and-mission-statements-63e0d89343b2.

Rodriguez, L. (2020, September 21). *5 laws Ruth Bader Ginsburg championed to support gender equality*. Global Citizen. https://www.globalcitizen.org/en/content/gender-equality-laws-quotes-ruth-bader-ginsburg/.

Rowland, C. (2020, September 23). *Apple Inc.'s mission statement and vision statement (an analysis)*. Panmore Institute. https://panmore.com/apple-mission-statement-vision-statement.

Scelfo, J. (2017, January 16). On MLK Day, honor the mother of the Civil Rights Movement, too. *Time*. https://time.com/4633460/mlk-day-ella-baker/.

Shamir, B., House, R. J., & Arthur, M. B. (1993). The motivational effects of charismatic leadership: A self-concept based theory. *Organization Science, 4*(4), 577–594. https://doi.org/10.1287/orsc.4.4.577.

SHRM. (2020a). *About*. https://www.shrm.org/about-shrm/Pages/default.aspx.

SHRM. (2020b). *Developing organizational leaders*. https://www.shrm.org/resourcesandtools/tools-and-samples/toolkits/pages/developingorganizationalleaders.aspx.

SHRM. (2020c). *SHRM competency model*. https://www.shrm.org/learningandcareer/career/pages/shrm-competency-model.aspx.

Skogstad, A., Einarsen, S., Torsheim, T., Aasland, M. S., & Hetland, H. (2007). The destructiveness of laissez-faire leadership behavior. *Journal of Occupational Health Psychology, 12*(1), 80. https://doi.org/10.1037/1076-8998.12.1.80.

Soutwest Airlines. (2020). *Culture*. https://careers.southwestair.com/culturetemplate.

STU Online. (2018, October 17). *What is laissez-faire leadership? How autonomy can drive success*. https://online.stu.edu/articles/education/what-is-laissezfaire-leadership.aspx.

Tabors, C. (2018). A voice for the "least of these": Eleanor Roosevelt's servant leadership. *Servant Leadership: Theory & Practice*, *5*(1), 13–24. Retrieved from: https://csuepress.columbusstate.edu/sltp/vol5/iss1/2.

Tesla. (2011). *Tesla Motors company overview*. https://ir.tesla.com/static-files/43b9fc69-df93-421b-86b7-4f65e2d44594.

Thielen, D., & Thielen, S. (1999). *The 12 simple secrets of Microsoft management: How to think and act like a Microsoft manager and take your company to the top*. McGraw-Hill.

Thompson, S. (2018, January 12). *3 skills Martin Luther King Jr. mastered to become a transformational leader*. Inc. https://www.inc.com/sonia-thompson/3-essential-martin-luther-king-jr-leadership-skills-all-good-leaders-should-master.html.

Williams, A. (2019, March 2). *Walt Disney company's mission statement & vision statement (an analysis)*. Panmore Institute. https://panmore.com/walt-disney-company-mission-statement-vision-statement-analysis.

World History EDU. (2019, July 14). *9 great achievements of Abraham Lincoln*. https://www.worldhistoryedu.com/9-great-achievements-of-abraham-lincoln/.

Yukl, G. A. (2013). *Leadership in organizations* (8th ed.). Pearson.

CHAPTER 10

Closing Thoughts and Additional Resources

Abstract In this chapter, we conclude with a summary of LMX and its value, critiques of the theory, and offer additional resources such as practical skills-based takeaways and suggested readings for leaders and members. One area that will be of particular interest to researchers and scholars will be measuring and studying LMX. A brief section of this chapter will offer readers suggestions on methodological and statistical techniques, in addition to pointing interested parties to useful resources.

Keywords Critique · Limitations · Future research · Resources

The Value of LMX

LMX is the processual development of the leader–member relationship that flourishes or flounders through a series of communicative exchanges. Like any long-term relationship, this requires daily effort on the end of both parties, and the connection is subject to change, which is not necessarily a negative thing. For example, through continued efforts, thoughtful communication, and two-way feedback, a member who feels (or whose leader feels) they got off on the wrong foot, can help to rectify the relationship through intentional communication. Relatedly, suppose

L. M. Omilion-Hodges and J. K. Ptacek, *Leader-Member Exchange and Organizational Communication*, New Perspectives in Organizational Communication, https://doi.org/10.1007/978-3-030-68756-4_10

one of the parties begins to take the other for granted or ceases to perform basic relational maintenance. In that case, the relationship may be redefined and reclassified at a lower quality. Relational maintenance strategies include positivity (e.g., kindness), assurances (e.g., affirming the strength or importance of the relationship), openness (e.g., limits self-disclosure or engaging in furtive behavior), shared tasks (e.g., withdraws from common interests), and social networks (e.g., spends less time with shared friends, colleagues).

The heart of leader–member exchange (LMX) theory is quite simple. Leaders develop relationships of varying quality with each follower. Some of these are of higher quality, and some are of lower quality. Yet, it is in everyone's best interest to attempt to develop a highly functional exchange relationship for each leader–member dyad. Why? Because effective leader–member dyads lead to increased output, and stronger coworker exchange relationships, which leads to a higher level of cohesion and effectiveness at the group level.

This helps to illustrate why this modest leadership theory is so critical. High-quality leader–member exchange relationships, an agreement between leader and member of the quality of these relationships, and high group consensus of LMX lead to leadership excellence (Schyns & Day, 2010). Operating from a place of leadership excellence presumes that all workgroup members, including the leader, are clear about their role expectations, likely due in large part to effective workgroup communication. Leadership excellence, or high LMX across the board, indicates effective exchange among members (vertically and horizontally), and a well-developed social and group identity. What does this mean? Because leader–member, coworker, and team exchange relationships are dynamic, members can inspire each other to perform at even higher levels in a situation of leadership excellence.

The decades of empirical research is another strength of leader–member exchange theory. These stocks of knowledge address antecedents and outcomes of the pivotal relationship that transpires between leader and member. Scholars have also considered LMX at the group and organizational levels in addition to the dyadic level. LMX has been studied in various contexts, such as with multiple leaders in virtual or co-located teams and across cultural and demographic differences. More recently, this line of inquiry has shifted to a more relational or communicative approach. This pivot has lent a greater depth and sophistication to understand how these critical workgroup relationships develop, function, impact other associations, and grow or dissolve. Since relationships stem from the "interacts" between leader and member, a communicative lens helps illuminate otherwise overlooked aspects of the association.

Omilion-Hodges and Baker (2013) conducted a multi-part study to tease out the specific communicative exchanges in these dyads. This resulted in a more complex understanding of the unique relationships that a leader develops with each follower. That is, instead of using binary shortcuts such as "high" or "low" LMX, considering the specific communicative exchanges helps to uncover the differences found within homogeneous LMX dyads (high/high, low/low) to reveal the unique relational processes and interactions that leaders undertake in pursuit of meeting organizational goals. This moves the field away from an either/or view (e.g., either a member has high or low LMX) and into a place to consider relationships in gradients rather than stock categories. This recent turn helps to address some of the critiques lobbied against LMX, many of which have persisted for decades.

Critiques of LMX

It has recently been suggested that LMX research needs to return to square one owing to measurement, analysis, and conceptual concerns (Gottfredson et al., 2020). These concerns are not new (i.e., Dulebohn et al., 2012; Schriesheim et al., 1999) as reviews and metanalyses have continued to flag issues related to misalignment between theory, hypotheses, measurement, and takeaways. Case in point, Gooty and Yammarino (2013) found that nearly 90% of studies on dyadic LMX measured and analyzed the data in ways that inappropriately captured the dyadic level. Why is this problematic? Talking about the relationship in one way, measuring it another, and then offering pragmatic and theoretical advances that match one or the other or neither of the previous conceptualizations, muddies what we think we know about leader–member exchange theory. Similarly, it has also recently been pointed out that when we seek to understand various perspectives of the leader–member relationship, such as individual followers or the team, those different perspectives likely call for different approaches to measurement (Martin et al., 2018).

Additional critiques of the theory relate to measurement and methods. In particular, the vast majority of LMX research is measured from the perspective of the member, which may be at the expense of the leader.

Relatedly, what we know about the leader–member dyad is often a result of cross-sectional studies, limiting the dynamism of relationships. This is paradoxical in the sense that the heart of theory rests on interpersonal relationships, which ebb and flow. Though in measuring the relationship at one point in time, studies may fail to capture the unique context in which these relationships exist. Moreover, part of the dynamism of leader–member dyads is considering the synchrony or divergence of the actors (Butler, 2015; Hofmans et al., 2019). If we are interested in understanding these relationships in situ, it is essential to think about how these experiences may be symmetrical or discrepant at various times.

Similarly, studies often rely solely on member-centered data. This may mean that our understanding of LMX from the leader-perspective is still in its infancy or, at the very least, not as nuanced as our understanding of members' experiences. Foregrounding the member perspective also conceals or obscures what is known about leader agency in the relationship development and maintenance processes. Research has found modest links in data with matched leader–member ratings, resulting in correlations ranging from 0.29 to 0.37 (Gerstner & Day, 1997; Sin et al., 2009). However, as scholars are quick to point out (Schyns & Day, 2010), this does not mean that leader and member ratings are the same (i.e., high-high, low-low), but rather that they are related.

A final lasting critique is that some consider LMX a shorthand for leader likeability or favoritism. The leader likeability critique opens the doorway for related criticism, especially in terms of the absence of a sophisticated understanding of the complex relationships at hand. In the oft-used "high" or "low" LMX shortcuts, on the surface, the theory can appear to only offer researchers and organizational members a binary designation: Either you have a high-quality relationship with your leader, or you have a low-quality relationship with your leader. This either/or relationship categorization is a slippery slope that can perpetuate monolithic or rudimentary thinking: this is a good relationship, or this is a bad relationship (Hofmans et al., 2019). This view may stem from the fact that LMX is often operationalized from measures of interpersonal exchange between leader and member. Foundational LMX research (Liden & Maslyn, 1998) forwarded mutual liking or affect, respect, loyalty, and contribution as reliable indicators of leader–member relationship quality. Indeed, this makes sense since social exchange theory provides the scaffolding for the theory, yet it continues to represent a soft spot that remains game for critique. However, proponents of the theory return to the roots of social exchange theory to remind others that reciprocity is the mechanism by which interpersonal relationships, such as that between superior and subordinate, are developed and maintained. Relationships are often built or continue to mature because parties develop mutual affection and trust, and therefore, it is faulty to assume that measurement of a high-quality (or a low-quality) leader–member relationship would function otherwise.

Besides suggesting a back to square one approach, others have also offered insights to resolve the methodological stalemate (Hofmans et al., 2019) and move dyadic research, such as LMX, forward (Tse & Ashkanasy, 2015). Hofmans et al. (2019) suggest that focusing on the emergence of relationship patterns, or the dynamism within and between dyads, is one concrete means of rectifying previous concerns. This suggestion echoes those issued by leadership communication scholars (Omilion-Hodges & Baker, 2017; Sheer, 2015) who have encouraged scholars to study the literal social and work exchanges between leader and member, rather than to talk about them in broad strokes. Focusing on communicative interactions (Omilion-Hodges & Baker, 2017; Sheer, 2015), such as workplace communication and social communication, may yield a more realistic and more in-depth understanding of the complex relational phenomena imbued within these unique dyadic relationships.

A focus on methods and expanding beyond traditional survey approaches may also open the door to more nuanced understandings and help address methodological concerns. Hofmans et al. (2019) have suggested that using repeated measures, journaling or diary methodology, experience sampling, and lab experiments may be useful for extending this storied theory even further. Additionally, innovative methods can add greater depth and new understanding as extant LMX research is predominantly quantitative in nature. The addition of qualitative or experimental work, for example, will undoubtedly yield new insights, perhaps uncovering why specific trends or patterns continued to be found in quantitative-based LMX inquiry.

LMX Takeaways

This section addresses significant findings and pragmatic takeaways from leader–member exchange theory literature for three distinct audiences: titled leaders, employees, and teacher-scholars. This approach allows us to translate key implications for those who are actively managing others, for those who are being managed/led by others, for those who are in a position to either conduct-related research or help those on the cusp of entering industry.

For Titled Leaders

Leader–member exchange can be a resource and a source of strength, or it can be a hindrance that prevents the workgroup from performing at its highest level. Leaders should always focus on the collective functioning of the group. They can do this by being mindful of the relationships they share with individual members, their resource distribution practices, and remaining aware of how their relationships and distribution of resources are perceived by the group. It may seem as though you've read this bit of advice a time or two (or twenty) throughout this text, but if leaders are concerned for the well-being of their group, it really is as simple as being intentional about: relationships, resources, and member perceptions of relationships and resources (Omilion-Hodges & Baker, 2017). This advice is easy to access, though it requires an unyielding commitment to adept communication and flexibility on the part of the leader. Yet, why does the guidance continue to trail back to these recommendations? Research continues to find that in instances where the leader is not intentional or mindful of their relationships or how they distribute resources among members, that it implicates how members view their leader in terms of justice, fairness, and equity (Henderson et al., 2008; Hooper & Martin, 2008; Omilion-Hodges & Baker, 2017; Sias & Jablin, 1995). In instances when members perceive leader favoritism, or it seems as though members are unfairly earning a leader's resources (e.g., praise, attention, professional development, etc.), members will come together to make sense of the events. While this may help affirm member perceptions of a leader's perceived inequality, it does not bode well for the collective functioning of the workgroup. In separate focus groups with titled managers and with employees, the outcome was the same: everyone, regardless of rank, is aware that their leader develops relationships of varying quality with members (Omilion-Hodges & Baker, 2017). This can also lead to members engaging in coalition-building against the leader's "pet" employees.

Not only can mismanagement or perceptions of mismanagement take employees away from their role responsibilities to engage in sensemaking via back channels, but perceived breaches to individual leader–member relationships can permanently damage the dyad. Researchers have found that leader-led breaches to the leader–member relationships can cause employees to reassess the relationship and may also prevent members from further exchange with the leader (Kangas & Kangas, 2019). Moreover, since these relationships are part of an interconnected web, it would be naive to presume a strained LMX relationship wouldn't bleed over and impact other workgroup relationships (e.g., coworkers, team cohesion and performance).

For Employees

The most important thing for employees to be mindful of is that the LMX relationship is built and maintained over time. This means that one bad day, a less than stellar presentation, or getting off on the wrong foot is not the end of the world. This also means that having a big "win" on a rare occasion is also not likely enough to develop a high-quality relationship based on trust and mutual respect. What does this leave? This means that daily interactions color the quality of the relationship. Put simply, making a daily effort to check-in or update your manager and inquire about ongoing projects can go a long way in establishing rapport. The point is, you want to show (not tell) your manager that you are doing the work and that you are committed to the overall functioning of the team. Assuming that radio-silence means that you are hard at work is not an effective or proactive way to illustrate industriousness to your leader.

While we won't undercut the importance of effective leader–member relationships, we will not undersell the value of trusted coworker exchange relationships. High-quality peer relationships can serve as a buffer to a moderate or trying leader–member relationship by providing additional resources in the form of friendship, support, and feedback, among other important resources. As has long been asserted (Chiaburu & Harrison, 2008), peers make the place. Yet, there may be some instances where regardless of the strength of the coworker bonds, it may be necessary for employees to consider other employment options if the leader–member relationship is proving to be an insurmountable obstacle.

In the absence of a satisfactory leader–member relationship, employees may feel that they need to transfer to another department or move to a new company to continue growing professionally. Leaders have been likened to gatekeepers for a reason. Depending on their position power and the organization's culture, some leaders may block members from promotions and limit their earning potential. Some leaders may even feel that they are acting in the organization's best interest, yet as research indicates, there are times when members have an unfairly low LMX (Omilion-Hodges & Baker, 2013). In a simulation using an experimental design, Omilion-Hodges and Baker (2013) presented participants with various scenarios where a member's performance matched or did not match the leader's treatment of them. For example, in matched scenarios, an employee with a low-performance review was perceived to have low LMX, and those with high-performance reviews had earned high LMX. Though in conditions where the employee appeared to be a high performer, but in the simulation the leader treated them as a low LMX member, study participants reported the leader was unjust. This research indicates that leaders are people too and at times, their view of others may be obscured by biases, or personality differences. Moreover, when employees speak up and their ideas are dismissed or remain unaddressed, members often stop offering new ideas and withdraw from the organization. This can result in diminished well-being at work, which can also seep over to impact an employee personally as well.

Taken together, the leader–member exchange relationship is not necessarily the be all, end all of workplace relationships. Peer and team relationships can go a long way in bolstering an employee's social support needs as can securing formal and informal mentors. However, in some cases it may be more fruitful for an employee to seek a new opportunity with a new leader if the relationship appears to be beyond repair.

For Teacher-Scholars

Recent research (Omilion-Hodges et al., 2019) uncovered that students receive realistic job previews but tend to dismiss them in favor of embracing what they hope their work experience will be. This means that teacher-scholars can better prepare students for the workplace by helping them sort out wants and best-case scenarios from more realistic expectations. A focus on being communicatively adept is also recommended.

Suppose students are coached to adapt their communication style to fit their audience and the context. In that case, they will fare far better than new hires who expect their new manager and peers to tailor their communication approaches for them. This recommendation puts the onus on students/new hires, but it also means that they are better positioned to form effective workplace relationships by adapting to their audience. With effective two-way communication, they are more likely to develop a high-quality leader–member relationship as they interact while accomplishing organizational goals. Though it would be nice to expect the manager or others with more experience to bend their communication style to accommodate the expectations of new hires, it is not a realistic assumption. Waiting for the leader to communicate the exact way they had hoped is likely to leave new hires in a position to hope to develop moderate LMX at best. It may also help students learn about their personal attachment style as this may also impact their communication tendencies and their expectations for their leader–member relationship (Maslyn et al., 2017).

LMX Resources

The following readings are recommended for titled leaders, employees, students, and teacher-scholars. These recommendations are organized by topic area and are cross-listed where necessary for reader convenience.

Background/Foundational Understanding

Bauer, T. N., & Erdogan, B. (Eds.). (2016). *The Oxford handbook of leader-member exchange*. Oxford University Press.

Graen, G. B., & Uhl-Bien, M. (1995). Relationship-based approach to leadership: Development of leader-member exchange (LMX) theory of leadership over 25 years: Applying a multi-level multi-domain perspective. *The Leadership Quarterly, 6*, 219–247. https://doi.org/10.1016/1048-9843(95)90036-5.

Hooper, D. T., & Martin, R. (2008). Beyond personal leader–member exchange (LMX) quality: The effects of perceived LMX variability on employee reactions. *The Leadership Quarterly, 19*(1), 20–30. https://doi.org/10.1016/j.leaqua.2007.12.002.

Martin, R., Thomas, G., Legood, A., & Dello Russo, S. (2018). Leader-member exchange (LMX) differentiation and work outcomes: Conceptual clarification and critical review. *Journal of Organizational Behavior, 39*(2), 151–168. https://doi.org/10.1002/job.220.

Omilion-Hodges, L. M., Ptacek, J. K., & Zerilli, D. H. (2016). A comprehensive review and communication research agenda of the contextualized workgroup: The evolution and future of leader-member exchange, coworker exchange, and team-member exchange. *Annals of the International Communication Association, 40*(1), 343–377.

Communication Perspective/Functions

Fairhurst, G. T., & Connaughton, S. L. (2014). Leadership: A communicative perspective. *Leadership, 10*(1), 7–35. https://doi.org/10.1177/1742715013509396.

Johansson, C., Miller, V. D., & Hamrin, S. (2014). Conceptualizing communicative leadership: A framework for analysing and developing leaders' communication competence. *Corporate Communications, 19*(2), 147–165. https://doi.org/10.1108/CCIJ-02-2013-0007.

Kelley, K. M. (2014). Leaders' narrative sensemaking during LMX role negotiations: Explaining how leaders make sense of who to trust and when. *The Leadership Quarterly, 25*(3), 433–448. https://doi.org/10.1016/j.leaqua.2013.10.011.

Omilion-Hodges, L. M., & Baker, C. R. (2013). Contextualizing LMX within the workgroup: The effects of LMX and justice on relationship quality and resource sharing among peers. *The Leadership Quarterly, 24,* 935–951. https://doi.org/10.1016/j.leaqua.2013.10.004.

Omilion-Hodges, L. M., & Baker, C. R. (2017). Communicating leader-member relationship quality. *International Journal of Business Communication, 54*(2), 115–145. https://doi.org/10.1177/232948841668705.

Sheer, V. C. (2015). "Exchange lost" in leader-member exchange theory and research: A critique and a reconceptualization. *Leadership, 11*(2), 213–229. https://doi.org/10.1177/1742715014530935.

Sias, P., & Jablin, F. M. (1995). Differential superior-subordinate relations, perceptions of fairness, and coworker communication. *Human Communication Research, 22*(1), 5–38. https://doi.org/10.1111/j.1468-2958.1995.tb00360.x.

New Hires and Millennials

Anderson, H. J., Baur, J. E., Griffith, J. A. & Buckley, M. R. (2017). What works for you may not work for (gen) me: Limitations of present leadership theories for the new generation. *The Leadership Quarterly, 28*(1), 245–260. https://doi.org/10.1016/j.leaqua.2016.08.001.

Omilion-Hodges, L. M., & Ptacek, J. K. (2019). Personal factors, wants, and needs: Exploring vocational anticipatory socialization through young adults' preferences for managerial communication behaviors. *International Journal of Business Communication.* https://doi.org/10.1177/2329488419893745.

Omilion-Hodges, L. M., Shank, S. E., & Packard, C. M. (2019). What young adults want: A multistudy examination of vocational anticipatory socialization through the lens of students' desired managerial communication behaviors. *Management Communication Quarterly, 33*(4), 512–547. https://doi.org/10.1177/0893318919851177.

Diversity and Inclusion

Ayman, R., & Korabik, K. (2010). Leadership: Why gender and culture matter. *American Psychologist, 65*(3), 157–170. https://doi.org/10.1037/a0018806.

Mor Barak, M. E. (2013). *Managing diversity towards a globally inclusive workplace* (3rd ed.). Sage.

Randolph-Seng, B., Cogliser, C. C., Randolph, A. F., Scandura, T. A., Miller, C. D., & Smith-Genthôs, R. (2016). Diversity in leadership: Race in leader-member exchanges. *Leadership & Organization Development Journal, 37*(6), 750–773. https://doi.org/10.1108/LODJ-10-2014-0201.

Sanchez-Hucles, J. V., & Davis, D. D. (2010). Women and women of color in leadership: Complexity, identity, and intersectionality. *American Psychologist, 65*(3), 171–181. https://doi.org/10.1037/a0017459.

Shore, L. M., Chung-Herrera, B. G., Dean, M. A., Ehrhart, K. H., Jung, D. I., Randel, A. E., & Singh, G. (2009). Diversity in organizations: Where are we now and where are we going? *Human*

Resource Management Review, 19(2), 117–133. https://doi.org/10.1016/j.hrmr.2008.10.004.

Critiques

Gottfredson, R. K., Wright, S. L., & Heaphy, E. D. (2020). A critique of the leader-member exchange construct: Back to square one. *The Leadership Quarterly*. https://doi.org/10.1016/j.leaqua.2020.101385.

Schyns, B., & Day, D. (2010). Critique and review of leader–member exchange theory: Issues of agreement, consensus, and excellence. *European Journal of Work and Organizational Psychology, 19*(1), 1–29. https://doi.org/10.1080/13594320903024922.

Sheer, V. C. (2015). "Exchange lost" in leader–member exchange theory and research: A critique and a reconceptualization. *Leadership, 11*(2), 213–229. https://doi.org/10.1177/1742715014530935.

Measurement and Analysis Resources

Bernerth, J. B., Armenakis, A. A., Feild, H. S., Giles, W. F., & Walker, H. J. (2007). Leader-member social exchange (LMSX): Development and validation of a scale. *Journal of Organizational Behavior, 28*, 979–1003. https://doi.org/10.1002/job.443.

Chaudhry, A., Vidyarthi, P. R., Liden, R. C., & Wayne, S. J. (2020). Two to tango? Implications of alignment and misalignment in leader and follower perceptions of LMX. *Journal of Business and Psychology*, 1–17. https://doi.org/10.1007/s10869-020-09690-8.

Graen, G. B., & Scandura, T. A. (1987). Toward a psychology of dyadic organizing. In B. M. Staw & L. L. Cummings (Eds.), *Research in organizational behavior* (pp. 175–208). JAI Press.

Liden, R. C., & Maslyn, J. M. (1998). Multi-dimensionality of leader-member exchange: An empirical assessment through scale development. *Journal of Management, 24*(1), 43–72. https://doi.org/10.1016/S0149-2063(99)80053-1.

Omilion-Hodges, L. M., & Baker, C. R. (2017). Communicating leader-member relationship quality: The development of leader communication exchange scales to measure relationship building and maintenance through the exchange of communication-based goods. *International Journal of Business Communication, 54*(2), 115–145. https://doi.org/10.1177/2329488416687052.

References

Butler, E. A. (2015). Interpersonal affect dynamics: It takes two (and time) to tango. *Emotion Review, 7*(4), 336–341. https://doi.org/10.1177/1754073915590622.

Chiaburu, D. S., & Harrison, D. A. (2008). Do peers make the place? Conceptual synthesis and meta-analysis of coworker effects on perceptions, attitudes, OCBs, and performance. *The Journal of Applied Psychology, 93*(5), 1082–1103. https://doi.org/10.1037/0021-9010.93.5.1082.

Dulebohn, J. H., Bommer, W. H., Liden, R. C., Brouer, R. L., & Ferris, G. R. (2012). A meta-analysis of antecedents and consequences of leader-member exchange: Integrating the past with an eye toward the future. *Journal of Management, 38*(6), 1715–1759. https://doi.org/10.1177/0149206311415280.

Gerstner, C. R., & Day, D. V. (1997). Meta-analytic review of leader-member exchange theory: Correlates and construct issues. *Journal of Applied Psychology, 82*(6), 827–844.

Gooty, J., & Yammarino, F. J. (2013). The leader-member exchange relationship: A multisource, cross-level investigation. *Journal of Management, 42*(4), 915–935. https://doi.org/10.1177/0149206313503009.

Gottfredson, R. K., Wright, S. L., & Heaphy, E. D. (2020). A critique of the leader-member exchange construct: Back to square one. *Leadership Quarterly*. https://doi.org/10.1016/j.leaqua.2020.101385.

Henderson, D. J., Wayne, S. J., Shore, L. M., Bommer, W. H., & Tetrick, L. E. (2008). Leader-member exchange, differentiation, and psychological contract fulfillment: A multilevel examination. *The Journal of Applied Psychology, 93*(6), 1208–1219. https://doi.org/10.1037/a0012678.

Hofmans, J., Dóci, E., Solinger, O. N., Choi, W., & Judge, T. A. (2019). Capturing the dynamics of leader–follower interactions: Stalemates and future theoretical progress. *Journal of Organizational Behavior, 40*(3), 382–385. https://doi.org/10.1002/job.2317.

Hooper, D. T., & Martin, R. (2008). Beyond personal leader-member exchange (LMX) quality: The effects of perceived LMX variability on employee reactions. *Leadership Quarterly, 19*(1), 20–30. https://doi.org/10.1016/j.leaqua.2007.12.002.

Kangas, H., & Kangas, H. (2019). Spanning leader-subordinate relationships through negative interactions: An examination of leader-member exchange breaches. *Standard Article Leadership*, 1–18. https://doi.org/10.1177/1742715020952676.

Liden, R. C., & Maslyn, J. M. (1998). Multidimensionafity of leader-member exchange: An empirical assessment through scale development. *Journal of Management, 24*, 43–72. https://doi.org/10.1177/014920639802400105.

Martin, R., Thomas, G., Legood, A., & Dello Russo, S. (2018). Leader-member exchange (LMX) differentiation and work outcomes: Conceptual clarification and critical review. *Journal of Organizational Behavior, 39*(2), 151–168. https://doi.org/10.1002/job.2202.

Maslyn, J. M., Schyns, B., & Farmer, S. M. (2017). Attachment style and leader-member exchange. *Leadership & Organizational Development Journal, 38*(3), 450–462. https://doi.org/10.1108/LODJ-01-2016-0023.

Omilion-Hodges, L. M., & Baker, C. R. (2013). Contextualizing LMX within the workgroup: The effects of LMX and justice on relationship quality and resource sharing among peers. *The Leadership Quarterly, 24*(6), 935–951. https://doi.org/10.1016/j.leaqua.2013.10.004.

Omilion-Hodges, L. M., & Baker, C. R. (2017). Communicating leader-member relationship quality: The development of leader communication exchange scales to measure relationship building and maintenance through the exchange of communication-based goods. *International Journal of Business Communication, 54*(2), 115–145. https://doi.org/10.1177/2329488416687052.

Omilion-Hodges, L. M., Shank, S. E., & Packard, C. M. (2019). What young adults want: A multistudy examination of vocational anticipatory socialization through the lens of students' desired managerial communication behaviors. *Management Communication Quarterly, 33*(4), 512–547. https://doi.org/10.1177/0893318919851177.

Schriesheim, C. A., Castro, S. L., & Cogliser, C. C. (1999). Leader-member exchange (LMX) research: A comprehensive review of theory, measurement, and data-analytic practices. *The Leadership Quarterly, 10*(1), 63–113. https://doi.org/10.1016/S1048-9843(99)80009-5.

Schyns, B., & Day, D. (2010). European journal of work and organizational psychology critique and review of leader-member exchange theory: Issues of agreement, consensus, and excellence. *Organizational Psychology, 19*(1), 1–29. https://doi.org/10.1080/13594320903024922.

Sheer, V. C. (2015). "Exchange lost" in leader-member exchange theory and research: A critique and a reconceptualization. *Leadership, 11*(2), 213–229. https://doi.org/10.1177/1742715014530935.

Sias, P. M., & Jablin, F. M. (1995). Differential superior-subordinate relations, perceptions of fairness, and coworker communication. *Human Communication Research, 22*(1), 5–38. https://doi.org/10.1111/j.1468-2958.1995.tb00360.x.

Sin, H. P., Nahrgang, J. D., & Morgeson, F. P. (2009). Understanding why they don't see eye to eye: An examination of leader-member exchange (LMX) agreement. *Journal of Applied Psychology, 94*(4), 1048–1057. https://doi.org/10.1037/a0014827.

Tse, H. H. M., & Ashkanasy, N. M. (2015). The dyadic level of conceptualization and analysis: A missing link in multilevel OB research? *Journal of Organizational Behavior, 36*(8), 1176–1180. https://doi.org/10.1002/job.2010.

Glossary

Active Listening: The practice of giving your conversational partner(s) your full attention. This includes demonstrating immediacy behaviors that indicate that you are listening including nodding, asking questions, and paraphrasing.

Authentic Leadership: This approach to leadership emphasizes embracing one's natural communication and relational tendencies as they work with others to accomplish group goals. Unlike other styles or approaches to leadership, authentic leadership suggests that leaders will be most effective by embracing their natural strengths and dispositional factors rather than attempting to enact styles or communication tendencies that do not come naturally.

Charismatic Leadership: Charismatic leaders are naturally skilled communicators who are especially dynamic and persuasive in their interpersonal encounters. Owing to their adept communication skills, charismatic leaders often form especially close relationships with followers and inspire great levels of loyalty.

Communication Channel: Communication channels refer to the mediums that messages are transmitted over. Channels include traditional face-to-face communication and the myriad computer-mediated communicationchannels available such as email, text, and video conferencing.

L. M. Omilion-Hodges and J. K. Ptacek, *Leader-Member Exchange and Organizational Communication*, New Perspectives in Organizational Communication, https://doi.org/10.1007/978-3-030-68756-4

Coworker Exchange Theory (CWX): CWX describes the relationship between two peers who report to the same manager.

Diversity and Inclusion: While these terms are often used interchangeably, they describe related yet different phenomena. Diversity refers to characteristics that make individuals unique and are often considered in terms of demographicdifferences. Inclusion refers to behaviors and policies meant to encourage and facilitate an environment that is equitable for all.

Emotional Exhaustion: Emotional exhaustion can stem from a number of factors, including an overdemanding role, unsupportive environment, and challenging or contentious workplace relationships, among others. Emotional exhaustion can lead to serious mental health issues and is often associated with burnout.

Emotional Intelligence: Emotional intelligence has long been linked to effective leadership as highly emotional intelligent individuals are skilled at recognizing their emotions and the emotions of others. This skill can help leaders to connect with followers, adapt to work environments, and create a workplace that is healthy for themselves and others.

Ethical Leadership: Ethical leadership involves committing to honest, transparent, and moral behavior and facilitating an environment that rewards others who engage in these same behaviors. The reverse is also true in that ethical leaders will respond to unethical behavior with swift and harsh ramifications.

Formal/Titled Leadership: Formal and titled leaders are those who are in managerial positions and oversee at least one other employee. This contrasts with the idea of self-leadership or informal leadership where everyone regardless of title is encouraged to communicate and behave as a leader.

Informal leadership: In contrast to formal or titled leaders, informal leadership is when an individual, regardless of title or rank, influences others through their communication and behaviors.

In-Group: In-group members are employees who share a high-quality exchange relationship with their leader. These employees tend to befriend other in-group members and enjoy a variety of rewards such as increased mentoring, additional attention from their leader, and increased access to organizational information.

Laissez-Faire Leadership: This approach to leadership is often considered in two distinct veins: abdication and guided freedom. Leadership who abdicates their responsibilities are seen as ineffective at best and unethical at worst. Leadership may enact a guided freedom approach when they oversee employees who are highly specialized and require little to no direct oversight.

Leader-Member Exchange Theory (LMX): LMX describes the tendency for leaders to develop relationships of varying quality with each member. This theory emerged in direct response to Average Leadership Styles which suggested that managers approached all members in an identical fashion.

Mission Statement: A formal statement of purpose, values, and aims.

Organizational Citizenship Behavior (OCB): OCB describes instances when employees engage in helping behaviors that are above those described in their formal role description. These may include staying late to help a colleague or volunteering to help socialize a new colleague.

Organizational injustice: Failing to treat employees equitably.

Out-Group: Out-group members are those who have a lower-quality relationship with their manager. This does not necessarily mean that it is a poor relationship, but more likely one that is transactional in nature. Out-group members tend to form workplace friendships with other out-group members and often report having access to fewer organizational resources including limited mentoring opportunities.

Self-Managed Work Team/Autonomous Workgroups: This approach to work distributes authority and power from a traditional leadership role across the workgroup. This means that group members collaborate to make hiring and promotion decisions and weigh-in to determine how to best organize the functioning of their unit collectively.

Situational Leadership: Situational leadership is a model that accounts for the structure of the task and follower maturity. In considering these two factors, the model offers leaders prescriptive advice for how to communicatively navigate the various pairings of follower readiness with the structure of the task at hand.

Team-Member Exchange Theory (TMX): TMX refers to the collective communicative and relational environment for all members who report to the same direct manager.

Transactional Leadership: Transactional leadership describes situations where leaders approach management largely through the distribution of rewards and or punishments. This is considered a classic approach to leadership and does not account for the importance or impact of relationships as more contemporary leadership theories do.

Transformational Leadership: Widely considered the antithesis of transactional leaders, transformational leaders work to inspire and form effective, two-way relationships with followers. Transformational leadership is often described by four behaviors: intellectual stimulation, inspirational motivation, idealized influence, and individualized consideration.

Turnover: Turnover describes the rate at which employees leave a workplace. Turnover can be extremely costly to organizations financially and can have a negative impact on employee morale.

Virtual Teams: Virtual teams are those that complete their duties remotely and rely on technology and computer-mediated communication to do so. Virtual groups are often geographically dispersed, though the only criterion of a virtual team is that they do not complete their work in a traditional face-to-face fashion.

Vision Statement: A statement that describes an idealized, future state. This statement is often part and parcel with strategic planning as vision statements describe what the organization or individual is working to achieve.

Index

L. M. Omilion-Hodges and J. K. Ptacek, *Leader-Member Exchange and Organizational Communication*, New Perspectives in Organizational Communication, https://doi.org/10.1007/978-3-030-68756-4

D

E

The manufacturer's authorised representative in the EU is Springer Nature Customer Service Centre GmbH, Europaplatz 3, 69115 Heidelberg, Germany. If you have any concerns regarding our products, please contact ProductSafety@springernature.com

Printed and bound by CPI Group (UK) Ltd, Croydon, CR0 4YY

30/09/2026

02225457-0006